SUPPLY CHAIN STRATEGY

The Logistics of Supply Chain Management

Edward Frazelle

McGraw-Hill
New York   Chicago   San Francisco   Lisbon   London
Madrid   Mexico City   Milan   New Delhi   San Juan
Seoul   Singapore   Sydney   Toronto

Library of Congress Cataloging-in-Publication Data

Frazelle, Edward.
    Supply chain strategy : the logistics of supply chain management / by Edward Frazelle.
      p. cm
    ISBN 0-07-137599-6
    1. Business logistics.   2. Industrial procurement.   I. Title
    HD38.5.F735 2001   2001045282

McGraw-Hill

*A Division of The **McGraw·Hill** Companies*

6 7 8 9 0 DOC/DOC 0 7

ISBN 0-07-137599-6

The sponsoring editor for this book was Catherine Dassopoulos.
It was set in Times New Roman by MacAllister Publishing Services, LLC.

Printed and bound by R.R. Donnelley & Sons Company.

*This book is dedicated to Jesus Christ—my Lord, Savior, and best friend;
Pat—the most noble and beautiful wife a husband could ever be blessed with;
and Kelly and Andrew—the most encouraging children a father could ever know.*

Contents

Section III Implementing Logistics Systems 275

Preface

*S*UPPLY *C*HAIN *S*TRATEGY: *The Logistics of Supply Chain Management* teaches the best practices and basics in logistics and supply chain management. The book is richly illustrated with 238 figures featuring logistics principles in action at the world's best logistics organizations. In a conversational style, the book presents best-practice, common-sense, high-tech, high-touch, and analytical solutions for logistics challenges spanning the entire supply chain. From customer service to inventory planning to supply to transportation to warehousing, *Supply Chain Strategy* puts the logic back in logistics!

The book is organized according to Dr. Edward Frazelle's Logistics Master Planning methodology for developing supply chain strategy. Three major sections address the investigation, innovation, and implementation of logistics solutions to supply chain problems. In so doing, the book presents simultaneously a methodology for planning and managing logistics activities while illustrating world-class practices and systems in use by logistics organizations around the globe. In addition, each chapter stands alone in addressing the major issues in logistics data mining, logistics performance measurement, customer response, inventory planning and management, supply management, transportation, warehousing, logistics information systems, and logistics organization design and development.

Acknowledgments

IN THE LAST TEN YEARS, God has led me through a series of consulting and research projects literally spanning the globe to work with the world's best logistics organizations in all areas of logistics management. During that time, He taught me a framework for logistics management and problem solving that is the essence of this book. He also showed me examples of the world's best logistics practices. Those illustrations are sprinkled throughout the book.

I have been blessed with a career overflowing with support and encouragement from family, mentors, business partners, staff, consulting clients, and students of all ages. Because this book is a summary of my consulting and research in logistics, all those kind folks have contributed to this book. It would take another book just to name all the individuals involved in the projects covered in this book. I don't have time or space to name each individual, but I do want to say a special thanks to several individuals and organizations who have made significant contributions.

Even though my mother was an English teacher, I still need an inordinate amount of support with editing. Ms. Freida Breazeal with The Logistics Institute at Georgia Tech, Tammy Artosky with Logistics Resources International, and Steve Erbe with Walt Disney World assisted me with reviewing and editing the manuscript.

This book could not come to life if it were not for a variety of organizations willing to allow me to share lessons learned during my work with them. My most sincere appreciation goes out to Hal Welsh, Lynn Barratt, Steve Erbe, Tom Nabbe, Bruce Terry, and Karen Hall with Walt Disney World Distribution Services; Carliss Graham with BP; Tony Fuller and Matthew Anderson with the U.S. Armed Services Velocity Management Program; Mike Graska with Swagelok; Jack Gross with Applied Materials; Roosevelt Tolliver with Avon Products; Bill Hightower with BellSouth; Joe Neal and Jerel Williams with Payless ShoeSource; Will Walker with NORTEL; Mike Harry with Lifeway Christian Resources; Brad Morris with NuSkin International; Bob Hribernik with Techdata; and Raul Mendez with Coca-Cola.

This book could also not come to life if it were not for my partners in logistics consulting who encourage and teach me daily and keep me involved on the frontlines of logistics problem solving. Thanks to Hugh Kinney, Hugh Kinney Jr., Juan Rubio, Ricardo Sojo, Ron Gable, and Masaji Nakano.

THE DEFINITION, EVOLUTION, AND ROLE OF LOGISTICS IN BUSINESS

"But many who are first will be last, and many who are last will be first."

Matthew 19:30

FTER WINNING BACK-TO-BACK World Series titles, Sparky Anderson, then manager of the Cincinnati Reds, was asked what it felt like to be on top of the world. His simple reply was, "Every dog has his day." As logistics professionals, once the lowest professionals on the corporate totem pole, we are having our day.

During this past year, *logistics* has been featured on the cover of the *Wall Street Journal, Forbes, Fortune,* and *Business Week* magazines. It is no wonder.

- Logistics expenditures represent about 10 percent of the U.S. gross domestic product and are approximately $1 trillion annually (see Figure 1-1).

- Global logistics expenditures exceed $3.5 trillion annually and represent nearly 20 percent of the sum total of the world's GDP (see Figure 1-2).

FIGURE 1-1   U.S. logistics expenditure 1989–1999.
Source: Cass Logistics

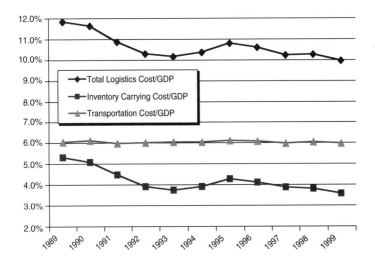

FIGURE 1-2   Global logistics expenditures.
Source: Michigan State University

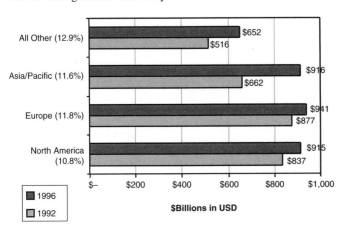

- Most U.S. corporations spend between 8 percent and 15 percent of sales revenue on logistics activities (see Figure 1-3).

Logistics is being recognized as perhaps the last frontier for major corporations to significantly increase shareholder and customer value. An excellent example is the Coca-Cola corporation. With the world's most recognized brand, Coke is the envy of the world in marketing. With a route dri-

FIGURE 1-3   **Logistics expenditures versus sales for various industries.**
Source: Herb Davis & Associates

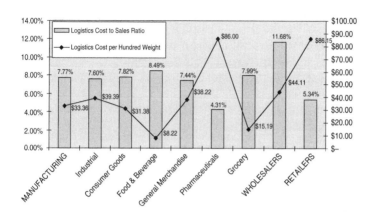

ver or order taker appearing in nearly every customer location, nearly every day, Coke's customer service is outstanding. With a product made for over a century by the same mixing of sugar, water, carbonation, and flavoring, theoretical capacities for production quality and efficiency are being reached. The linking of those world-class marketing, customer service, and production processes, *logistics*, is the next great frontier for Coca-Cola and many other enterprises.

Logistics and its younger cousin, supply chain management, are popular but greatly misunderstood topics. Logistics and supply chain management are new concepts in private industry. A minority of the professionals who work in logistics have formal training in logistics. Logistics and supply chain management cut across and draw from personnel in a multiplicity of disciplines. It is no wonder that confusion abounds and that a majority of logistics projects never reach their intended goals or wind up as catastrophic failures. Add to this a marketplace that includes more than one thousand vendors of logistics software, three thousand transportation providers, and one thousand providers of third-party logistics, and we have a situation ripe for unmet promises and potential. The unmet potential is evidenced by the fact that less than 30 percent of all logistics projects ever achieve their intended goals (if the project involves software, the success rate drops to less than 15 percent) and that logistics productivity in the United States in the last few years has remained flat. We believe (and our benchmarking supports) that the underlying cause of recent failures in logistics is that the tools, technology, and training available to logistics professionals are not keeping pace with growing logistics complexities. *In short and ironically, there is not nearly enough logic in logistics!*

This observation is based on my work with Fortune 1000 clients in a wide variety of industries and by statements made to me by many of the participants in our professional education programs. This observation motivated me in 1992 to organize The Logistics Institute at Georgia Tech, to develop the Logistics Management Series of courses, to form Logistics Resources International, and to author this book—each endeavor with the common motivation to teach and illustrate the following:

- A *definition* of logistics (Chapter 1, "The Definition, Evolution and Role of Logistics in Business")
- A *methodology* for logistics problem solving (Chapter 1)
- A *profile* of logistics activity (Chapter 2, "Logistics Activity Profiling and Data Mining")
- A *scoreboard* of logistics performance measures (Chapter 3, "Logistics Performance, Cost, and Value Measures")
- A *standard* for world-class logistics practices in customer response (Chapter 4, "Customer Response Principles and Systems"), inventory management (Chapter 5, "Inventory Planning and Management"), supply (Chapter 6, "Supply Management"), transportation (Chapter 7, "Transportation and Distribution Management"), and warehousing (Chapter 8, "Warehousing and Fulfillment Operations")
- An *architecture* for logistics and supply chain management systems (Chapter 9, "Logistics and Supply Chain Management Systems")
- A *development program* for logistics organizations (Chapter 10, "Logistics Organization Design and Development")

that consistently yields higher levels of customer service, higher corporate valuations, and lower logistics costs. That definition, along with methodology, scoreboard, standard, architecture, and development program we call *The Logistics of Supply Chain Management*.

The story begins here with the definition, evolution, and role of logistics in business. This chapter presents

- A *formal definition* of logistics and supply chain management (Section 1.1, "The Definition of Logistics")
- The *evolution* of logistics and supply chain management (Section 1.2, "The Evolution of Logistics and Supply Chain Management")
- *Descriptions* of the five interdependent logistics activities (Section 1.3, "Logistics Activities")
- *Logistics optimization* (Section 1.4, "Logistics Optimization")

- *Logistics master planning* (LMP) methodology (Section 1.5, "Logistics Master Planning")
- *Logistics conditions* around the world (Section 1.6, "Logistics Around the World")

1.1   THE DEFINITION OF LOGISTICS

I was recently asked by a large food manufacturer to help them develop a formal logistics organization. At the kickoff meeting, the participants spent the first 2 hours arguing with one another about who should be represented in the new organization. As utter frustration was setting in and the first meeting was about to adjourn by default, it finally dawned on me why we were not able to make any progress. Each person in the room came to logistics without a formal degree in logistics and from a different professional discipline. One came from marketing, another from sales, another from material management, another from manufacturing, another from warehousing, another from transportation, and another was the nephew of the chairman of the board. As a result, each had his or her own different definition of logistics. It is impossible to develop anything, let alone an organization, for a process that is not even defined, and where each of the major players speaks a different language.

Remember what God did to humble the people who were trying to build a monument to themselves reaching all the way to Heaven? He gave them all a different language, so that the people could not communicate with each other. As a result, they could not complete the construction of the tower. We are the same way in logistics; if we can't speak the same language, we can't start, let alone finish a project.

Our definition of logistics is simple. *Logistics is the flow of material, information, and money between consumers and suppliers.* The confusion in the definition enters when logistics is placed in context, when it is confused with many of the buzzwords that incorporate logistics, when it is mixed up with the objectives of logistics, and/or confused with the interdependent processes that make up logistics. To help clear up some of the potential confusion, we're going to now review five different contexts for logistics that also serve as a presentation of the evolution of logistics.

1.2   THE EVOLUTION OF LOGISTICS
AND SUPPLY CHAIN MANAGEMENT

Paralleling advances in management theory and information systems, logistics has evolved in scope and influence in the private sector since the mid to late 1940s. In the 1950s and '60s, the military was the only organization using the term logistics. There was no true concept of logistics in private industry at that time. Instead, departmental silos including material handling, warehousing, machining, accounting, marketing, and so on, were the norm.

The five phases of logistics development—workplace logistics, facility logistics, corporate logistics, supply chain logistics, and global logistics—are plotted in time in Figure 1-4.

Workplace Logistics
Workplace logistics (see Figure 1-5) is the flow of material at a single workstation. The objective of workplace logistics is to streamline the movements of an individual working at a machine or along an assembly line. The principles and theory of workplace logistics were developed by the founders of industrial engineering working in WWII and post-WWII factory operations. A popular name today for workplace logistics is ergonomics.

Facility Logistics
Facility logistics (see Figure 1-6) is the flow of material between workstations within the four walls of a facility (that is, interworkstation and intra-facility). The facility could be a factory, terminal, warehouse, or distribution center. Facility logistics has been more commonly referred to as material handling. The roots of facility logistics and material handling are in the mass production and assembly lines that distinguished the 1950s and 1960s. In those times and even into the late 1970s, many organizations maintained material-handling departments. Today, the term material handling has fallen out of favor because of its association with nonvalue added activities.

FIGURE 1-4   The evolution of logistics.

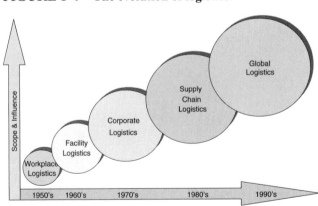

FIGURE 1-5   **Workplace logistics.**
Source: Bertlesmann

FIGURE 1-6   **Facility logistics.**
Source: Lifeway Christian Resources

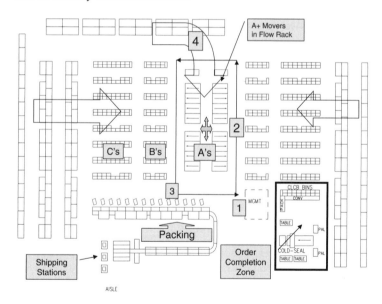

In the 1960s, material handling, warehousing, and traffic were grouped together to become known as physical distribution; procurement, marketing, and customer service were grouped together to become known as business logistics. (Even today in many academic institutions, logistics is still divided along these lines; where logistics is taught in the business school, it is taught as business logistics, and in the engineering schools as physical distribution.)

Corporate Logistics

As management structures advanced and information systems accordingly, our ability to assimilate and synthesize departments (material handling, warehousing, and so on) into functions (physical distribution and business logistics) in the 1970s permitted the first application of true logistics within a corporation. Corporate logistics became a process with the common objective to develop and maintain a profitable customer service policy while maintaining and reducing total logistics costs.

Corporate logistics (see Figure 1-7) is the flow of material and information between the facilities and processes of a corporation (inter-workstation, inter-facility, and intra-corporate). For a manufacturer, logistics activities occur between its factories and warehouses; for a wholesaler, between its distribution centers; and for a retailer, between its distribution centers and retail stores. Corporate logistics is sometimes associated with the phrase physical distribution that was popular in the 1970s. In fact, the *Council of Logistics Management* (CLM) was called the *National Council of Physical Distribution Management* (NCPDM) until 1982.

Supply Chain Logistics

Supply chain logistics (see Figure 1-8) is the flow of material, information, and money between corporations (interworkstation, interfacility, intercorporate, and intrachain).

There is a lot of confusion surrounding the terms logistics and supply chain management. I distinguish the two by explaining that the supply chain is the network of facilities (warehouses, factories, terminals, ports, stores, and homes), vehicles (trucks, trains, planes, and ocean vessels), and *logistics information systems* (LIS) connected by an enterprise's supplier's suppliers and its customer's customers. Logistics is what happens in the supply chain. Logistics activities (customer response, inventory management, supply, transportation, and warehousing) connect and activate the objects in the supply chain. To borrow a sports analogy, logistics is the game played in the supply chain arena.

It is unfortunate that the phrase supply chain management has been so readily and commonly adopted as a reference to excellence in logistics. First, it is not supply (or demand) that should dictate the flow of material, information, and money in a logistics network. Actually, there are some links in the chain and some circumstances in which supply should dictate flow and

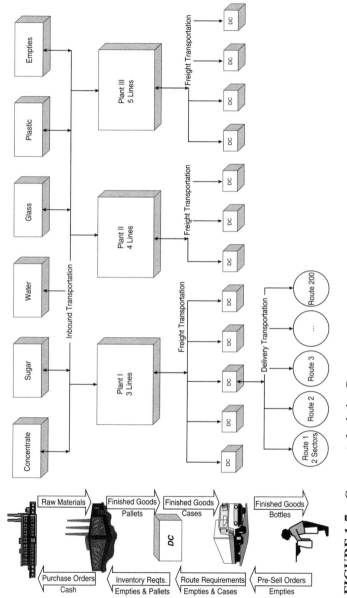

FIGURE 1-7 Corporate logistics flows.

FIGURE 1-8 Supply chain logistics.

Supply Chain Flows

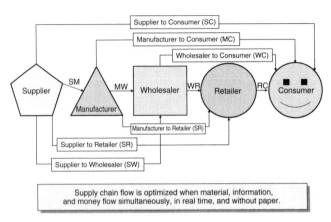

Supply chain flow is optimized when material, information, and money flow simultaneously, in real time, and without paper.

some in which demand should dictate flow. Second, if you drew lines connecting all the trading partners in a typical supply chain, what you would see would not look anything like a chain. You would see something that looks more like a complex web of links.

A chain stretched full is a line. The danger in the choice of the term *chain* is that the term oversimplifies the complexities in logistics management and leads to inflated expectations for what can be achieved by supply chain management systems. Finally, the term *management* suggests that a single party in the chain can truly manage and dictate the operations of the supply chain. Instead, the best any party can do is to collaboratively plan the operations of the chain. Consider the computing industry supply chain with players like HP, Microsoft, Intel, UPS, FEDEX, Sun, Ingram-Micro, Compaq, CompUSA, and so on. There is not a single one of those parties who can or should manage the entire computing industry supply chain.

Global Logistics

Global logistics (see Figure 1-9) is the flow of material, information, and money between countries. Global logistics connects our suppliers' suppliers with our customers' customers internationally. Global logistics flows have increased dramatically during the last several years due to globalization in the world economy, expanding use of trading blocs, and global access to Web sites for buying and selling merchandise. Global logistics is much more complex than domestic logistics, due to the multiplicity of handoffs, players, lan-

FIGURE 1-9   **Global logistics flows.**

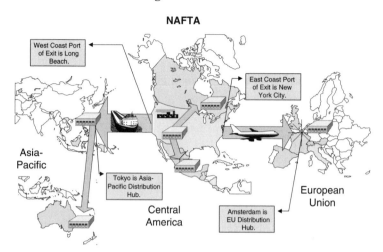

guages, documents, currencies, time zones, and cultures that are inherent to international business.

Next-Generation Logistics

There are many theories as to the next phase of logistics development. Many logisticians believe that *collaborative logistics*, logistics models built with continuous and real-time optimization and communication between all supply chain partners, will be the next phase of evolution. Other camps in the logistics community believe the next phase of evolution will be *virtual logistics* or *fourth-party logistics*, where all logistics activities and management will be outsourced to third-party logistics providers who are in turn managed by a *master* or *fourth-party logistics* providers acting kind of like a general contractor. I used to joke that *interplanetary logistics* would be the next phase of evolution until the director of logistics for NASA and the international space station program showed up in our Logistics Management Series and began asking my advice on how to get parts to Mars to support their next mission.

The only thing I can predict with confidence about the future of logistics is that it will continue to play a major role in the success or failure of most corporations, and that it will continue to expand in scope and influence as management theories and information systems continue to advance. I can also predict with confidence that each stage of logistics development is and will be a prerequisite to success in the other stages. Many organizations have left behind the proven disciplines and best practices learned in

the early stages of logistics development and are finding it difficult to succeed in the more advanced stages. I personally believe that poor execution
of the basics of logistics management is the fundamental reason for the business failure of so many dotcoms and pure e-tailers, and that consistent execution of the basics of logistics management is the reason traditional
brick-and-mortar companies have withstood and flourished during the
e-wave. A wise prophet once said that when we are faithful with the small
things, we will be blessed with the larger things.

1.3   LOGISTICS ACTIVITIES

In our definition, logistics is comprised of five interdependent activities: customer response, inventory planning and management, supply, transportation,
and warehousing. Each activity and its objective is described briefly in Figure
1-10 and in detail in Chapters 4 through 8.

Customer Response

Customer response links logistics externally to the customer base and internally to sales and marketing. Customer response is optimized when the *customer service policy* (CSP) yielding the lowest cost of lost sales, inventory
carrying, and distribution is identified and executed.

FIGURE 1-10   Interdependent logistics activities.

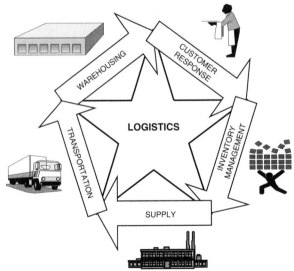

The logistics of customer response includes the activities of

- Developing and maintaining a customer service policy
- Monitoring customer satisfaction
- *Order Entry* (OE)
- *Order Processing* (OP)
- Invoicing and collections

Definitions, illustrations, measures, and world-class practices for each of these customer response activities will be presented in Chapter 4.

Inventory Planning and Management

The objective of *inventory planning and management* (IP&M) is to determine and maintain the lowest inventory levels possible that will meet the customer service policy requirements stipulated in the customer service policy. The logistics of inventory planning and management includes

- Forecasting
- Order quantity engineering
- Service level optimization
- Replenishment planning
- Inventory deployment

Definitions, illustrations, measures, and world-class practices for each of these inventory management activities will be presented in Chapter 5.

Supply

Supply is the process of building inventory (through manufacturing and/or procurement) to the targets established in inventory planning. The objective of supply management is to minimize the *total acquisition cost* (TAC) while meeting the availability, response time, and quality requirements stipulated in the customer service policy and the inventory master plan. The logistics of supply include

- Developing and maintaining a *Supplier Service Policy* (SSP)
- Sourcing
- Supplier integration
- Purchase order processing
- Buying and payment

Definitions, illustrations, measures, and world-class practices for each of these supply activities will be presented in Chapter 6.

Transportation

Transportation physically links the sources of supply chosen in sourcing with the customers we have decided to serve chosen as a part of the customer service policy. We reserve transportation for the fourth spot in the logistics activity list because the deliver-to points and response time requirements determined in the customer service policy and the pick-up points determined in the supply plan must be in place before a transportation scheme can be developed.

The objective of transportation is to link all pick-up and deliver-to points within the response time requirements of the customer service policy and the limitations of the transportation infrastructure at the lowest possible cost. The logistics of transportation includes

- Network design and optimization
- Shipment management
- Fleet and container management
- Carrier management
- Freight management

Definitions, illustrations, measures, and world-class practices for each of these transportation activities will be presented in Chapter 7.

Warehousing

I present warehousing as the last of the five logistics activities because good planning in the other four activities may eliminate the need for warehousing or may suggest the warehousing activity be outsourced. In addition, a good warehouse plan incorporates the needs of all the other logistics activities. Good or bad, the warehouse ultimately portrays the efficiency or inefficiency of the entire supply chain.

The objective of warehousing is to minimize the cost of labor, space, and equipment in the warehouse while meeting the cycle time and shipping accuracy requirements of the customer service policy and the storage capacity requirements of the inventory play. The logistics of warehousing includes

- Receiving
- Putaway
- Storage
- Order picking
- Shipping

Definitions, illustrations, measures, and world-class practices for each of these warehousing activities will be presented in Chapter 8.

Figure 1-11 summarizes our definition of logistics and its related activities. This definition of logistics has proven successful in a wide variety of industries and locales and is the basis for all of our consulting, teaching, research, and decision support tool development.

1.4   LOGISTICS OPTIMIZATION

My experience with logistics problems is that a mix of optimization techniques, common sense, business-best practices, and political savvy is required to develop and implement a workable solution. My experience is also that there is typically plenty of common sense, business-best practices, and political savvy to go around in most organizations. What is often lacking are the analytical resources required to model and solve logistics problems.

Because logistics problems tend to be complex and cross-functional, optimization techniques are and should be used to develop and quantify an ideal solution. Executed properly, the optimization process tends to de-politicize a project and focuses a project team's attention on the solution that maximizes total corporate performance. Hence optimization is a key ingredient in our logistics master planning methodology.

I will describe many optimization techniques and examples of applied optimization in this book, including customer service policy optimization, computing optimal purchase order quantities, determining optimal product sources, choosing optimal locations for distribution centers, and optimizing the placement of products in a warehouse. In each case, the fundamental principle is the same—there is a quantifiable objective function that should be minimized/maximized, and a set of quantifiable constraints that make it difficult to minimize/maximize the objective function. For example, to determine the optimal customer service policy, the objective is to minimize the *total logistics costs* (TLC), including inventory carrying costs, response time costs (warehousing and transportation), and lost sales costs. The constraints are the availability of inventory and the response time requirements that make up the core of the customer service policy. Mathematically, we can write the following:

Minimize:

Total logistics costs = Inventory carrying costs + Response time costs
+ Lost sales cost

Constraints:
1.   Inventory availability > Customer service inventory target
2.   Response time < Customer service response time target

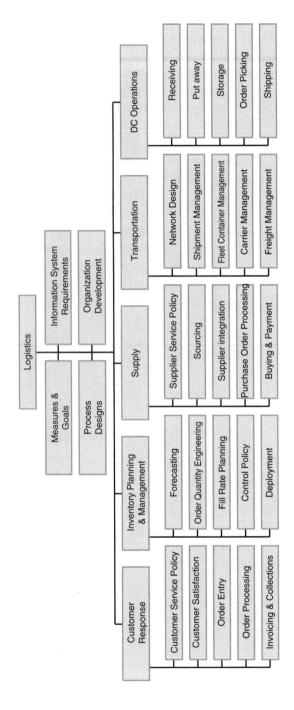

FIGURE 1-11 Logistics framework of activities.

16

A major advance in logistics optimization is the graphical representation of supply chains and related tradeoffs. The customer service optimization problem is presented and solved pictorially in Figure 1-12. The figure is an illustration of the tradeoffs involved in choosing an optimal customer service policy addressing inventory availability and response time. With inventory availability expressed as the unit fill rate, the greater the fill rate, the lower the lost sales cost, but the higher the inventory levels and associated inventory carrying cost required. In response time, we can reduce lost sales cost by responding faster; however, we will incur a higher response cost either for more expensive transportation modes or for more warehousing space located in close proximity to our customer base.

In the example, the total logistics cost is minimized with a customer service policy providing next-day response and 99.5 percent inventory availability. The optimization should be conducted for each item-customer pair because the parameters vary greatly with each item and customer's unique demand profile.

1.5   LOGISTICS MASTER PLANNING

Once an optimal solution has been defined, we need a roadmap to get there. LRI calls that mapping process *logistics master planning* (LMP). LMP is a planning process that develops short- and long-term metrics, process definitions, information system requirements, and organizational requirements for logistics as a whole and for customer response, inventory management, supply, transportation, and warehousing individually. No matter the level of detail, we always move through the phases in the same order: investigate, innovate, implement (see Figure 1-13).

FIGURE 1-12   **Logistics optimization.**

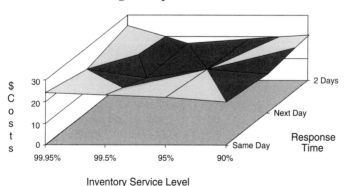

FIGURE 1-13   Logistics master planning methodology.

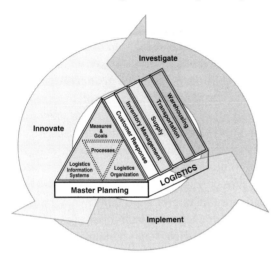

FIGURE 1-14   Investigate, innovate, and implement.

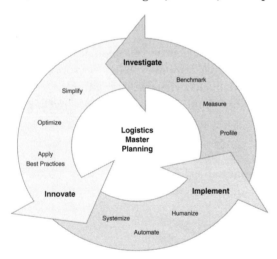

These three steps—investigate, innovate, implement—are the foundation of our LMP methodology (see Figure 1-14). This methodology can and has been used in a wide variety of industries, countries, and operating scenarios. *Logistics master planning is the logic applied to logistics that is often missing.*

Investigate

In the *investigation* phase, we

- *Profile* current logistics activity
- *Measure* current logistics performance
- *Benchmark* performance and practices versus world-class standards

In so doing, we utilize our logistics audit programs to assess the current performance, practices, and systems versus world-class standards developed over years of data collection and research. The result is a logistics gap analysis revealing current strengths, weaknesses, and the financial opportunities available for closing the revealed gaps.

Logistics activity profiling is the subject of Chapter 2. The gap analysis techniques will be described and illustrated in Chapter 3. An example gap analysis is provided in Figure 1-15.

Innovate

In the *innovation* phase, we

- *Simplify* (eliminate and combine work activities)
- *Optimize* (apply decision support tools to determine optimal resource requirements)
- *Apply world-class practices* (tailor the world's best logistics practices to the particular setting and circumstance)

to determine the most appropriate design for each logistics activity. We also use a variety of supply chain imagineering and optimization tools to create

FIGURE 1-15   **Example of logistics gap analysis.**

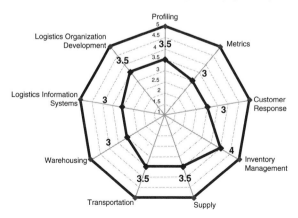

and evaluate alternative plans of action. These tools will be described and illustrated in Chapters 4 through 8.

Implement

In the *implementation* phase, we

- *Systemize* (develop and document detailed procedures)
- *Automate* (justify, select, and implement appropriate systems)
- *Humanize* (design, populate, and develop organization plans for human resources)

In so doing, we use a variety of logistics templates to develop detailed action plans and to choose appropriate vendors. An example logistics implementation plan is provided in Figure 1-16. Logistics implementation principles are the subject of Chapters 9 and 10.

In addition to defining logistics and supply chain management and presenting world-class practices for each logistics activity, this book is a trip through the LMP methodology. While teaching logistics, I want to teach you how to solve logistics problems. One of my goals in writing this book is to

FIGURE 1-16   **Logistics implementation plan.**

MxM Logistics Master Plan

Initiative	Recommendation	Est. Expense	Est. Duration	System Reqts.
Store Service				
Store Service Metrics	Create and implement store service performance measures.		3	LS
Store Service Segmentation	Segment store service policy by channel, store, commodity group, and SKU.		2	CAP
Store Service Optimization	Optimize store fill rate.	$24	4	FRP
	Optimize store delivery frequency.	$24	3	DFP
Supply				
Store Replenishment	Implement vendor managed inventory or automated continuous replenishment to close the order entry gap.	$500	12	EDI
Inventory Management				
Inventory Performance Metrics	Implement inventory performance metrics.		3	LS
Intelligent Forecasting	Implement intelligent forecasting methodologies.		6	
	Establish dedicated forecasting personnel.		2	
	If required, select and implement forecasting package.	$200	6	
Supply Performance Metrics	Implement financial, productivity, quality, and response time metrics for supply partners.		3	LS
	Implement productivity metrics for the supply process.		3	LS
Supply Flow Optimization	Determine DSD, XD, and DC flow paths based on total logistics cost and service implications.	$80	9	CAPS
	Determine potential benefits of inbound transportation consolidation, cross-trucking, backhauling, and mini-DCs.		3	CAPS
Collaborative Planning & Supply Chain Scheduling	Meet with key supply partners on an on-going basis to jointly plan logistics schedules and backhaul opportunities.		3	
	Share point-of-sale data with key suppliers.		4	POS
	Integrate continuous replenishment with supplier production scheduling.		6	EDI
	Implement receiving appointment scheduling.		3	WMS EDI
	Establish annual supplier logistics conference.		1	
Transportation				
Transportation Performance Metrics	Implement and institute a formal transportation performance measures program.		3	TS
Optimal, Dynamic Routing	Implement a on-line, real-time, routing optimization software (e.g. Road show, CAPS Logistics, MANUGISTICS, Blast).	$80	6	RS
Roll Cages	Utilize collasible roll cages for order picking and store shelf restocking.		3	
DC Operations				
Pre-Receiving	Eliminate receiving inspection for "green-light" vendors and sample receiving inspection for "yellow-light" vendors.		6	EDI
Slotting Optimization	Implement a PC-based tool for assigning SKUs to storage modes, allocating space with in each mode, and locating an SKU with in the mode.	$40	4	SP
WMS	Analyze WMS requirements beyond SAP capabilities.	$300	3	WMS
Pick and Price	Investigate the costs and benefits and pricing product during the picking process.	$20	3	

equip you to develop a logistics master plan for the organization you are currently working for or will work for in the future.

1.6   LOGISTICS AROUND THE WORLD: NECESSITY IS THE MOTHER OF INVENTION

I have traveled to more than 50 countries. I have noticed during those travels that as in any industry, necessity is the mother of invention in logistics. Logistics conditions around the world are quite unique and in some cases severe. Those conditions—the necessity—force creative logistics solutions —the inventions. Those inventions provide rich lessons in logistics design strategy and logistics management for logistics managers around the world. Because our clients are located throughout North America, South America, Western Europe, and Japan, we are forced to research and document these logistics conditions and the appropriate response. A summary of unique logistics conditions around the world is provided in Table 1-1.

With these solutions in mind, a truly world-class logistics organization would borrow from and have implemented the best of each. With that in mind, a world-class logistics organization would be characterized by

- Extensive use of logistics key performance and financial indicators
- Supply chain integration
- Use of integrated logistics information systems
- Strategic use of logistics service and education providers
- A sense of urgency to leapfrog to world-class status
- Strategic use of third-party logistics providers
- Human-friendly logistics via logistics ergonomics and green logistics
- Order and discipline
- Justifiable use of automated storage and handling systems
- Excellent land and building utilization

We hold our clients accountable to these standards, and you will see a variety of applications of these standards written into and illustrated throughout this text.

Understanding these conditions and the proper strategic response is especially important to U.S. companies. In the United States, we have been spoiled over the years with enough market demand and reasonably priced production capacity to fuel a healthy economic growth. However, we must remember than only 4 percent of the world's population lives in the United States. We may have reached the capacity of our own population to produce and consume products at a rate fast enough to fuel our historical economic

TABLE 1-1   World-Wide Logistics Conditions and Solutions

Region	Logistics Condition(s)	Logistics Solution(s)
North America	• Short-term focus on shareholder return and return on capital • Excellent infrastructure	• Extensive logistics finance and performance measures • Supply chain integration and logistics information systems to reduce capital assets
Latin America	• Limited to no logistics infrastructure and/or logistics service providers	• Leapfrog to world-class status • Import logistics service providers and education • High security designs
Western Europe	• Transportation heritage • Individual rights	• Transportation heritage makes 3PL providers commonplace • Focus on individual rights yields human-friendly logistics via excellent logistics ergonomics and green logistics
Japan	• Lack of land and/or human resources and high logistics transaction requirements	• Logistics culture of discipline and order • Automated storage and handling systems • Multistory logistics facilities

growth. Hence, it is now our time to turn to international markets and sources to fuel our economic growth. Other countries around the world have been playing and excelling at international trade to support their own economic growth. In general, we are behind many other countries in our ability to succeed in international trade and the accompanying global logistics issues. Understanding and tailoring logistics strategies to different regions of the world and the variety of worldwide logistics is one of the keys to success.

S E C T I O N

INVESTIGATING LOGISTICS PERFORMANCE AND PRACTICES

2

LOGISTICS ACTIVITY PROFILING AND DATA MINING

"They will . . . die without knowledge."

Job 36:12

S UPPOSE YOU WERE SICK and went to the doctor for a diagnosis and prescription. When you arrived at the doctor's office, he already had a prescription waiting for you, without even talking to you, let alone looking at you, examining you, or doing blood work. In effect, he diagnosed you with his eyes closed and a random prescription generator. Needless to say, you would not be going back to that doctor for treatment.

Unfortunately, the prescriptions for many sick logistics operations are written and implemented without much examination or testing. For lack of knowledge, lack of tools, and/or lack of time, many logistics reengineering projects commence without any understanding of the root cause of the problems and without exploration of the real opportunities for improvement.

Logistics activity profiling is the systematic analysis of item and order activity. The activity profiling process is designed to quickly identify the root cause of material and information flow problems, to pinpoint major opportunities for process improvements, and to provide an objective basis for project-team decision making.

Logistics activity profiling is the first step in logistics master planning because it is in the initial stages of considering improvements to any activity that we have the greatest opportunity for improvement and the lowest costs of making design changes (see Figure 2-1). In the initial phases of a project, the cost of making a design change is the cost of tearing up a piece of paper or erasing a white board. Later on, the cost to make significant design changes are prohibitive since hardware and software may be installed, and people may have changed positions. In the initial phases of a project, the opportunity for improvement is nearly infinite since there are no set-in-stone commitments to ideas, procedures, or systems. That opportunity for improvement declines rapidly as commitments are made.

Unfortunately, many organizations rush through this phase of a project. Media hype, the pace of change, and the increase in competition make it more and more difficult to be patient in the planning phase of major initiatives. It is a little bit like doing homework before a big exam or practicing before a big game. In the end, however, it is the ones who study the hardest and practice with the most diligence who ace the exam and win the game. A wise prophet once reminded us of the embarrassment suffered by the builder of a castle who failed to count the cost before he started building and was left with a half-finished project.

We will start with some of the major motivations and potential roadblocks to successful profiling. Then we will review a full set of example profiles and their interpretations. The examples will serve to teach the principles of profiling and as an outline for the full set of profiles required for re-engineering logistics. We will finish with the data gathering, data compilation, data analysis, and data presentation process required in profiling.

FIGURE 2-1   **Cost of design changes during a logistics project.**

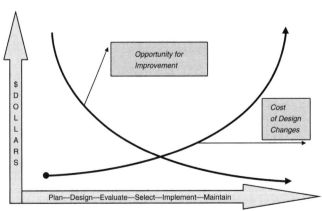

2.1 PROFILING MOTIVATIONS AND MINEFIELDS

Profiling Pays

Done properly, profiling quickly reveals logistics design and planning opportunities that might not naturally be in front of you. Profiling quickly eliminates options that really aren't worth considering to begin with. Many logistics re-engineering projects go awry because we work on a concept that never really had a chance in the first place.

Profiling provides the right baseline to begin justifying new investments. Profiling gets key people involved. During the profiling process, it is natural to ask people from many affected groups to provide data, to verify and rationalize data, and to help interpret results. My partner Hugh Kinney says that, "People will only successfully implement what they design themselves." To the extent people have been involved, they feel that they have helped with the design process.

Finally, profiling permits and motivates objective decision making as opposed to biased decisions made with little or no analysis or justification. I worked with one client whose team leader we affectionately called Captain Carousels. No matter what the data said, no matter what the order and profiles looked like, no matter what the company could afford, we were going to have carousels in the new design. You can imagine how successful that project was!

You Can Drown in a Shallow Lake—On Average!

You will see a lot of complex statistical distributions in our journey through logistics activity profiling. Why go to all the trouble?

Imagine we are trying to determine the average number of items on an order. Suppose we did the analysis based on a random sampling of 100 orders. In Figure 2-2, 50 orders are for one line, zero are for two items, and 50 are for three items. What is the average number of items per order? It's two. How often does that happen? It never happens! If we are not careful to plan and design based on distributions as opposed to averages, the entire planning and design process will be flawed. That is why it is so important to go to the extra step to derive these profile distributions.

Wallowing in the Data Stimulates Creative Thinking

When I write a new article or book, one of the first things I do to stimulate my own thinking is to read what other people have written about the particular topic. If I am preparing to teach a Sunday School class or a seminar, I do the same thing; I review what other people have prepared on the topic to stimulate my thinking and to avoid reinventing the wheel. You know the

FIGURE 2-2   Example items per order distribution.

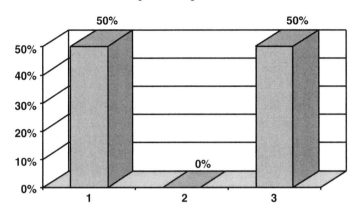

difference between plagiarism and research. Plagiarism is when you borrow from a single author; research is when you borrow from many.

Activity profiling works the same way. As you start to look at the profiles of customer orders, purchase orders, item activity, and inventory levels, the creative juices begin to flow for everyone on the project team. Everyone on the project team starts making good decisions and generating new ideas.

A Picture Is Worth a Thousand Words
When you see a picture of a mother coddling her newborn baby, you experience a thousand simultaneous thoughts. We are aiming for the same effect in logistics activity profiling as we paint a picture of what is going on throughout the supply chain. In profiling, we are trying to capture the activity of logistics in pictorial form so we can present the information to management and so we can make quick consensus decisions as a team.

You Can Drown in Your Own Profiles
One warning before we begin to profile the supply chain (as an engineer and logistics nerd, I fall into this trap a lot): you can drown in your own profiles. Some people call this paralysis of analysis. If you are not careful, you can get so caught up in profiling that you forget to solve the problem. You have to be careful to draw the line and say, *that is enough.*

2.2   LOGISTICS ACTIVITY PROFILES
A logistics activity profile is comprised of the profiles of the flow of material, information, and money in each of the major logistics activities: customer response, inventory management, supply, transportation, and

warehousing. Hence, we outline and define below five corresponding activity profiles:

- Customer activity profile (CAP)
- Inventory activity profile (IAP)
- Supply activity profile (SAP)
- Transportation activity profile (TAP)
- Warehouse activity profile (WAP)

A couple of example profiles are provided in the following sections. A variety of example profiles for each logistics activity are shared within the chapter dedicated to each logistics activity.

Customer Activity Profile

The *customer activity profile* (CAP) captures and illustrates sales activity by customer and by item in dollars, the number of orders, the number of order lines, units, weight, cube, truckloads, pallets, and cases. The customer activity profile is a key ingredient in developing one of the most important elements of a logistics strategy: the customer service policy. Because not all customers and not all items create the same level or type of logistics demand, the logistics strategy should reflect the unique logistics requirements of each customer and each item.

One of the most useful customer activity profiles is the customer-item sales profile (see Figure 2-3). The profile reveals the amount of sales accomplished on A items going to A customers, A items going to B customers . . . C items going to C customers. It highlights the dramatic differences in the logistics activities in different channels of the same enterprise. For example, typically very few customers or items can be found in the AA segment, yet it has high volumes, high revenues, and intense competition. Many customers and items can typically be found in the CC category, yet it is characterized by low volumes, low revenues, and little to no competition. The logistics strategy should reflect these stark contrasts. The tailoring of a logistics strategy along these lines will be one of the key points in Chapter 4, "Customer Response Principles and Systems."

The population, interpretation, and use of customer activity profiles is the subject of Section 4-2, "Customer Activity Profiling."

Inventory Activity Profile

My experience with inventory reduction initiatives is that there is rarely a single, major source of inventory buildups. Instead, inventory piles up in many places for many reasons, some valid and some not. It is a lot like the

FIGURE 2-3   **Example of a customer-item sales activity profile.**

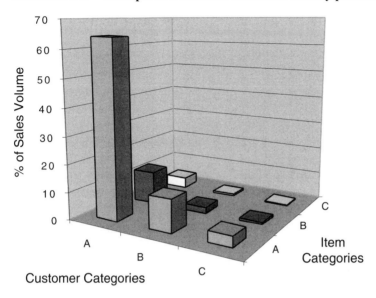

way "stuff" piles up in a house—bits and pieces everywhere, most with very little explanation.

The *inventory activity profile* (IAP) pinpoints the major opportunities to reduce inventory and improve customer service at the same time. It identifies places in the supply chain and/or categories of merchandise where excess has accumulated. The inventory profile reports the turns, days-on-hand, and inventory investment for each item, item category, and vendor for each facility and region, in-transit and in total.

An example inventory activity profile is included in Figure 2-4. The ABC inventory valuation analysis is a little like drilling for oil, in that the analysis helps reveal where the pockets of excess inventory investment have accumulated. The analysis considers A, B, and C *stock-keeping units* (SKUs) purchased domestically and internationally, *cross-docked* (XD) or moved through the warehouse (WHC), and located in-transit, in the warehouse, or in a retail store location. This analysis helps reveal the most significant opportunities for reducing inventory investments.

Inventory activity profiling is also the subject of Section 5.2, "Inventory Activity Profiling." A variety of inventory activity profiles are illustrated and interpreted there.

FIGURE 2-4   **ABC inventory valuation analysis.**

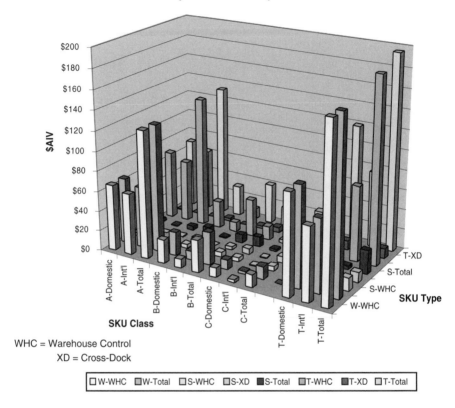

WHC = Warehouse Control
XD = Cross-Dock

□ W-WHC ▨ W-Total □ S-WHC □ S-XD ■ S-Total ▨ T-WHC ■ T-XD □ T-Total

Supply Activity Profile (SAP)

The *supply activity profile* (SAP) reveals opportunities for purchasing improvements by reporting purchasing activity in dollars, units, cases, pallets, truckloads, weight, volume, orders, and order lines by SKU, SKU category, supplier, and supplier location. (Another phrase for supply activity profiling is spend analysis.) The supply activity profile also serves as the basis for categorizing suppliers, supplier rationalization programs, inbound logistics planning, make-buy analysis, and purchase order profiling.

Transportation Activity Profile

The *transportation activity profile* (TAP) reveals opportunities for transportation strategy and process improvements by reporting for each transportation lane the units, cases, pallets, truckloads, weight, volume, and dollars moved in addition to lane statistics on carrier availability, carrier performance, on-time percentage, damage rates, and claims rates. The transportation activity profile is used in carrier rationalization programs, carrier performance measurements, transportation network design, routing and scheduling, and consolidation opportunities assessments. A variety of transportation activity profiles are illustrated and interpreted in Section 7.2, "Transportation Activity Profiling."

Warehouse Activity Profile

The *warehouse activity profile* (WAP) reveals patterns in item activity and customer orders that lead to improvements in storage system design, warehouse layout, and order picking policy design. The warehouse activity profile includes an item activity profile and an order activity profile. The item activity profile reports for each item and item category the requests, units, cases, pallets, dollars, cube, and weight shipped per day, week, month, and year. The item activity profile is used in choosing and designing the storage system and housing for each item. The order activity profile is a distribution of the units, cubes, cases, pallets, dollars, weight, and number of items per order and order type (that is, regular, emergency, and so on). The order activity profile is used in designing order picking and shipping systems. A variety of warehouse activity profiles are presented, explained, and interpreted in Section 8.2, "Warehouse Activity Profiling."

2.3   LOGISTICS DATA MINING

Have you ever wondered how your telephone company knew to call you to offer a new promotion just before you were about to switch to another carrier? At least one carrier, MCI-Sprint, uses a technique called data combing to analyze your calling patterns. Based on those patterns, they can anticipate from your history which pattern has led to a customer switching. When they see those switching patterns emerge, they preempt the switch by devising and offering a custom calling plan. The process of analyzing the calling patterns is data-intensive and is called data mining.

Wal-Mart is another large user of data mining technology. One of the analyses conducted by Wal-Mart via data mining is market basket analysis in which they learn from customer purchases the types of products that a customer is likely to purchase together. One of the most famous results is the sick customer basket that includes orange juice and cough syrup. (If a customer buys cough syrup there is at least a 30 percent chance that they will also buy orange juice.) These types of results can be used strategically in product placement throughout the store to promote cross-selling and/or to promote certain traffic patterns through the store.

We have used the same kind of analysis in designing slotting schemes for distribution center operations. We call it order completion and demand correlation analysis. The item-order completion profile (see Figure 2-5)

FIGURE 2-5   Example of an item-order completion profile.

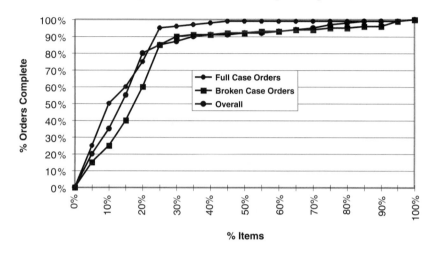

identifies small groups of items that can fill large groups of orders. Those small groups of items can often be assigned to small *order completion zones* in which the productivity, processing rate, and processing quality are two to five times better than that found in a general warehouse.

The design principle is similar to that used in agile manufacturing, where we look for small groups of parts that have similar machine routings. Those machines and those parts make up a small group technology cell wherein the manufacturing efficiency, quality, and cycle time are dramatically improved over those found in the factory as a whole.

I recently worked with a large media distributor of compact discs, cassettes, and videos and helped to identify 5 percent of its 4,000 SKUs, which could complete 35 percent of the orders. We assigned those 5 percent to carton flow rack pods (three flow rack bays per pod and one operator per pod) at the front of the distribution center. Operators could pick-pack orders from the flow rack at nearly six times the overall rate of the distribution center. The distribution center has won its industry's productivity award for the last two years.

The demand correlation profile (see Figure 2-6) indicates the affinity of demand between individual items and between families of items. Just like a minority of the items in a warehouse make up a majority of the picking activity, certain items in the warehouse tend to be requested together. As an example, pairs of items are ranked based on their frequency of appearing together on orders. We are looking for general patterns. Let's say we are examining data from a mail order apparel company. The first three digits represent the style of the item (crew neck sweater, V-neck sweater, turtle neck

FIGURE 2-6   Demand correlation profile (style-size-color) example.

Item Number	Item Number	Pair Frequency
189-2-4	189-2-1	58
493-2-1	493-2-8	45
007-3-3	007-3-2	36
119-2-1	119-2-7	30
999-1-8	999-1-6	22
207-4-2	207-4-24	15
662-1-9	662-1-1	12
339-7-4	879-2-8	9
112-3-8	112-3-4	6

shirt, pleated pants, and so on), the middle digit represents the size of the item (1=small, 2=medium, 3=large, 4=extra large), and the last digit represents the color (1=white, 2=black, 3=red, 4=blue, 5=green).

What do you think people tend to order together from this mail order apparel catalog operator? (I thought it would be shirts and pants that looked good together in the catalog.) What does the distribution in Figure 2-6 suggest? In this case, customers tend to order items of the same style and size together. The explanation is that customers tend to get comfortable with a certain style and tend to order in multiple colors to add variety to their wardrobe. Of course, they order the same size unless they will return one for fitting. This was a surprise to me. More importantly, it was a surprise to the marketing people. That is the most important reason to go through the profiling process—to surface the truth. Unfortunately, our intuition about logistics issues is often off-base. The myriad of SKUs, order patterns, suppliers, and interdependent decisions make it difficult to form reliable intuition about logistics operations.

How do we take advantage of this demand-correlation information in slotting the warehouse? We are looking for the lowest common denominator of correlation, the factor that will create the largest family of items. In this case, it is the size of the item. So, we zone the warehouse by item size first, creating a zone for the smalls, mediums, larges, and extra larges of all styles. Within each size area, we store items of the same style together, mixing colors within a style. This zoning strategy enables us to create picking tours based on size and style. As a result, order pickers can pick many items on short-distance picking tours. At the same time, we will manage congestion by spreading out the sizes. Golden zoning is used to store the most popular color for each style at or near waist level.

Logistics data mining is key to the success of any logistics improvement initiative, but it is normally the activity in a logistics project that our clients are the least enthusiastic about and the internal I/T group is least likely to want to support. To help overcome both barriers, we have developed a streamlined methodology and some Web-based tools to facilitate logistics data mining.

We begin with a standard representation of logistics data warehouse and data mining requirements. Those requirements are presented in Table 2-1. Those data and profile elements also spell out the underlying requirements for the logistics data structure and decision support capabilities. If the I/T group is unable to develop these profiles due to limited resources or technology constraints, we often create the logistics activity profiles for our clients via a Web-based data mining service (see Figure 2-7). Organizations transfer the specified files, and the Web-based tools produce an online logistics activity profile. The profile is updated as often as the client resends the required files. In that role, we are an example of a *logistics application service provider* (LASP). We will talk more about ASPs in the section on Web-based logistics.

FIGURE 2-7   **Web-based logistics data mining and activity profiling.**

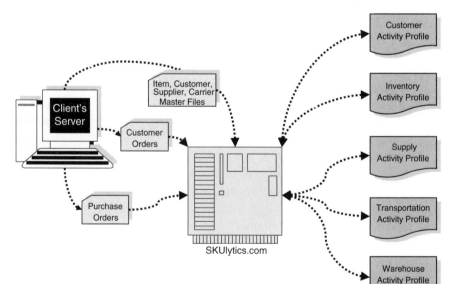

TABLE 2-1 Logistics Activity Profiling, Data Mining, and Data Warehousing Requirements

Profile	Files/Sources	Queries	Profiles	Decisions
Customer Activity Profile	• Customer order, history • POS data • Customer master file • Item master file	• **Sales by customer and customer location** in dollars, pallets, cases, pieces, weight, volume, frequency, orders, lines, deliveries • **Sales by SKU** in dollars, pallets, cases, pieces, weight, volume, lines • **Sales by customer and SKU** in dollars, pallets, cases, pieces, weight, volume	• **Customer activity**: ABC customers by sales and volume • **SKU activity**: ABC SKUs by sales and volume • **Customer-SKU activity**: ABCxABC customers and SKUs by sales and volume • **Customer order profile**: Sales, volume, cube, weight, and lines per order	• Customer response measures • Customer classifications • SKU classifications • Customer-SKU classifications • Customer service policy design
Inventory Activity Profile	• Item master file, snapshots of on-hand inventory • POS data • Customer order file	• **On-hand inventory** in turns, days-on-hand, dollar value, cubes, space, pieces by location and commodity by vendor, SKU popularity, SKU usage, and SKU age • **Forecasting** lead time, demand variability and forecast accuracy by SKU by location	• **Demand variability** by SKU popularity and SKU age • **On-hand inventory** by location and commodity by SKU popularity ranking, SKU age ranking, SKU popularity and age rankings, and vendor rankings	• Inventory management performance measures • SKU categories for inventory management • Inventory turnover and fill rate targets by logistics segments • Forecasting models by SKU category • Inventory reduction opportunities by logistics segment

(continued)

TABLE 2-1 Logistics Activity Profiling, Data Mining, and Data Warehousing Requirements

Profile	Files/Sources	Queries	Profiles	Decisions
Transportation Activity Profile	• Purchase order history file • Supplier master file	• **Purchasing by supplier** and supplier location in dollars, weight, pieces, cases, volume, frequency, orders, lines, deliveries • **Purchasing by SKU** in dollars, cases, pieces, weight, volume, lines • **Purchasing by supplier and SKU** in dollars, pallets, cases, pieces, weight, volume	• **Supplier activity**: ABC by purchase dollars, volume, the number of SKUs • **SKU activity**: ABC by purchasing dollars, volume, frequency • **Supplier-SKU activity**: ABCxABC by purchasing dollars, volume, SKUs • **Purchase order profile**: purchasing, volume, cube, weight, and lines per purchase order	• Supplier performance measures • Supplier categories • SKU categories for supply planning • Supplier-SKU rationalization • Sole versus primary-secondary versus competitive sourcing • Make-buy analysis • Supplier service policy design
Supply Activity Profile	• Shipping manifest history file • Carrier master file • Customer master file • Supplier master file	• **From-to matrix** between all pickup and deliver-to points including frequency, volume, weight, dollar value, carriers, carrier capacity, carrier availability, distance, time, freight paid, on-time delivery, damages, claims	• **Lane activity profile**: ABC lanes by freight dollars, volume, claims • **Carrier activity**: ABC carriers by freight dollars, volume, shipments • **Inbound transportation activity**: ABC by freight dollars, volume, value, frequency	• Transportation performance measures • Logistics hierarchy design • Logistics network design • Inbound freight management • Consolidation design

Profile	Files/Sources	Queries	Profiles	Decisions
Warehouse Activity Profile	• Item master file • Customer order history file • Purchase order history file	• SKU activity by popularity, usage, cases, pallets, cubes, weight • Orders by dollar value, lines, cube, units	• **Outbound transportation activity:** ABC by freight dollars, volume, value, frequency • **Carrier-shipment activity:** ABCxABC by purchasing dollars, volume, SKUs • **Manifest profile:** shipping, volume, cube, weight, and lines per manifest • **Order profile:** lines, cubes, pieces, dollar value, and weight per order distribution • **Lines and cube per order distribution** • **Item activity profile:** ABC SKUs by picks, usage, and volume by SKU • **Item-order completion profile** • **Inbound activity profile**	• Routing and scheduling • Fleet configuration • Mode and carrier selections • Potential roles for third parties • Warehouse performance measures • SKU categories for warehouse master planning • Slotting • Storage mode selection • Order picking policies • Warehouse layout

3

LOGISTICS PERFORMANCE, COST, AND VALUE MEASURES

"You must have accurate and honest weights and measures . . ."

Deuteronomy 25:15

W E OFTEN PLAY A GAME in our seminars called the Question of the Day game. The student who asks the best question during the day receives a special prize. A few months ago Roger with QWEST Communications asked what was perhaps the question of the year. He asked me in our experience with our clients, what is the simplest, least expensive, and least time-consuming initiative an organization can put in place to bring its logistics up to world-class standards? I responded without hesitation that implementing a set of world-class logistics performance indicators is a prerequisite to any organization being able to achieve world-class logistics. The reason is simple: *people behave based on the way they are measured.* World-class measures lead to world-class behaviors.

If you accept that description of human nature, the design and selection of the logistics performance measures dictates the overall performance and practices in logistics. If there are no measures, there will be no performance. If the measures are oriented toward cost reduction, the practices will follow. If the measures are oriented toward service, the practices will be service-oriented. If the measures are balanced between service and cost (and they should be), the practices will follow.

Another aspect of human nature is that *what gets measured gets improved.* That's the good news. The bad news is that if there is not a holistic set of logistics performance measures in place, we may improve the wrong things. We worked recently with a large retail client. The distribution organization was measured on the cost paid per unit to pick and ship each store order. This client had and still has one of the most efficient picking and shipping functions in their industry. One of the practices used to achieve this efficiency was the batching of orders for release to the warehouse floor and the holding of outbound trucks to achieve maximum cube utilization. These practices did yield a low picking and transportation cost. Unfortunately, the store orders were delayed to the point that out of stocks were costing the company more than $300 million per year. A fairly simple restructuring of the picking and shipping schedule recovered the lost sales and had only a minor impact on picking and shipping costs.

It is hard to win a game without a scoreboard. It's hard to even know what game you are playing without a scoreboard. Yet many logistics organizations are run and managed without a formal set of logistics performance measures, let alone a set that is aligned with overall business objectives for cost and service. In fact, a recent study revealed that less than 10 percent of logistics organizations operate with a formal logistics performance measurement program. For those organizations that do have a measurement program in place, many change the measures and/or the targets in mid-stream, essentially nullifying the impact of the metrics. My daughter is famous for playing the same game with my son. If she loses a game of kickball, she concludes that the objective was to score the fewest runs!

One reason so few organizations have or use a logistics scoreboard is the lack of standardization in logistics performance metrics. This chapter and an associated measurement system (the Logistics Scoreboard™) presents a holistic set of logistics performance indicators and provides a framework for collecting and benchmarking logistics performance measures. The defined metrics enable you to see yourself as your customers and constituents see you. In addition to your customers, your stockholders, employees, and suppliers have a major stake in the performance of your logistics system. The published metrics must address their major concerns.

The recommended measures also point to the need for single-point accountability for logistics performance in value, cost, productivity, quality, and time. As a result, the Logistics Scoreboard measurement system also begins to suggest the design for a unified logistics organization.

Because any logistics organization is in competition with their competitor's logistics organization and third-party logistics services, it is critical to hold the logistics organization accountable to business-like performance measures. Since businesses compete on the basis of financial performance (covered in Section 3.1, "Financial Measures of Logistics Performance"), productivity performance (covered in Section 3.2, "Productivity Measures or Logistics Performance"), quality performance (covered in Section 3.3, "Quality Measures of Logistics Performance"), and cycle time performance (covered in Section 3.4, "Cycle Time Measures of Logistics Performance"), our measures fall into those same four categories.

The secondary categorization for the measures is by logistics process. Recall that our definition of logistics includes five interdependent processes: *customer response* (CR), *inventory planning and management* (IP&M), supply, *transportation and distribution* (T&D), and warehousing or *DC operations* (DCO). Our framework for logistics performance measures stems from the four categories of measures and five interdependent processes. The Logistics Scoreboard framework is presented in Table 3-1.

The logistics benchmarking and goal-setting process described here also permits a quantitative assessment of the opportunity for improvement in each *logistics key performance indicator* (LKPI). In addition, our *logistics performance gap analysis* (LPGA) technique (covered in Section 3.5, "Logistics Performance Gap Analysis") yields an estimate of an annual financial benefit related to the quantified opportunity for improvement. With that annual benefit (dollars per year) in hand, and in relation to the corporate required payback period, it is easy to compute an estimate of the affordable investment available for process improvements. This estimate further defines the possible alternatives and resources available for process improvements.

To assist in understanding and implementing a set of logistics performance measures, we are including a checklist summary of the key logistics performance indicators and screen shots from the Logistics Scoreboard™.

3.1 FINANCIAL MEASURES OF LOGISTICS PERFORMANCE

Logistics is playing an increasingly important role in value creation, revenue enhancement, capital consumption, and expense control. As a result, logistics financial performance is playing a bigger role in corporate financial performance. Measuring and improving logistics financial performance is increasingly important in measuring and improving corporate financial performance.

In addition, since logistics is often in competition with other business processes for capital projects, the better the overall financial reporting we do in logistics, the better chance we have to justify our logistics projects.

TABLE 3-1 Logistics Performance Measures Matrix

	Financial Indicators	Productivity Indicators	Quality Indicators	Response Time Indicators
Customer Response	Total response cost Response cost per customer order	Customer orders per person hour	Order entry accuracy Status communication accuracy Invoice accuracy	Order entry time Order processing time
Inventory Planning & Management	Total inventory cost Inventory cost per SKU	Inventory turns SKUs per planner	Fill rate Forecast accuracy	
Supply	Total supply cost Supply cost per PO	POs per person-hour SKUs per nuyer	Perfect PO percentage	Purchase order cycle time
Transportation	Total transportation cost Transportation cost per mile	Stops per route Fleet yield Container capacity utilization	On-time arrival percentage Damage percentage Miles between accidents	In-transit time
Warehousing	Total warehousing cost Warehousing cost per piece Warehousing cost per square foot	Units per person hour Storage density	Inventory accuracy Picking accuracy Shipping accuracy Damage percentage Hours between accidents	Warehouse order cycle time
TOTAL LOGISTICS	**Logistics expenses Logistics profit Logistics asset value Logistics asset turnover Logistics capital charges Total logistics cost Logistics cost-sales ratio Return on logistics assets Logistics value added**	**Perfect orders per logistics FTE**	**Perfect order percentage**	**Total logistics cycle time**

The most important principal to remember in developing and implementing logistics financial performance measures is that nearly every generally accepted corporate financial measure has a corresponding logistics financial measure. Some key corporate financial measures and their corresponding logistics financial measures are described in Table 3-2. Detailed descriptions of each indicator follow in the section below.

Logistics Expenses (LE)
Logistics expenses are dominated by labor expenses but also include telecommunications, inbound and outbound freight, fuel, fees to third parties, and leased or rented space.

Logistics Profit (LP = R − LE)
Logistics profit is computed simply as revenue minus logistics expenses. The computation of logistics profit per item, per category, or per location is helpful in determining the business viability of an item, category, or location.

TABLE 3-2   Logistics Financial Measures

Corporate Financial Measures	Notation	Logistics Financial Measures	Notation
Revenue	R		
Expenses	E	Logistics expenses	LE
Profit	$P = R - E$		
Asset value	AV	Logistics asset value	LAV
Asset turnover	$AT = R/AV$	Logistics asset turnover	$LAT = R/LAV$
Asset carrying rate	ACR		
Corporate capital charges	CCC	Logistics capital charges	$LCC = LAV \times ACR$
Total corporate cost	$TCC = E + CCC$	Total logistics cost (TLC)	$TLC = LE + LCC$
Cost-sales ratio	$CSR = (E+CCC)/R$	Logistics cost-sales ratio	$LCSR = TLC/R$
Return on assets	$ROA = P/AV$	Return on logistics assets	$ROLA = LP/LAV$
Economic value added	$EVA = P - (AV \times ACR)$	Logistics value added	$LVA = P - (LAV \times ACR)$

Logistics Asset Value (LAV)

The *logistics asset value* is the sum total of the value of assets deployed in logistics including inventory, logistics facilities, transportation fleets, material handling systems, logistics information systems, and so on. The valuation is typically based on book value, replacement value, and/or the capitalization of logistics assets. An example of a LAV calculation is provided in Figure 3-1.

Return on Logistics Assets (ROLA = P/LAV)

The *return on logistics assets* is computed simply as the ratio of corporate *profit* (P) to LAV. The ratio can demonstrate the difference between the return on logistics assets versus the return on overall corporate assets or the assets deployed in the other areas of the business.

Logistics Asset Turnover (LAT = R/LAV)

Logistics asset turnover measures the overall utilization of logistics assets and is computed as the ratio of corporate revenue to the investment in logistics assets.

FIGURE 3-1 Logistics asset value analysis.
Source: LRI's Logistics Scoreboard

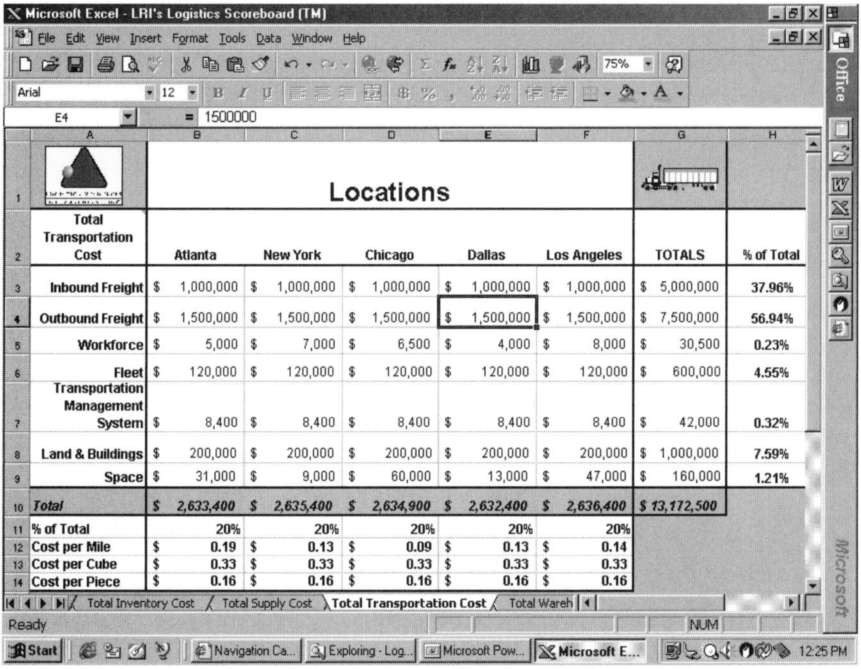

Total Transportation Cost	Atlanta	New York	Chicago	Dallas	Los Angeles	TOTALS	% of Total
Inbound Freight	$ 1,000,000	$ 1,000,000	$ 1,000,000	$ 1,000,000	$ 1,000,000	$ 5,000,000	37.96%
Outbound Freight	$ 1,500,000	$ 1,500,000	$ 1,500,000	$ 1,500,000	$ 1,500,000	$ 7,500,000	56.94%
Workforce	$ 5,000	$ 7,000	$ 6,500	$ 4,000	$ 8,000	$ 30,500	0.23%
Fleet	$ 120,000	$ 120,000	$ 120,000	$ 120,000	$ 120,000	$ 600,000	4.55%
Transportation Management System	$ 8,400	$ 8,400	$ 8,400	$ 8,400	$ 8,400	$ 42,000	0.32%
Land & Buildings	$ 200,000	$ 200,000	$ 200,000	$ 200,000	$ 200,000	$ 1,000,000	7.59%
Space	$ 31,000	$ 9,000	$ 60,000	$ 13,000	$ 47,000	$ 160,000	1.21%
Total	*$ 2,633,400*	*$ 2,635,400*	*$ 2,634,900*	*$ 2,632,400*	*$ 2,636,400*	*$ 13,172,500*	
% of Total	20%	20%	20%	20%	20%		
Cost per Mile	$ 0.19	$ 0.13	$ 0.09	$ 0.13	$ 0.14		
Cost per Cube	$ 0.33	$ 0.33	$ 0.33	$ 0.33	$ 0.33		
Cost per Piece	$ 0.16	$ 0.16	$ 0.16	$ 0.16	$ 0.16		

Logistics Capital Charges (LCC = LAV × ACR)

Logistics capital charges are computed as the product of the investment in logistics assets and the *asset carrying rate* (ACR). The ACR is used to annualize the holding cost of fixed assets.

Total Logistics Cost (TLC = LE + LCC)

Total logistics costs (TLC) is defined to include expense and capital costs in the five logistics processes: customer response, inventory planning and management, supply, transportation, and warehousing. The total logistics costs are made up of the following: *total response cost* (TRC), *total inventory costs* (TIC), *total supply costs* (TSC), *total transportation costs* (TTC), and *total warehousing costs* (TWC).

$$TLC = TRC + TIC + TSC + TTC + TWC$$

An example of a TLC analysis developed for a large grocer is illustrated in Figure 3-2.

Customer response (CR) costs (or *total response costs* [TRC]) include the cost of labor, telecommunications, and space required for the personnel and systems used in order processing and order status communication.

FIGURE 3-2   **Total logistics cost analysis example.**
Source: LRI's Logistics Scoreboard

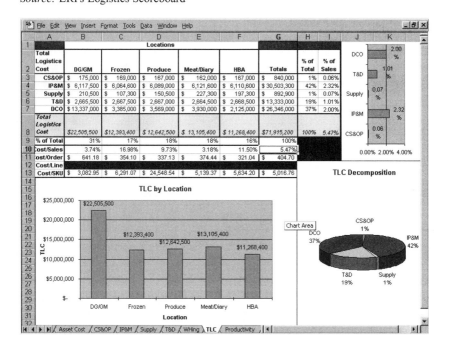

The TIC includes the inventory carrying cost and the cost of personnel, office space, and systems employed in managing inventory. Inventory carrying cost is computed as the product of the *average inventory value* (AIV) and the *inventory carrying rate* (ICR).

$$ICC = AIV \times ICR$$

The ICR is an annual percentage applied to the AIV to estimate inventory carrying charges. The rate includes the opportunity cost of capital (every dollar invested in inventory could theoretically be earning the opportunity interest rate), insurance, taxes, loss, and obsolescence. With this definition, the ICR typically ranges between 10 and 30 percent per year. In addition, storage and warehousing costs may also be included if they are not already being considered as a part of total logistics cost. If warehouse operating costs are included, the ICR typically ranges between 15 and 40 percent. In most cases, corporations underestimate their inventory investment and associated carrying charges. Often, corporations do not even have a standard inventory carrying rate.

The AIV for an item, *i*, should be estimated as the product of the *average inventory level* (AIL) in units and the *unit inventory value* (UIV). The UIV is the investment in or cost of creating each unit of inventory at its current status (raw material, work in process, or finished goods). The UIV is typically the selling price less the margin. The AIV is computed as follows:

$$AIV_i = AIL_i \times UIV_i$$

Total supply costs (TSC) include the cost of labor, space, systems, and telecommunications used in planning, approving, executing, and tracking purchase orders.

Total transportation costs (TTC) include inbound and outbound transportation costs. If the company operates a private fleet, the costs of fueling, maintaining, acquiring, and staffing the fleet must be included. If carriers are used, the freight bills can be used to compute freight transportation costs. An example of TTC calculation is illustrated in Figure 3-3.

Total warehousing costs (TWC) include the cost of labor, space, material-handling systems, and information-handling systems. The cost of labor is simply the product of the *annual working hours* (AWH, hours/year) and the *warehouse wage rate* (WWR, dollars/hour with fringes). The cost of space is the product of the *total floorspace* (TFS, in square feet) and the *space occupancy rate* (SOR, dollars/SF $\times$ year). The cost of material-handling systems is the product of the *material handling systems investment* (MHSI, dollars) and the *systems capitalization rate* (SCR, percent per year). Similarly, the cost of information-handling systems is the product of the

FIGURE 3-3 Total transportation cost analysis.
Source: LRI's Logistics Scoreboard

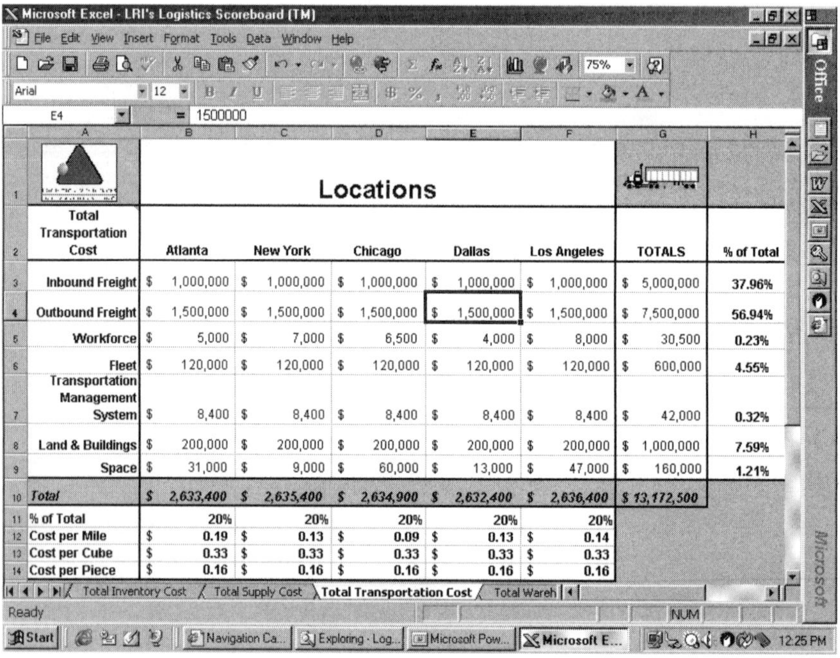

Total Transportation Cost	Atlanta	New York	Chicago	Dallas	Los Angeles	TOTALS	% of Total
Inbound Freight	$ 1,000,000	$ 1,000,000	$ 1,000,000	$ 1,000,000	$ 1,000,000	$ 5,000,000	37.96%
Outbound Freight	$ 1,500,000	$ 1,500,000	$ 1,500,000	$ 1,500,000	$ 1,500,000	$ 7,500,000	56.94%
Workforce	$ 5,000	$ 7,000	$ 6,500	$ 4,000	$ 8,000	$ 30,500	0.23%
Fleet	$ 120,000	$ 120,000	$ 120,000	$ 120,000	$ 120,000	$ 600,000	4.55%
Transportation Management System	$ 8,400	$ 8,400	$ 8,400	$ 8,400	$ 8,400	$ 42,000	0.32%
Land & Buildings	$ 200,000	$ 200,000	$ 200,000	$ 200,000	$ 200,000	$ 1,000,000	7.59%
Space	$ 31,000	$ 9,000	$ 60,000	$ 13,000	$ 47,000	$ 160,000	1.21%
Total	*$ 2,633,400*	*$ 2,635,400*	*$ 2,634,900*	*$ 2,632,400*	*$ 2,636,400*	*$ 13,172,500*	
% of Total	20%	20%	20%	20%	20%		
Cost per Mile	$ 0.19	$ 0.13	$ 0.09	$ 0.13	$ 0.14		
Cost per Cube	$ 0.33	$ 0.33	$ 0.33	$ 0.33	$ 0.33		
Cost per Piece	$ 0.16	$ 0.16	$ 0.16	$ 0.16	$ 0.16		

information-handling systems investment (IHSI, dollars) and the SCR. An example of warehousing cost calculation is presented in Figure 3-4.

Logistics Cost-Sales Ratio (LCSR = TLC/R)

The *logistics cost-sales ratio* is the ratio of TLC to corporate revenue. TLC as a percentage of sales is a popular measure of logistics cost performance. A representative sample of logistics cost ratios for a variety of industries is shown in Figure 3-5.

Some other helpful unit costs are the *logistics cost per order* (LCPO), the *logistics cost per line* (LCPL), and the *logistics cost per item* (LCPI). The ratios are computed simply as the ratio of TLC to the *orders shipped per year* (OPY), the *lines shipped per year* (LPY), and the number of items (or SKUs) stocked (NIS). The equations for each of these costs are shown here:

$$LCPO = TLC / OPY$$

$$LCPL = TLC / LPY$$

$$LCPI = TLC / NIS$$

FIGURE 3-4   Total warehousing cost calculation example.
Source: LRI's Logistics Scoreboard

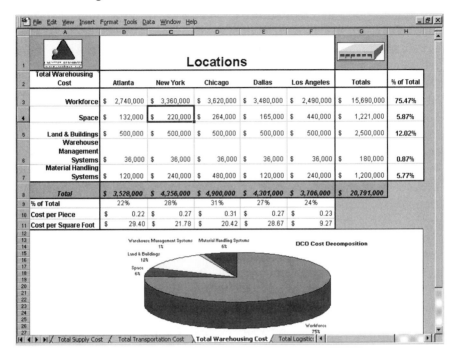

FIGURE 3-5   Logistics costs as a percentage of sales for various industries.
Source: Herb Davis & Associates

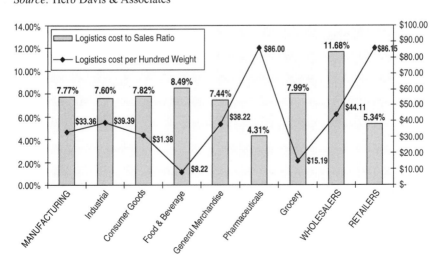

Unfortunately there is no large database providing industry norms for these three cost ratios.

Though popular, these logistics cost ratios can be misleading. First, there may be large swings in the denominator. Sales, orders, lines, and/or the number of stocking units may increase/decrease dramatically indicating large reductions/increases in the ratios, which may have little to do with improvements in logistics performance or practices. Second, logistics managers and engineers have little or no influence on some of the major elements of the cost equation, including wage rates, occupancy rates, inventory carrying rates, and system capitalization rates. Hence, large increases/decreases in those factors may show large increases/decreases in cost without any real improvement in logistics performance and/or practices. Third, the ratios do not consider the major customer service indicators: inventory availability and response time. Hence, improvements in cost ratios can come at the expense of customer service. These ratios cannot be used in isolation to measure and monitor logistics performance. Instead, these measures can and should be used in combination with productivity and service indicators to present a comprehensive and meaningful picture of the state of logistics performance in an organization.

Logistics Value Added (LVA = P − LCC)

Logistics value added is computed in similar fashion to the *economic value added* (EVA) of a corporation, subtracting logistics capital charges from after-tax profitability. Since EVA is the most reliable predictor of future shareholder value (according to Stern-Stewart), LVA is an excellent measure of the contribution of logistics to future shareholder value. In addition, by incorporating the impact on revenue, expenses, and capital charges, LVA is a good indicator of the overall value of logistics initiatives. A summary presentation of logistics financial indicators is provided in Figure 3-6.

3.2 PRODUCTIVITY MEASURES OF LOGISTICS PERFORMANCE

A danger in focusing too much attention on logistics costs is that certain cost elements cannot be controlled by logistics managers and engineers. For example, logistics managers have limited control over some of the major cost factors, including wage rates, fuel costs, occupancy cost, inventory carrying rates, and systems capitalization rates. Instead, logistics managers have direct control over the amount of inventory in the system, the amount of working hours expended, the amount of occupied space, and the number of transportation miles traveled. Essentially, logistics managers and analysts have influence over the amount of logistics resources consumed in providing target customer service levels (see Figure 3-7). Hence, a fair set of per-

FIGURE 3-6   **Logistics financial performance analysis.**
Source: LRI's Logistics Scoreboard

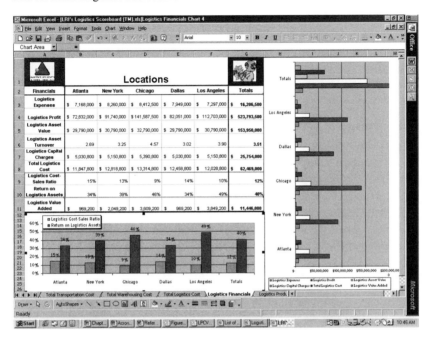

FIGURE 3-7   **An input-output perspective on logistics productivity.**

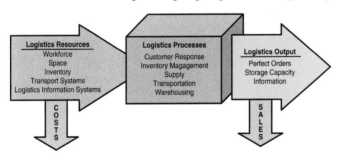

formance indicators will include measures of logistics resource utilization and productivity. Those measures are the focus of this section, which describes utilization and productivity measures for the logistics workforce, transportation capacity, logistics facilities, and inventory.

The productivity of a specified resource(s) is generically measured as the ratio of the output of the resource(s) to the consumption of the resource(s):

$$\text{Productivity}_r = \text{Output}_r / \text{Consumption}_r$$

The utilization of a specified resource(s) is generically measured as the ratio of the output of the resource(s) to the capacity of the resource:

$$\text{Utilization}_r = \text{Output}_r / \text{Capacity}_r$$

A recommended set of key logistics productivity and resource utilization measures is outlined in Table 3-3. The table reports the recommended measures by logistics process.

More detailed descriptions of the indicators follow.

Logistics Workforce Productivity Indicators

The logistics workforce includes the operators, supervisors, planners, analysts, and managers employed in customer response, inventory planning and management, supply, transportation, and warehousing.

The principle mission of the logistics workforce is order fulfillment. Hence, the output of the logistics workforce is typically measured in orders. The consumption unit for the logistics workforce is typically measured as the number of *full-time equivalents* (FTEs) and/or working hours. As a result,

TABLE 3-3   Logistics Productivity Indicators

Process	Output	Resource	Productivity Indicator
Customer response	Customer orders processed	Person-hours	Customer orders per person-hour
Inventory planning and management	Sales	Investment in inventory	Inventory turnover
	SKUs	IP&M headcount	SKUs per head
Supply	Purchase orders placed	Person-hours	Purchase orders per person-hour
	SKUs	SUPPLY headcount	SKUS per head
Transportation	Volume occupied	Volume availability	Vehicle utilization
	Sales shipped	Fleet investment	Fleet yield
Warehousing	Inventory on hand	Square footage	Storage density = inventory per square foot
	Units shipped	Person-hours	Units per person-hour

logistics workforce productivity (LWFP) is computed as the ratio of the *total orders shipped* (TOS) to the number of full-time equivalents working in logistics (LWF):

$$\text{LWFP} = \text{TOS} / \text{LWF}$$

Two popular variants on this indicator are the *logistics hours per order* (LHPO) and the *sales per logistics employee* (SPLE). The LHPO is computed as the ratio of the number of hours worked in logistics to the total orders shipped. This is the inverse of LWFP with the consumption of the logistics workforce measured in hours as opposed to FTEs. The indicator is an effective benchmark for determining the labor requirements and *labor cost per order* (LCPO). LHPO and LCPO are calculated as follows:

$$\text{LHPO} = (\text{LWF} \times \text{FHPY}) / \text{TOS}$$
$$\text{LCPO} = \text{LHPO} \times \text{LWR}$$

The deployment of electronic commerce technologies and paperless logistics should dramatically reduce the LHPO, and this measure can be used in the justification of those technologies.

The *sales per logistics employee* (SPLE) is computed as the total sales revenue divided by the number of FTEs in the logistics workforce:

$$\text{SPLE} = \text{TSR} / \text{LWF}$$

Customer Response (CR) Productivity Indicators
The primary productivity indicator for CR is the number of customer orders processed per person-hour. Through customer service automation methods, including Internet ordering, EDI, automated contact management, call center automation, and/or touchtone ordering, the productivity and quality of CR can be improved.

Inventory Management Productivity
The most popular indicators for inventory management productivity are inventory turnover and the productivity of the inventory planners. The productivity of the inventory planners is computed simply as the number of SKUs planned per planner. Inventory turnover computations are more varied and sophisticated.

Since the output of inventory is sales and the consumption is investment, by far the most popular measure of inventory productivity is *inventory turnover* (IT). IT may be computed as the ratio of *total sales revenue at cost*

(TSR) to the *average inventory value* (AIV) or the *total unit sales* (TUS) to the *average inventory level* (AIL):

$$IT = TSR / AIV$$
$$IT = TUS / AIL$$

IT may be computed for a facility, a country, a supplier, or globally:

Supply Productivity

Supply productivity measures are focused on the buying and procurement organization. Three common measures of supply productivity are

- The number of purchase orders per person-hour
- The number of SKUs managed per full-time-equivalent
- The dollar value managed per full-time-equivalent in procurement

Transportation Productivity

The principal output of transportation is delivered dollars, orders, weight, and/or cubic volume. The principal resources consumed in transportation are operating (vehicle and/or driver) hours, container capacity, and fuel. (These resources are of principal concern if the corporation operates a private fleet.) The useful productivity ratios resulting from these inputs and outputs relate in ratio the delivered dollars, orders, pounds, or cubic volume to the available operating hours, cubic capacity, weight capacity, or fuel. Table 3-4 is a table of helpful transportation productivity ratios.

Warehouse Operations Productivity

The principal missions of a logistics facility (warehouses, distribution centers, logistics centers, and/or terminals) are throughput and storage. The principal resource consumed in achieving the throughput mission is the labor and systems deployed in material handling. The overall labor productivity for a distribution center is computed as the ratio of the number of units processed per year to the number of person-hours consumed per year.

For material-handling systems, we measure consumption as the annualized investment cost in material-handling systems. The annualized *material handling systems investment* (MHSI) is estimated by multiplying the estimated replacement cost of MHSI by the *systems capitalization rate* (SCR). The principal material-handling output is the number of units and/or weight moved. The *material handling unit cost* (MHUC) is computed as a ratio of the annualized investment in material handling systems to the *total units moved* (TUM) measured in pallets, cases, containers, and/or pieces):

$$MHUC = (MHSI \times SCR) / TUM$$

TABLE 3-4   Transportation Productivity Ratios

Resource	Input	Output	Productivity Ratio	Utilization Indicator
Vehicle operators	Operating hours	Delivered dollars, orders, pounds, cube	Dollars per hour, orders per hour, pounds per hour, cube per hour	Percent of time in value-added activities
Vehicles	Operating hours	Delivered dollars, orders, pounds, cube	Dollars per hour, orders per hour, pounds per hour, cube per hour	Percent of time in value-added activities
Containers	Weight capacity, cube capacity	Delivered dollars, orders, pounds, cube	Dollars per available lb. or CF, orders per available lb. or CF	Weight capacity utilization, Cube capacity utilization
Fuel	Gallons	Delivered dollars, orders, pounds, cube	Dollars per gallon, orders per gallon, pounds per gallon, CF per gallon	Percent of empty miles, percent of idle time

The reason we have storage space is to house inventory, and the principal consumed resource is floorspace. Hence, space productivity, often referred to as *storage density* (SD), is computed as the ratio of the AIV or AIL- to- *total floorspace* (TFS). Ideally, the AIL is expressed in a common material handling unit of measure such as pallets or cases.

$$SD = AIV / TFS$$
$$SD = AIL / TFS$$

Logistics Productivity Gap Analysis

Once a set of logistics productivity indicators have been developed, we use logistics productivity gap analysis to compare the overall logistics productivity of an organization with world-class standards. In addition, by incorporating wage rates, occupancy rates, transportation rates, and inventory carrying rates, we compute the annual benefit of closing the gap with world-class productivity performance. An example follows.

Figure 3-8 illustrates the logistics productivity gaps for a major food manufacturer. Each axis represents one key performance indicator. A score of 5 represents world-class performance, or an A on the logistics productivity report card. A score of 3 represents middle-class performance, or a C on the logistics productivity report card. A score of 1 represents no-class performance, or a failing grade.

FIGURE 3-8   Logistics productivity gap analysis.

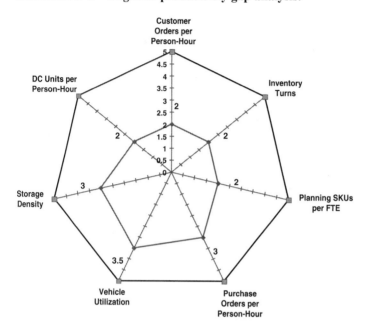

The specific benchmarks, the annual benefit associated with closing the gap and project justification, are computed in Table 3-5.

3.3 QUALITY MEASURES OF LOGISTICS PERFORMANCE

How do you measure logistics quality? Unfortunately, no industry standard exists for doing so. In fact, so many different measures are available that many managers have given up trying. The issue is so complex that universities around the country have entire research projects devoted to identifying the right set of logistics accuracy indicators.

In our experience, the most effective indicator of logistics accuracy or quality is the *perfect order percentage* (POP), which ties together the indices for logistics quality in each of the logistics activities. The perfect order percentage and its components are defined in the following section.

Perfect Order Percentage (POP)

According to the *American Heritage Dictionary*, accurate means deviating only slightly or within acceptable limits from a standard (accuracy is the quality or state of being accurate.) Logistics encompasses customer service, inventory planning, manufacturing and procurement, transportation, and warehousing. Defining the right measurement focus, defining the right

TABLE 3-5 Logistics Project Justification Using Logistics Productivity Gap Analysis

	Customer Orders per Person-Hour	Inventory Turns	Planning SKUs per FTE	Purchase Orders per Person-Hour	Vehicle Utilization	Storage Density	DC Units per Person-Hour
Annual Volume	300,000 orders	$700,000,000 sales/year	23,000 SKUs	47,000 POs	3,500 loads/year	35,000 pallets on-hand	1,200,000 cases/year
Current Performance	40 orders/PH	3 turns/year	1,000 SKUs/FTE	22 POs/PH	0.82 vehicle utilization	8 SF/pallet	12 cases/PH
Current Resource Requirement	7,500 person-hours	$233,333,333 $on-hand	23 FTEs	2,136 person-hours	4,268 loads	280,000 square feet	100,000 person-hours
World-Class Performance	50 orders/PH	5 turns/year	1,500 SKUs/FTE	30 POs/PH	0.95 vehicle utilization	5 SF/pallet	20 cases/PH
World-Class Resource Requirement	6,000 person-hours	$140,000,000 $on-hand	15 FTEs	1,567 person-hours	3,684 loads	175,000 square feet	60,000 person-hours
Resource Savings	1,500 person-hours	$93,333,333 $on-hand	8 FTEs	570 person-hours	584 loads	105,000 square feet	40,000 person-hours
Rate	$30 $/PH	30% % per year	$60,000 $/year	$30 $/PH	3,000 $/load	$25 $/SF*year	$25 $/PH
Annual Savings	$45,000	$28,000,000	$480,000	$17,091	$1,752,246	$2,625,000	$1,000,000

Total Savings ($s/year)	$33,899,337
Payback Period (Years)	2
Justifiable Investment	$67,798,675

55

standard, and defining the acceptable limits of deviation from the standard for an integrated set of activities as broad as logistics are complex tasks.

Let's consider each issue in turn. First, the right measurement focus. The link and common deliverable of customer service, inventory planning, manufacturing and procurement, transportation, and warehousing is an order. Logistics exists to fill orders. Second, the standard. The standard has to be perfection; otherwise, the pursuit of the standard will not yield the order of magnitude improvements needed in all areas of logistics. The focus—an order—the standard: perfection. Alas, the perfect order. The perfect order is logistically perfect, meaning it is

- Perfectly *entered* (the entry is exactly what the customer wants) by the means (telephone or direct entry) the customer desired in a single entry
- Perfectly *fillable* with the exact quantity of each item available for delivery within the customer-specified delivery window
- Perfectly *picked* with the correct quantities of the correct items
- Perfectly *packaged* with the customer-designated packaging and labelling
- Perfectly *shipped* without damage
- Perfectly *delivered* in the customer-designated time window and to the customer-designated location
- Perfectly *communicated* with order status reports available 24 hours a day
- Perfectly *billed* with on-time payment
- Perfectly *documented* with customer-specified documentation means, including paper, fax, EDI, and/or Internet

Suppose each of these nine logistics activities were performed correctly (assuming performance-independence) 90 percent of the time. Then more than 60 percent of the orders would be *imperfect*. If each of these activities were performed correctly 95 percent of the time, 40 percent of the orders would be imperfect. If each of the activities were performed correctly 99 percent of the time, 10 percent of the orders would be imperfect. If each of these activities were performed correctly 99.95 percent of the time, then 0.5 percent of the orders would be imperfect.

To get an idea of your own perfect order percentage, take the product of your performance in each area you define as making up perfect order performance. Formally, with P_n, the performance in one of n elements of perfect order performance, the POP is computed as

$$POP = \Pi_{(n = 1 \text{ to } N)} P_n$$

FIGURE 3-9 Perfect order percentage calculations.

Source: LRI's Logistics Scoreboard

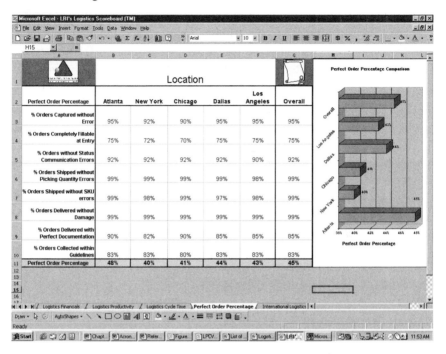

An example of a POP for a logistics organization is provided in Figure 3-9. Many lessons can be learned in this little exercise. First, you may not even track performance in the nine activities described earlier. It is difficult to improve something that you don't measure. Second, you may not recognize the interdependence of these logistics activities. They all contribute to the ultimate logistics objective of filling a customer order perfectly. In fact, POP can only be as high as the lowest performance in its composite elements. Third, you may not believe how low the number is. Most of our clients have a POP lower than 50 percent. If you want to know why your customers always seem dissatisfied, here's the reason. Imagine walking into your boss's office and telling him or her that you got less than half the orders right last month. What kind of conversation would that be? Very short or the last one.

Unfortunately, very little data exists on perfect order performance. Admittedly, it is difficult because so many parties are involved in perfect order performance, including suppliers, manufacturers, wholesalers, inventory planners, carriers, and third-party logistics companies. But that is the point. To deliver a perfect order requires integrated and coordinated performance by and across all of these parties. World-class logistics requires this same degree of integration and coordination. The first step to improving something is to measure it. Do you measure perfect order performance? If so, what is your performance? If not, why not?

The POP is a composite index of the quality performance in each of the five interdependent logistics activities. We review some of the key quality measures for each logistics process in the following section.

Customer Response (CR) Quality Measures

The principal indicators of quality in *customer response* (CR) are

$$\text{Order entry accuracy (OEA)} = \frac{\text{Orders entered exactly as specified by the customer}}{\text{Total orders entered}}$$

$$\text{Order status communication accuracy} = \frac{\text{Orders for which order status is communicated correctly}}{\text{Total orders with status communication requests}}$$

$$\text{Invoice accuracy} = \frac{\text{Invoices with perfect match of items, quantities, prices, and totals}}{\text{Total invoices}}$$

Inventory Management Quality Measures

The two most important indicators of inventory management quality are inventory availability (typically referred to as fill rate) and a related measure, forecast accuracy.

Fill Rate   Inventory availability performance is typically expressed as the demand fill rate. Fill rate can be expressed as the line, order, and/or unit fill rate. In each case, the fill rate measures the ratio of satisfied to total demand. The *line fill rate* (LFR) is the ratio of the number of order *lines completely satisfied* (LS) to the total order *lines requested* (LR):

$$\text{LFR} = \text{LS} / \text{LR}$$

The *order fill rate* (OFR) is the ratio of the number of *orders completely satisfied* (OS) without substitution or backorder to the number of *orders requested* (OR):

$$\text{OFR} = \text{OS} / \text{OR}$$

The *unit fill rate* (UFR) is the ratio of the *total units shipped* (TUS) to the *total units requested* (TUR):

$$UFR = TUS / TUR$$

In each case, the fill rate can be measured as the *first-time-fill-rate* (FTFR), which assesses the fill rate upon initial demand, or the *secondary fill rate* (SFR) achieved via substitutions and backorders. Unless stated otherwise, all references to the fill rate here will be to first-time fill rate.

If you only know one of the fill rate measures, the other two can be estimated as follows. The LFPR can be estimated by raising the UFR to the average *units per line* (upl) power. The OFR can be estimated by raising the LFR to the average *lines per order* (lpo) power. Formally, it is as follows:

$$LFR = UFR^{upl}$$
$$OFR = LFR^{lpo}$$

A summary of fill rate calculations is provided in Table 3-6.

Forecast Accuracy   The most popular measures of forecast accuracy are the algebraic deviation and percentage, the absolute deviation mean and percentage, and the standard deviation of forecast errors.

The measures related to the algebraic are as follows:

Algebraic deviation = Forecast demand − Actual demand
Algebraic deviation percentage = Algebraic deviation/actual demand

Absolute deviation = Forecast demand − Actual demand
Absolute deviation percentage = Absolute deviation/actual demand

Mean absolute deviation (MAD) =
Sum of absolute deviations over N periods/N

Mean absolute deviation percentage =
Sum of absolute deviation percentages over N periods/N

The standard deviation of forecast errors is often estimated as $1.25 \times$ MAD [Silver].

TABLE 3-6   **Fill Rate Calculations**

Measure	Definition	Conversion
Unit fill rate (UFR)	Units shipped/ Units requested	
Line fill rate (LFR)	Lines shipped complete/ Lines requested	$LFR = UFR^{upl}$
Order fill rate (OFR)	Orders shipped complete/ Orders requested	$OFR = LFR^{lpo}$

Some sample forecast accuracy computations follow in Table 3-7.

Supply Quality Indicators   Just like the perfect order percentage is the best indicator for our logistics quality, its counterpart, the *perfect purchase order percentage* (PPOP) is the best indicator of overall supply quality. The PPOP is computed just like the POP.

Transportation Quality Indicators   The most important transportation quality indicators for our own or for our carrier's fleet are the *on-time arrival percentage* (OTAP), *damage percentage* (DP), *claims-free shipment percentage* (CFSP), and *miles between accidents* (MBA).

$$\text{On-time arrival percentage} = \frac{\text{Orders arriving within agreed time window}}{\text{Total orders}}$$

$$\text{Damage percentage} = \frac{\text{Orders arriving without in-transit damage}}{\text{Total orders}}$$

$$\text{Claims-free shipment percentage} = \frac{\text{Shipments without claims}}{\text{Total shipments}}$$

$$\text{Miles between accidents} = \frac{\text{Total miles driven}}{\text{Number of accidents}}$$

These indicators can be summarized similar to the perfect order percentage to develop a perfect delivery percentage, the percent of deliveries arriving on-time without damage, claims, or accidents. One step further gets us to the perfect route percentage, the percentage of routes with 100-percent perfect deliveries.

Warehouse Operations Quality Indicators
The most critical quality indicators for DC operations are inventory accuracy, picking accuracy, shipping accuracy, and warehouse damage percentage.

$$\text{Inventory accuracy} = \frac{\text{Number of warehouse locations without discrepancies}}{\text{Total number of warehouse locations}}$$

TABLE 3-7 Example Forecast Accuracy Computations

Family	Actual Demand	Actual Mix%	Forecast	Forecast Mix %	Mix Error%	Algebraic Deviation	Absolute Deviation	MAD%
Housewares	$ 21,230	11	$ 24,100	10	−1	$ 2,870	$ 2,870	14
Sporting Goods	$ 13,150	7	$ 21,690	9	2	$ 8,540	$ 8,540	65
Paint Products	$ 19,300	10	$ 19,280	8	−2	$(20)	$20	0
Lumber	$ 7,720	4	$ 4,820	2	−2	$(2,900)	$ 2,900	38
Fasteners	$ 17,370	9	$ 26,510	11	2	$ 9,140	$ 9,140	53
Lawn & Garden	$ 34,740	18	$ 50,610	21	3	$15,870	$15,870	46
Tools	$ 28,950	15	$ 31,330	13	−2	2,380	$ 2,380	8
Electrical	$ 17,370	9	$ 19,280	8	−1	$ 1,910	$ 1,910	11
Plumbing	$ 15,440	8	$ 24,100	10	2	$ 8,660	$ 8,660	56
Heating	$ 17,370	9	$ 19,280	8	−1	$ 1,910	$ 1,910	11
Total	**$192,640**	**100**	**$241,000**	**100**	**0**	**$48,360**	**$54,200**	**25**

Tracking Signal: 8.92

Average MAD: 30

61

Picking accuracy =

$$\frac{\text{Number of lines picked without errors}}{\text{Total number of lines picked}}$$

Shipping accuracy =

$$\frac{\text{Number of lines shipped without errors}}{\text{Total number of lines shipped}}$$

Warehouse damage percentage =

$$\frac{\text{\$ Value of warehouse damages per year}}{\text{\$ Value shipped per year}}$$

3.4   CYCLE TIME MEASURES OF LOGISTICS PERFORMANCE

The *total logistics cycle time* (TLCT) includes *order entry time* (OET), *order processing time* (OPT), *purchase order cycle time* (POCT), if the product is not available from stock), *warehouse order cycle time* (WOCT), and *in-transit time* (ITT).

$$TLCT = OET + OPT + [POCT \times (1\text{-}OFR)] + WOCT + ITT$$

OET is the elapsed time from order placement until completed order entry and capture for processing. For orders received by mail, the order entry time includes ITT, waiting time for order entry, and OET. For orders received by fax, the OET includes fax transmission time, waiting time for order entry, and the keying and/or scanning time for order entry. For orders received by phone, the OET includes the waiting time for the customer, the conversation time, and the keying time for the order entry specialist. For orders received electronically, the OET is reduced to the transmission time for the order. A typical range of OETs by order type is provided in Figure 3-10.

The OPT clock starts when the order is entered in and captured by the order processing system and stops when the order is released to the warehouse (or factory) for picking. The OPT includes the time to verify customer information, verify for credit clearance, batch for schedule for release, and dwell for release to the warehouse for assembly.

The POCT is simply the customer order cycle time you receive from your supplier. The POCT clock starts when you place your order with your supplier and stops when the order is received at your designated location. POCT is included in the TLCT when the product is not available from stock.

FIGURE 3-10   Typical range of order entry times.

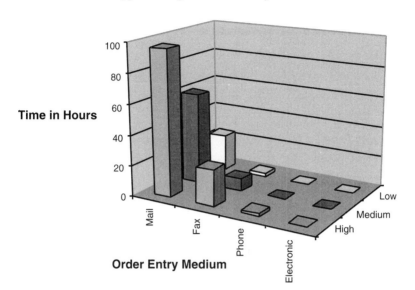

The WOCT clock starts when the order is released to the warehouse management system and stops when the order is picked, packed, and staged for shipping. The WOCT includes the time to schedule, pick, assemble, pack, and stage the order for shipping.

The ITT clock starts when the order is ready for shipping and stops when the order is delivered at the customer's designated location. ITT includes waiting for loading, travel time, and unloading time at the customer site.

3.5   LOGISTICS PERFORMANCE GAP ANALYSIS

Our methodology for logistics performance gap analysis brings together the key logistics performance indicators in cost, productivity, quality, and cycle time, and permits a single-view comparison across those indicators. The gap analysis typically spans financial, productivity, quality, and response time indicators, including the logistics cost-sales ratio, logistics workforce productivity, inventory turnover, storage density, fill rate, logistics cycle time, and the perfect order percentage. An example gap analysis is provided in Figure 3-11.

The logistics performance gap analysis is a formal way to assess logistics performance relative to world-class standards, industry norms, competitors, and/or internal organizations. Logistics performance gap analysis

FIGURE 3-11   Logistics performance gap analysis.

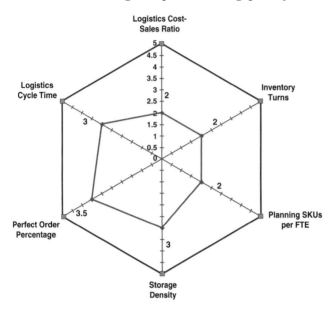

can be used to (1) identify logistics strengths and weaknesses in logistics audits, (2) benchmark performance versus internal and external organizations, (3) select from among competing vendor proposals, and/or (4) justify logistics projects.

Logistics Audits
The logistics performance gap analysis can be used to highlight logistics' strengths and weaknesses. We begin most logistics consulting engagements with a formal logistics audit to quantify the opportunity for improvement and to prioritize the initiatives in logistics process improvements. True world-class performers are strong in all areas with scores between 3 and 5 in every area. Middle-class performers are typically strong (3 to 5) in cost/productivity and weak (1 to 3) in service indicators (efficiency-oriented), or weak (1 to 3) in cost/productivity and strong (3 to 5) in service indicators (service-oriented). No-class performers, weak (1 to 3) in all areas, may not be in business much longer. Figure 3-12 illustrates this classification of logistics organizations.

Logistics Benchmarking
Benchmarking is a means to set the standards for the outer limits of the gap chart. (A benchmark is typically a quantitative assessment of some aspect

FIGURE 3-12   Logistics organization cost-service classification.

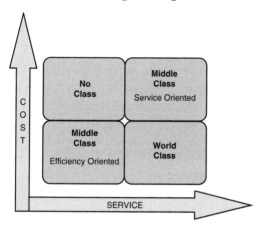

of performance of an enterprise.) Benchmarking is the process of gathering and sharing those assessments and developing an improvement plan of action based on the assessment. The process of benchmarking was popularized by the Xerox Corporation in the late 1980s and has been successfully applied to a variety of business functions and industries. The process is a key component of total quality management, and there now exists an International Benchmarking Clearinghouse supported by over 100 major corporations.

Logistics performance gap analysis can be used to compare and benchmark the performance of internal and/or external organizations. Ideal logistics benchmarking partnerships are formed between logistically similar organizations with offsetting strengths and weaknesses. An example of organizations with offsetting strengths is illustrated in Figure 3-13. With offsetting strengths, the organizations can share their methods for achieving excellence to help close the gaps for each organization. When weaknesses overlap, there is very little to be learned.

Logistically similar organizations are not necessarily in the same industry, but may have similar logistics profiles, including approximately the same number of SKUs, similar order profiles, similar success criteria, and similar operating scales. For example, one of the most successful logistics benchmarking partnerships was formed between the logistics organizations in L.L. Bean and Xerox service parts. Both carry tens of thousands of SKUs, both have approximately two lines per order, both place high priority on individual customers/technicians, and both operate logistics facilities in excess of 200,000 square feet.

FIGURE 3-13 Logistics performance gap analysis with offsetting strengths and weaknesses.

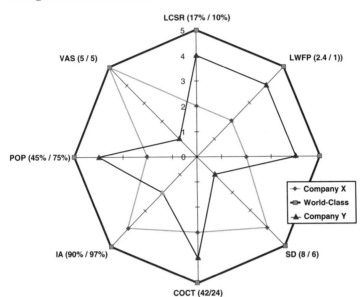

Logistics Project Justification

Another powerful use of logistics performance gap analysis is in logistics project justification. In each of the key performance indicators, a cost savings/avoidance and/or a revenue generation can be associated. By considering the annual benefit (cost savings and/or avoidance plus net revenue increases) of moving each indicator to or near world-class, an estimate of the total annual benefit of a world-class logistics initiative can be determined. With that in hand, and with the predetermined required payback period, the justifiable investment in a world-class logistics initiative can be computed. For example, suppose the annual benefit of moving to world-class performance was $24,000,000/year. If the company had a 2-year payback requirement, the company could justify an investment of up to $48,000,000. That investment is typically required to cover new logistics information systems, new material handling systems, new logistics facilities, associated professional fees, and training.

Another technique we use for logistics project justification is based on logistics cost ratios and assumes no erosion of customer service as cost reductions are implemented. The technique is illustrated on the following page where, based on specified initiatives in customer response, inventory

FIGURE 3-14   Logistics project justification analysis.

	1995 Annualized Logistics Costs	1996 Projected with Current Logistics Practices	1996 Projected with Improved Logistics Practices	1997 Projected with Current Logistics Practices	1997 Projected with Improved Logistics Practices	1998 Projected with Current Logistics Practices	1998 Projected with Improved Logistics Practices	3 Year Savings by Cost Category
CS&OP Total	$ 3.0	$ 3.9	$ 3.9	$ 5.1	$ 4.2	$ 6.6	$ 5.5	
CS&OP/Revenue	0.6%	0.5%	0.5%	0.6%	0.5%	0.6%	0.5%	
Annual CS&OP Savings			$ 0.65		$ 0.85		$ 1.10	$ 2.59
Transportation Total	$ 13	$ 17	$ 14	$ 22	$ 15	$ 28	$ 16	
Transportation/Revenue	2.6%	2.6%	2.2%	2.6%	1.8%	2.6%	1.5%	
Annual Transportation Savings			$ 3		$ 7		$ 12	$ 22
Inventory Carrying Cost Total	$ 65	$ 85	$ 75	$ 110	$ 85	$ 143	$ 93	
Inventory Carrying/Revenue	13.0%	13.0%	11.5%	13.0%	10.0%	13.0%	8.5%	
Annual Inventory Carrying Cost Savings			$ 10		$ 25		$ 49	$ 85
DC Operations	$ 4	$ 5	$ 5	$ 7	$ 4	$ 9	$ 5	
DC/Revenue	0.8%	0.8%	0.7%	0.8%	0.5%	0.8%	0.5%	
Annual DC Cost Savings			$ 1		$ 3		$ 3	$ 6
International	$ 3	$ 3	$ 3	$ 4	$ 4	$ 5	4.396	
Int'l/Revenue	0.5%	0.5%	0.5%	0.5%	0.4%	0.5%	0.4%	
Annual IO Savings			$ 0		$ 1		$ 1	$ 2
TOTAL	$ 87	$ 114	$ 96	$ 148	$ 107	$ 192	$ 120	
Revenues	$ 500	$ 650	$ 650	$ 845	$ 845	$ 1,099	$ 1,099	
GLC/Revenues	17.5%	17.5%	14.8%	17.5%	12.7%	17.5%	10.9%	
Annual Global Logistics Cost Savings			$ 14		$ 36		$ 66	$ 117

planning and management, transportation, and warehousing, an associated reduction in cost as a percentage of sales is computed. Those reductions combined with projected sales increases enable us to estimate the annual cost savings associated with the improved versus current logistics practices. An example 3-year savings assessment is provided in Figure 3-14. In the example, a 3-year savings of $117,000,000 is estimated. If the company has a 3-year payback requirement, then up to $336,000,000 could be justifiably invested in a world-class logistics initiative.

INNOVATING LOGISTICS PRACTICES AND SYSTEMS

C H A P T E R

CUSTOMER RESPONSE PRINCIPLES AND SYSTEMS

> " . . . whoever wants to become great among you must be your servant."
>
> *Matthew 20:26*

RECENTLY OVERHEARD a logistics manager in a large consumer products company say, "If it weren't for the customers, logistics would be easy." He was right; it would be easy, but making payroll and feeding the family would be a little tough.

Most organizations underestimate the value of good customer response and harm done by poor customer response. Consider the following aspects of customer behavior (*Fortune, One World Distribution*):

- Seventy-five percent of the reasons customers leave a company has nothing to do with the product.
- Of dissatisfied customers, 98 percent will never complain—they will just leave.
- Eighty-five percent of dissatisfied customers tell nine people; 13 percent tell 20 people. A satisfied customer tells five people.
- In the next 6 years, 80 percent of your customers will leave, 65 percent due to something you did.
- A 5 percent retention rate will increase profits from 25 to 55 percent.

Customer demand is the fountainhead for all logistics activities. Fulfilling customer orders creates the need for all logistics resources and activities. Customer response, including customer service and order processing, is the first of the five logistics processes (see Figure 4-1).

- Ahead of inventory planning and management because the objective of inventory management is to minimize the amount of inventory needed to satisfy the *customer* service policy
- Ahead of supply because the supply quality must meet *customer* expectations
- Ahead of transportation because the transportation system must deliver product within the *customer*-specified time windows
- Ahead of warehousing because the warehouse must respond within the *customer* service policy response time constraints, must support the fill rate objectives, and must offer the value added services specified by the *customer*

The objective of each of the other four logistics processes is to satisfy the customer response requirements at the lowest possible cost. Hence, the customer response requirements must be developed before the other logistics processes can be planned and executed.

Customer response is first because, without a profitable customer response strategy, the other logistics processes are worthless. Customer response is first because the customer response plan is the agreement between the logistics organization and its external and internal customers. It is first because it defines the constraints in the logistics optimization problem to

Minimize: Total logistics cost

Subject to: Customer service policy

4.1 CUSTOMER RESPONSE FUNDAMENTALS AND NOTATIONS

Before developing the customer response master plan, each organization must make a clear distinction between the customers and consumers of its products and services. The consumer is the last party in the logistics chain. The consumer is the party who uses the product for the purpose it was ultimately designed for. The customer is the party who buys the product from us.

The customer may or may not be the last party in the logistics chain. Depending on where you are in the supply chain, you may have no idea who is consuming your product, but you should always have a good relationship with the customer of the product.

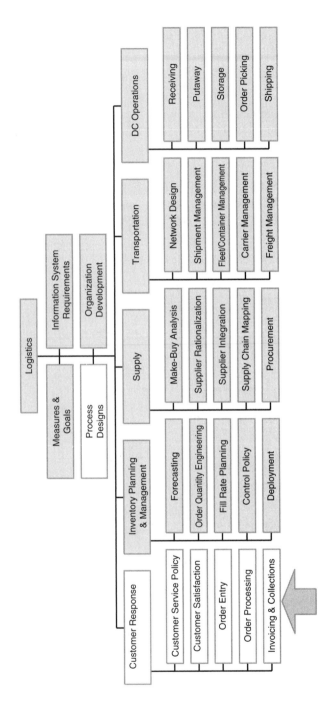

FIGURE 4-1 Customer response in the logistics framework.

72

If the product is food, consumers eat it; if the product is a beverage, consumers drink it. If the product is a television, consumers watch it. If we make TVs, if we are Phillips Corporation, and our customer is Circuit City, Circuit City doesn't consume the TV, they're just the customer. They sell it to one of us who consumes the television. For a manufacturer, the customer could be another manufacturer; it could be someone who assembles product, it could be a wholesaler, a distributor, a retailer, or a mail-order company, or the customer could even be the end consumer. Dell computer, for example, ships product directly from Austin, TX, to the end consumer.

If I'm a wholesaler or a distributor, my customer could be a manufacturer, someone who assembles something, another wholesaler or distributor, a mail-order company, or a retailer. In the United States, a typical supply chain is manufacturer, wholesaler, then retailer. In other countries, there are multiple levels of wholesaling. In Japan, it's very common for a wholesaler to be a customer of another wholesaler. (The excess handlings and markups due to extra layers of wholesaling in some Japanese supply chains have led the Japanese government to offer financial incentives to wholesalers who are reinventing themselves to become third-party logistics providers.) For a retailer or mail-order company, the customer is almost always an end consumer.

There are five activities in *customer response* (CR):

- Customer service policy design
- Customer satisfaction monitoring
- Order entry
- Order processing
- Invoicing and collections

The customer response master plan must address short, middle, and long-term designs for CR measures and goals, processes, systems requirements, and organization requirements (see Figure 4-2).

4.2   CUSTOMER ACTIVITY PROFILING

In the *customer activity profile* (CAP), we are trying to rank and categorize customers and SKUs in preparation for creating a customer service policy and to profile order sizes in anticipation of developing a logistics operations strategy. The three main customer activity profiles are the

- *Customer Sales Activity Profile* (CSAP)
- *Item Sales Activity Profile* (ISAP)
- *Customer-Item Sales Activity Profile* (CISAP)

FIGURE 4-2   Customer response master planning.

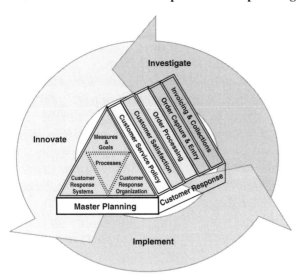

Customer Sales Activity Profile (CSAP)

The customer sales activity profile ranks the customers by sales and unit volume and classifies them into A, B, and C categories. The A category is typically comprised of the top 5 percent of customers and normally account for approximately 80 percent of the sales activity; the B category, the next 15 percent of customers normally accounting for approximately 15 percent of sales; and the C category, the remaining 80 percent of customers accounting for the last 5 percent of sales. These three categories often make up natural dividing points in the creation of a segmented customer service policy.

If possible, a *customer profitability profile* based on the cost to serve each customer may be used to weed out certain customers from the customer service profile.

Item Sales Activity Profile (ISAP)

The item sales activity profile ranks and classifies items based on dollars and unit sales. The A category is typically comprised of the top 5 percent of items and normally account for approximately 80 percent of sales activity; the B category, the next 15 percent of items normally accounting for approximately 15 percent of sales; and the C category, the remaining 80 percent of items accounting for the last 5 percent of sales. These three categories often make up natural dividing points in the creation of a segmented customer service policy.

FIGURE 4-3   Item profitability profile.

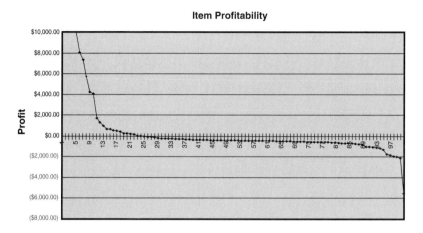

If possible, an item profitability profile can be used to weed out some items from the customer service profile. An example item profitability profile is provided in Figure 4-3. Note that in the analysis, less than one third of the items are profitable. Those are immediate candidates for purging. In many of our client studies, a majority of the items do not even cover their logistics costs.

Customer-Item Sales Activity Profile (CISAP)

One of the most useful customer activity profiles is the customer-item sales activity profile (see Figure 4-4). The customer-item sales activity profile is a joint distribution revealing the amount of dollars or unit sales accomplished in nine or more segments of business. The profile reveals the amount of sales accomplished on A items going to A customers, A items going to B customers, . . . , C items going to C customers. It highlights the dramatic differences in the logistics activities in different channels of the same enterprise. For example, there are typically very few customers, very few items, high volumes, high revenues, and intense competition in the AA segment. There are typically very many customers, very many items, low volumes, low revenues, and little-to-no competition in the CC category. The logistics strategy should reflect these stark contrasts.

A useful variation of the CISAP is the customer-item SKU activity profile (see Figure 4-5). This profile indicates the number of SKUs or items that are purchased in different business segments. It is often useful in weeding out items from the service profile. For example, in the illustration, we

FIGURE 4-4   Example of a customer-item sales activity profile.

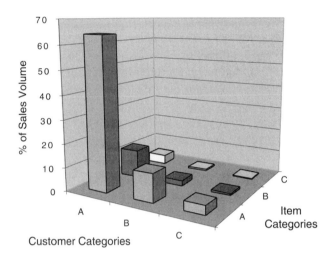

FIGURE 4-5   Customer-item SKU activity profile.

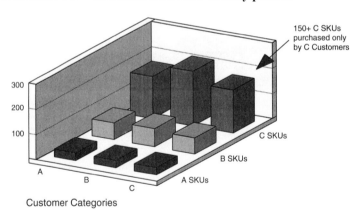

were able to identify 150 C items that were ordered only by C customers. Those are candidates for elimination.

4.3   CUSTOMER RESPONSE PERFORMANCE MEASURES

Customer response performance measures must incorporate financial, productivity, response time, and quality indicators.

Customer Response Financial Performance Indicators

The primary financial indicator for customer response performance is the *total response cost* (TRC), including the expense and capital charges for the customer response workforce, computer hardware and software, office space for customer response managers and operators, and telecommunications. An example total response cost computation and related ratios including the customer response cost per order is provided in Figure 4-6. In advanced logistics organizations, the customer response financial indicators extend to include the cost and profitability by customer, lane, region, and SKU.

Customer Response Productivity Performance Indicators

The primary productivity indicator for customer service and order processing is the number of customer orders processed per person-hour. Through customer service automation, methods including Internet ordering, EDI, automated contact management, call-center automation, and/or touchtone ordering the productivity and quality of customer service and order processing can be drastically improved. Federal Express estimates that without the implementation of its Web-enabled customer response system, they would need an extra 22,000 employees.

FIGURE 4-6   Example of total response cost computation.
Source: URI's Logistics Scoreboard

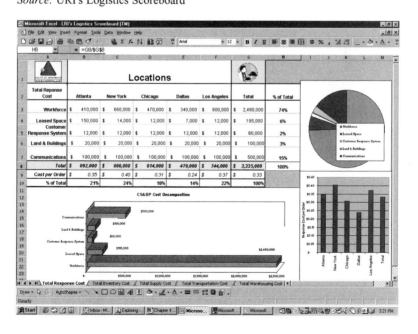

Customer Response Quality Performance Indicators

The principal indicators of quality in customer response are *order entry accuracy* (OEA), order status communication accuracy, invoice accuracy, *first-time-fill-rate* (FTFR), and the overall customer satisfaction (customer satisfaction index).

$$Order\ entry\ accuracy\ (OEA)\ =$$
$$\frac{\text{Orders entered exactly as specified by the customer}}{\text{Total orders entered}}$$

$$Order\ status\ communication\ accuracy\ =$$
$$\frac{\text{Orders for which order status is communicated correctly}}{\text{Total orders with status communication requests}}$$

$$Invoice\ accuracy\ =$$
$$\frac{\text{Invoices with perfect match of items, quantities, prices, and totals}}{\text{Total invoices}}$$

$$First\text{-}time\text{-}fill\text{-}rate\ =$$
$$\frac{\text{Total units shipped}}{\text{Total units requested}}$$

Customer Response Cycle Time Indicators

The principal response time indicators for customer response are the *order entry time* (OET) and the *order processing time* (OPT). The OET is the elapsed time from order initiation until the order is entered and captured by our business system. It includes any wait times that may be encountered by the customer over the phone or Internet and/or any system delays encountered by customer service representatives. The order processing time is the elapsed time from order entry until release to the warehouse for order picking.

4.4   CUSTOMER SERVICE POLICY DESIGN

I have heard it said, "Either manage the customers or they will manage you." The *customer service policy* (CSP) is the first step in proactive customer and demand management. The CSP is the contract between the logistics organization and the customer. It defines the service targets and objectives for logistics. The CSP sets the service requirements for each logistics process, including inventory management, supply, transportation, and warehousing.

The CSP is the foundation for logistics master planning. Nonetheless, many of our clients do not have a CSP or the one they have is defective.

CSPs usually reflect the culture and logistics maturity of the company. CSPs can be labeled as the following:

- **Ad-hoc**   There is no CSP ("We just do whatever the customer wants.").
- **Well-defined exuberance**   The CSP is stated but not quantified ("Our service rolls our customers' socks down.").
- **One-size-fits-all**   There is a stated and quantified CSP but no segmentation ("We will provide 100 percent availability for 100 percent of our SKUs for 100 percent of our customers 100 percent of the time and make our customers so excited about us that they will tell their friends and neighbors.").
- **Mature**   The CSP is stated, quantified, and segmented by customer and item classes.

A mature CSP quantifies fill rates, response times, and minimum order quantities. It formalizes policies for returns, consolidation, and value added services for item and customer classes. Though difficult to push through most sales and marketing paradigms, customer and item classes must be quantified and formalized. As described in Section 4.2, "Customer Activity Profiling," we use customer activity profiling extensively to support customer and item classification (see Figure 4-7).

In the example, one business is segmented into nine logistics categories: A items going to A customers, A items going to B customers, A items going to C customers, . . . , C items going to C customers. The extremes of the range are A items going to A customers (Segment I) and C items going to C customers (Segment IX). Segment I is highly competitive, focused on a few items going to a few customers and is the segment with most of the revenue and profit. Segment IX is a near monopoly, fragmented with a multiplicity of customers and items and offers limited revenue and profit. If the same customer service policy is used in both segments, either the policy is too weak, dissatisfying Segment I, or it is too strong, diverting precious resources into Segment IX that should be focused on a more strategic segment. This is an extreme example to support our recommendation that the customer service policy should be segmented and quantified.

Volume and revenue are not the only criteria used to classify items and customers. Customer classification should also consider customer loyalty, potential sales growth, strategic positioning, and payment history. Item

FIGURE 4-7   Customer activity profile.

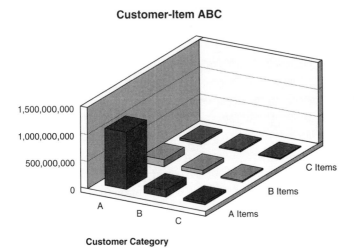

Customer-Item ABC

classification should also consider demand correlation with items in other classes, probability of failure in service parts, criticality for A customers, lead time, profitability, and value.

Once created, it is very difficult to maintain the discipline of the customer-item classification. There is a tendency to drift back to the comfortable status quo of giving the customer whatever he wants. Imbedding the customer service policy in the logistics information and customer response system is one key success factor for maintaining customer response discipline.

Another difficult practice in CSP maintenance is moving customers between classes. The tendency is to assign every customer to the A class. Instead, only a prespecified level of activity should be conducted with the A × A CSP. As a result, as customers grow or decline in loyalty, revenue, and/or volume, they must be continually reassigned to A, B, or C classes.

Most sales organizations fight the process of CSP design tooth and nail. Each salesperson wants to treat each customer as an A customer because his or her sales commission depends on the customer's treatment. As a result, actual customer service defaults to an internal and/or external personality and political contest. To lead the sales organizations along, we typically have to provide some prompting to overcome the initial inertia. One of those prompts is a template that facilitates the classification of customers (see Table 4-1).

TABLE 4-1   **Customer Segmentation Planning Template**

Customer Classification Criteria

1. Sales Volume	2. Profitability	3. Payment History	4. Future Growth	5. Relationship with Competition
Customer Segment	% Customers by Segment	% Sales by Segment	Numbers of Customers per Segment	Names of Customers in Segment
A	5%	80%	x	Name 1 . . .
B	15%	15%	y	Name 2 . . .
C	80%	5%	z	Name 3 . . .

Fill Rate—Response Time Computations

Fill rate and response time targets are the heart of the customer service policy. Computing fill rate and response time targets by customer-item class is the first and most important phase of logistics strategic planning. There are at least two ways to make the computation. First, we can consider *lost sales costs* (LSC) associated with not having sufficient inventory availability or not making it available in sufficient time. In theory, for every response time or inventory availability demand we cannot meet, there are lost sales consequences. The argument may be made that the extra transportation or warehousing cost required to meet higher response time demand is too costly, or that the inventory carrying cost required to satisfy higher inventory availability is too expensive. The argument may be resolved if we consider all the relevant costs together. In Figure 4-8, we consider all the related costs concurrently: total logistics cost and lost sales costs. The optimal logistics policy with respect to service levels and response time is the policy that minimizes total logistics cost including lost sales cost.

In this case, the optimal logistics policy is to provide 99.5 percent inventory availability and next-day response. The analysis can and should be performed for individual products, product lines, customer groups, the overall product line, and/or any meaningful subset of the business.

Another way to express the search for optimal logistics policy is in the form of a mathematical program. Simply, the optimal logistics policy minimizes total logistics cost while satisfying predetermined, quantified, and profit maximizing goals for customer service in inventory availability and response time.

FIGURE 4-8   Optimal logistics policy exchange curves.

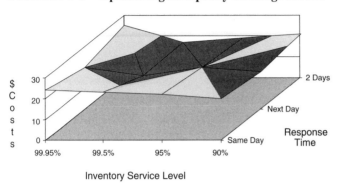

Inventory Service Level

Minimize: Total Logistics Cost (TLC) =
Total Response Cost (TRC) + Total Inventory Cost (TIC) +
Total Supply Cost (TSC) + Total Transportation Cost (TTC) +
Total Warehousing Cost (TWC)

Satisfy: Customer Service Policy (CSP) =
Inventory Availability (IA)   ≥ Profitable Target
Response Time (RT)   ≥ Profitable Target

The solution to this problem is the optimal logistics policy. By definition, those that find the solution have achieved world-class logistics. Unfortunately, most companies do not measure TLC and do not have a formal,
quantified CSP. It is very difficult to minimize something or satisfy something you can't see. The first step on the road to world-class logistics is measuring TLC and defining a quantifiable CSP.

With the optimal fill rate-response time combinations in hand, the
remainder of the customer service policy should be completed by a cross-
functional team comprised of representatives from sales and marketing, customer response, and logistics. A template for CSP definition follows (see
Table 4-2).

4.5   CUSTOMER SATISFACTION MONITORING

Once the customer service policy has been established, monitoring the performance to it and overall customer satisfaction are keys to maintaining customer intimacy—keeping the pulse on the customer. (The greatest business
failures can be traced to companies losing step with customer requirements.)
Customer satisfaction monitoring is a key discipline of customer response

TABLE 4-2   Customer Service Policy Definition Template

Service Segment	Customer-Item Class	Fill Rate	Response Time (Hours)	Returns Policy	Value Added Services	Minimum Order Quantity	Consolidation
I	A-A	99%	24	100%	Custom	None	Custom
II	A-B	95%	24	100%	Custom	None	Custom
III	A-C	85%	48	100%	Custom	None	Custom
IV	B-A	97%	24	50%	Limited	1000+	Partial
V	B-B	90%	48	50%	Limited	500+	Partial
VI	B-C	80%	72	0%	None	100+	Partial
VII	C-A	90%	48	50%	None	5000+	Partial
VIII	C-B	75%	72	0%	None	1000+	Partial
IX	C-C	50%	96	0%	None	500+	Partial

organizations and can be used to prioritize logistics initiatives and to maintain constructive customer communications.

Customer satisfaction surveys can be implemented over the Internet, over the telephone, and/or in person. In fact, some element of customer satisfaction should be monitored during each customer interaction. The survey process should begin by having the customers decide and rank the factors that define customer satisfaction for them. The survey should permit the customer to then rank our performance relative to expectations and relative to the competition with respect to the key factors identified by the customer.

The most valuable deliverable of the customer satisfaction monitoring process is the customer satisfaction grid (see Figure 4-9). The customer satisfaction grid helps us prioritize logistics initiatives. The factors requiring the most attention are those most important to the customer and where our performance is low. The factors requiring the least attention are those least important to the customer where our performance is high. Those factors with high performance and high importance and those with low performance and low importance should be maintained. In the example, the major points of emphasis for logistics improvements should be delivery quality, availability, and the friendliness of customer service representatives.

4.6   ORDER CAPTURE AND ENTRY

Order capture and entry is the activity of capturing customer demand and entering it into our own systems for processing. The main principle is to make order entry as customer-friendly as possible. There is nothing more frustrating for a customer than to have to work hard to order our products; in fact, to make it so is downright arrogant.

FIGURE 4-9   A customer satisfaction grid.

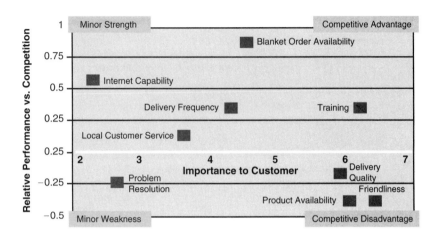

The order entry activity is the interface point with the customer, and it often makes the overall impression to the customer. The order entry experience should be pleasantly memorable. For example, the best CSRs in call centers know who is calling before they answer the phone and have extensive customer information on file and on the screen to prepare the CSR for the order entry conversation. Another important principle for customer order entry is to provide the customer with as many options for order entry as possible. (A bigger net catches more fish.) A variety of customer order entry methods are described in Table 4-3.

The order entry system should also provide real-time inventory visibility (for online inventory commitment), estimated transportation arrival times, one-stop and one-request ordering, advanced contact management, online customer satisfaction monitoring, and online survey information.

4.7   ORDER PROCESSING

Order processing is the set of activities occurring between order entry and order release to the warehouse. Order processing activities include

- Order pattern recognition
- Credit verification
- Order status communication and order changes
- Order batching and assignment for efficient transport and picking

TABLE 4-3 Order Entry Methods

Order Entry Method	Description	Keys to Success	Applications	Examples
Mail	Order forms received by mail and key-entered into logistics information system.	Scanning and imaging forms for automated order entry and customer database maintenance.	Where customers are uncomfortable with or do not have access to automated order entry methods.	Avon, Sears
Telephone—Customer Sales Representative	Orders entered over the phone by customer representatives.	On-line auditing of calls. Call centers benchmarking. Call management systems. Call queueing statistics. On-line Contact Management. Customer-Dedicated CSRs.	Where customers do not have access to order entry systems, and/or where specialized information is needed from a CSR, and/or where the customer contact culture calls for telephone ordering.	Lands' End, Computer Discount Warehouse, L.L. Bean, Corning
Telephone—Key Pad	Orders prompted and entered by telephone key pad.	Simple instructions and limited options.	Where the range of order entry options is limited.	Avon
Fax	Order forms submitted by fax.	OCR technology to enable direct order entry from fax forms.	Where customers have ready fax access and order entry information is easily captured on a single page.	
Modem Download	Orders downloaded directly from the customers' or CSR's computer to the order entry system.	Reliable, friendly, and fast download protocols and interfaces.	Where customers have easy access and good familiarity with computer modem communications protocol and computer forms transactions.	Dataslide
Internet	Orders entered directly by customers over the internet. Internet application walks customers through the order entry process.	Reliable Security. Friendly and Natural Interfaces (that is, shopping cart motif). Reliable Product Delivery (to increase trust in format). Online help to minimize customer frustration.	Where customers are Internet and computer literate and lack the time and/or patience to work through traditional order entry formats.	Boeing, Heineken, Amazon, Peapod

(continued)

TABLE 4-3 **Order Entry Methods** (*continued*)

Order Entry Method	Description	Keys to Success	Applications	Examples
Vendor Managed Inventory	Vendors monitor customer inventory levels and places orders on their behalf.	Consistent performance and continuous customer communication to increase trust in the system.	Where high-volume business-to-business transactions are prevalent with most SKUs holding consistent demand patterns.	Procter & Gamble, BOSE
Hand-Held Terminals	Customer service representatives review retail store levels and enter restocking quantities into hand-held terminals with real-time links to inventory systems.	On-line inventory availability and commitment. Integrated bar code scanning.	Retail replenishment.	Coca-Cola, Frito-Lay
On-Site Sales Reps with Laptops	Sales representatives go on-site with laptops and enter and download orders.	PC tools to present product and service lines to customer. Online inventory availability, commitment, and ETAs.	Sophisticated order entry requirements with need to go on-site.	Gordon Foods

Order Pattern Recognition

You may have had the same embarrassing experience I had recently in a jewelry store. I went into the store to purchase a gift for my wife. After I had selected a fairly expensive necklace and asked for it to be wrapped, the sales clerk disappeared for a long time. When she finally came back, she was holding the unwrapped necklace and a telephone. The clerk explained that my credit card company was on the phone and wanted to speak with me. (I felt like I was being arrested.) The credit card company wanted to confirm that I was the owner of the credit card and that I really wanted to buy the necklace. They had correctly recognized that I was using my corporate card that I normally use for business travel expenses to make a personal purchase. I explained that I was using the corporate card so my wife (who pays the credit card bills) would be surprised by the gift. The credit card company's order pattern recognition software had detected something unusual and wanted to give me a chance to verify the purchase. Order pattern recognition identifying requests for unusual items or quantities by a customer yields big customer service and inventory management dividends.

Credit Verification

For individual consumers, credit verification should take place before order release and inventory commitment. Credit verification should take place online and in near real-time. For large corporate customers, each customer should be classified as a

*   **Green-light customer**   Those customers with exemplary payment histories with orders released without credit checks.
*   **Yellow-light customer**   Those customers with good to average payment histories having a prespecified sample of orders checked or a check on all orders in excess of a prespecified value.
*   **Red-light customer**   Those with poor credit histories and all orders held for credit checks.

Order Batching and Assignment

Orders should be assigned to their optimal shipment and pick wave. The optimal shipment assignment (to a mode, carrier, and specific shipment) minimizes transportation cost yet satisfies the customer's response time requirements. The optimal pick wave assignment (to a group of orders picked together in a warehouse) minimizes the material handling cost yet satisfies the departure time requirement of the order's shipment. Order batching should be online and in real-time so that delivery time commit-

ments can be made online and communicated immediately to the customer. Once assigned, order release to the transportation management
shipment and warehouse management system should be automated in
real-time.

Order Changes and Status Communication

Customers and consumers should be allowed to change orders until the loading of the order into the transportation container and/or until the point the
change will delay the entire shipment. Order changes outside those parameters should be entered as new orders.

Order status communication should be proactive when there is an exception to the order contents, timing, or terms agreed upon at order entry. Order
status information should be updated in real-time and should be available
perpetually to the customer/consumer either by phone or online. If a telephone call is required, the communication should be completed with one
phone call and preferably made with a dedicated customer service representative or team member. Most corporate Web sites enable customers to
track the status of their orders.

4.8 DOCUMENTATION, INVOICING, AND COLLECTIONS

An order is not truly complete until it has been documented, invoiced, col-
lected, and archived. Documentation is made perfect by eliminating paperwork, handwriting, and key entry throughout the order flow documentation
process. Ideally, all customer orders, transportation documents, picking documents, and invoices are electronic and the number of required documents
is minimized. In some cases, the same document may serve all four purposes.

Invoicing is best conducted electronically and collections as well. EDI
and the Internet provide a natural platform for electronic invoicing and collections. When possible, collections should be immediate, permitting multiple payment options. Again, a bigger net catches more fish.

4.9 CUSTOMER RESPONSE SYSTEMS

Modern vernacular for a *customer response system* (CRS) is *customer relationship management* (CRM). For all the reasons outlined previously, CRM
software is one of the hottest software market spaces.

The CRS is one of five subsystems in a logistics information system.
The functionality in a customer response system includes

- Order entry
- Order processing

- Contact management
- Customer activity profiling
- Order pattern recognition
- Customer transaction databases
- Open order databases
- Customer service policy maintenance
- Customer service performance measurement
- Call/customer transaction management systems
- Customer satisfaction monitoring
- Infrastructure sufficient to provide real-time order and inventory status information even in peak demand periods
- Embedded CSP guidelines to maintain CSP disciplines
- Automated, single-point order entry
- Online order assignment to optimal shipments and pick waves

4.10   CUSTOMER RESPONSE ORGANIZATION DESIGN AND DEVELOPMENT

The theme for designing and developing a customer response organization should be customer intimacy—proactively able to anticipate and appreciate customer needs as opposed to reactively scrambling to each new customer request. Customer intimacy is a two-way street and is only achieved when an individual and his/her backup are dedicated to a customer and customer account. The world's best example may be the near magical relationship between Coca-Cola route drivers around the world and their retail customers in developing countries. The delivery experience includes the physical product delivery, order entry for the next delivery, marketing around future Coke promotions, order documentation, personal conversations, and collections for the current delivery. That dedicated relationship and resulting loyalty is one key success factor for Coca-Cola around the world. Whether in person at the customer's site, over the telephone, or over the Internet—customer intimacy is the aim.

Customer response is unique to the other logistics activities because it is the activity where most direct customer communications take place. That communications interface goes a long way toward determining overall customer satisfaction levels. As a result, there are a variety of practices we recommend to clients to help them maintain the most effective customer communications possible.

Customer Focus Groups

Customer focus groups are small groups of customers that represent the overall business. The groups come together in face-to-face or online meetings to act as a sounding board for new products or service offerings the enterprise is considering. It is essentially a customer board of directors. The feedback is invaluable for developing reliable input for customer response planning.

Dedicated, Personalized Account Teams

In the age of tele- versus personal communications, customers increasingly appreciate dedicated and personal response to their issues. Service personalization may be carried out by an individual or a group of individuals who are familiar with their concerns. The personalization program should be supported with advanced customer relationship management capability. Some transaction center management systems are sophisticated enough to route a call or incoming email automatically to the most appropriate individual to respond to the transaction.

Multilingual, Multicultural

Economic globalization, political globalization, and the World Wide Web make it increasingly likely that an order and a customer will be from somewhere other than the United States. In fact, it is projected that by the year 2005, English will be a minority language on the Internet. That said, a culturally tailored customer response is an increasingly important aspect of global customer response. Culturally tailored customer response requires speaking in the customers language and dialect, operating during their normal business hours ($7 \times 24 \times 365$), understanding the current and business events impacting them, and being respectful of their protocols.

Transaction Center Monitoring

Each customer interface should be monitored to record the length of the transaction, the wait time experienced by the customer, the number of balks due to wait time or down time, and the overall satisfaction with the transaction experienced by the customer.

INVENTORY PLANNING AND MANAGEMENT

HOW TO REDUCE INVENTORY AND IMPROVE CUSTOMER SERVICE AT THE SAME TIME

> "Go to the ant, . . . consider its ways and be wise!
> It has no commander, no overseer or ruler,
> yet it stores its provisions in summer and gathers its food at harvest."
>
> *Proverbs 6:6–8*

IF MONEY MAKES THE WORLD go 'round, inventory makes logistics go 'round. The planning, storing, moving, and accounting for inventory is the basis for all logistics. Inventory availability is the most important aspect of customer service. Inventory carrying costs are typically the most expensive costs of logistics. It is very difficult to convert physical inventory into a liquid asset, hence inventory is a very risky investment.

The goal of inventory management is to increase the financial return on inventory while simultaneously increasing customer service levels (see Figure 5-1).

FIGURE 5-1   How to reduce inventory and increase service at the
same time.

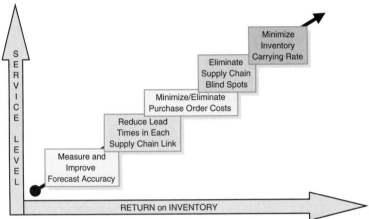

In my experience and in all of my research, I have found five initiatives
that lead to increased return on inventory and increased inventory availability
at the same time:

1. Improved forecast accuracy
2. Reduced cycle times
3. Lower purchase order/setup costs
4. Improved inventory visibility
5. Lower inventory carrying costs

These five initiatives are the foundation of any lasting progress in logistics and supply chain management. There are many fancy names applied to
these basics, but the basics remain so. We will explore the metrics and practices that yield progress in these five areas in this chapter (see Figure 5-2).

Recognition of the critical role of inventory has launched a variety of
industry wide inventory reduction initiatives, including *efficient consumer
response* (ECR) and *efficient foodservice response* (EFR) in the food and grocery industry, *quick response* (QR) in the textiles industry, *continuous flow
manufacturing* (CFM) in electronics manufacturing, and *just-in-time* (JIT) in
auto manufacturing. Despite all of these initiatives to reduce inventory in the
supply chain, there remain legitimate, value-added forms of inventory in the
supply chain, including service inventory, pipeline inventory, contingency
inventory, safety stock, efficient manufacturing inventory, and efficient procurement inventory.

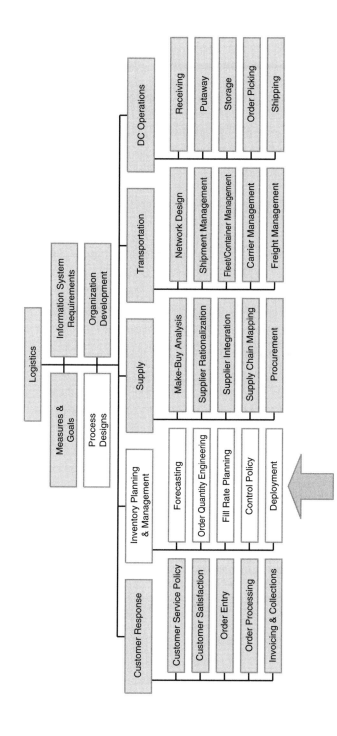

FIGURE 5-2 Inventory planning and management in the logistics framework.

Service inventory (SI) is in place to provide acceptable response time to customers. *Pipeline inventory* (PI) is in transit to/from customers and suppliers. *Contingency inventory* (CI) protects against unusual occurrences including strikes and natural disasters. *Safety stock* (SS) is in place to provide acceptable customer service levels in the face of random demand during replenishment lead times. *Efficient manufacturing inventory* (EMI) is in place to leverage the cost of manufacturing setups. *Efficient procurement inventory* (EPI) is in place for special opportunities to procure product at lower prices than normal. Table 5-1 enumerates several types of inventory and the beneficial role each type of inventory plays in the supply chain.

The challenge facing inventory managers is to insure that efficient inventory levels are in place in each of these inventory categories. Inventory levels should be minimized while satisfying customer service requirements. This chapter describes the inventory planning and management principles required to achieve these often conflicting objectives.

In spite of all the efforts to reduce inventory, the amount of inventory in the U.S. supply chain has remained fairly constant over the last few years.

TABLE 5-1   Inventory Types and Roles for Inventory in the Supply Chain

Inventory Type	Role	Benefits
Lot-size/ cycle stock	Order in batches versus one at a time to achieve economies of scale in setups, purchases, transport, and so on.	• Purchase discounts • Reduced setups • Lower freight, material handling, and administration costs
Safety stock (demand fluctuation)	Insurance against unexpected high/low demand and high/low lead times.	• Reduced lost sales and backorders • Increased customer service • Lower freight • Reduced customer response costs
Contingency/ supply fluctuation	Insurance against interrupted supply (that is, strikes, natural disasters).	• Reduced downtime and overtime • Reduced lost sales cost
Anticipation	Level out production (that is, to meet seasonal sales, promotions, and so on).	• Reduced overtime, subcontracting • Higher manufacturing capacity utilization
In-transit/ pipeline	Moving/staging between/ within facilities.	• Mobile warehousing
Hedge/ opportunity	Provide hedge against price increases.	• Lower material costs

(Figure 5-3 depicts the cost of logistics [transportation, inventory carrying, and order administration], transportation, and inventory carrying as a portion of the U.S. gross domestic product from 1989 to 1998.) There have been reductions at some points and for some organizations in the chain. For example, Dell Computer (see Figure 5-4) and Wal-Mart maintain large leads in financial performance over their competitors through significant advantages in inventory turnover. However, the inventory turn advantage of those enterprises

FIGURE 5-3 **Total Logistics Cost (TLC), Inventory Carrying Cost (ICC), and Transportation Cost (T&D) versus U.S. Gross Domestic Product (GDP).** *Source:* Adapted from Bob Delaney, Cass Logistics

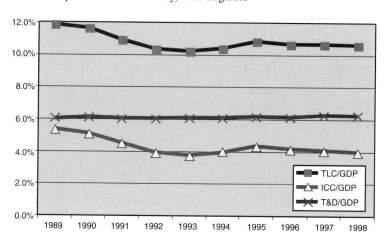

FIGURE 5-4 **Return on invested capital figures for select companies in the computing industry.** *Source:* Business Week

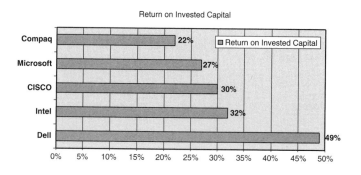

closest to the consumer have typically come at the expense of suppliers further up the chain. In addition, trends such as SKU proliferation, global logistics, ERP implementations, home delivery, and supply chain disruptions have made inventory reductions more difficult to achieve than ever. My concern is that in the midst of all those trends and the implementation of high-tech solutions, we may be losing touch with some of the fundamental and proven principles of inventory management. Those principles of inventory performance measurement, forecasting, order quantity engineering, fill rate planning, inventory control, inventory deployment, inventory management systems, and inventory organization development are the focus of this chapter. Those principles, implemented in the prescribed order, comprise LRI's inventory master planning methodology (see Figure 5-5). The goal of the methodology is to help our clients reduce inventory levels and improve customer service at the same time.

5.1 INVENTORY FUNDAMENTALS

With the many academic advances in inventory management have come a variety of notation sets. My favorite is the use of three-letter acronyms (as opposed to Greek notations) that offer some association between the term and what it represents. (I'm sure you have enough three-letter acronyms to work with, but this is better than lambdas, alphas, and betas—LBAs.) These

FIGURE 5-5   Inventory master planning methodology.

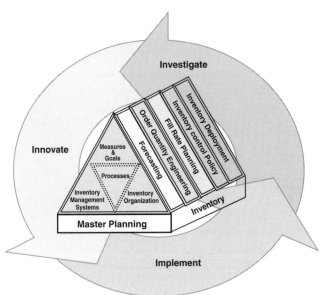

terms and notations will be used throughout our discussion of inventory management. The terms cover six aspects of inventory management:

- Inventory levels
- Stockouts
- Planning parameters
- Financial terms
- Demand terms
- Decision variables

Inventory Levels

Inventory levels are expressed with a variety of terminology and from a variety of perspectives. Common reference terms include *on-hand stock* (OHS), *net stock* (NS), and *net inventory position* (NIP).

On-hand stock is the number of units of inventory physically in storage. For a distribution center, the OHS is the number of units on-hand in the distribution center. For a domestic company, the *corporate on-hand stock* (COHS) is the inventories physically on-hand in all distribution centers. For an international company, the sum of all inventory on-hand in the international network of distribution centers is the *global on-hand stock* (GOHS).

Net stock (NS) is the OHS less *units on backorder* (UOB).

$$NS = OHS - UOB$$

The NIP is the OHS plus *units on order* (UOO), plus *pipeline inventory* (PI) less units UOB less *allocated inventory* (AI).

$$NIP = OHS + UOO + PI - UOB - AI$$

Stockout Conditions

Never being out of stock is like having an insurance policy with no deductible. The inventory carrying cost for never being out of stock is infinite, literally. As a result, not all demand can or should be satisfied directly from the shelf (see Figure 5-6). Because stockouts are costly situations in terms of customer service and material handling, managing unsatisfied demand is a critical dimension of inventory management.

There are three possible responses to unsatisfied demand: backordering, substitutions, and lost sales. The appropriate response depends on the unique characteristics of each item and customer.

In *backordering*, the quantity requested by the customer is placed on a separate order called a backorder, and the special order is filled as soon as the product is available from internal and/or external sources. In some cases, the backorder is shipped directly from its original source to the customer.

FIGURE 5-6   **Example of a stockout scenario.**

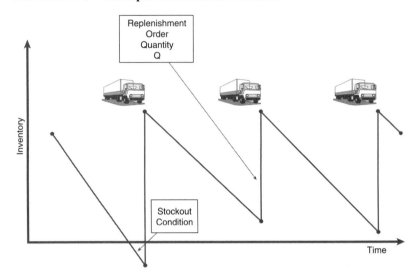

Backordering is commonplace when there is no other source for a product (that is, in captive markets).

Substitutions occur when a product acceptable to the customer is substituted for the product that is not available.

Lost sales occur when the unsatisfied demand is lost. Lost sales are common in retail situations where there are many alternative outlets for a product. Lost sales are critically expensive for A+ and A items where the unsatisfied demand may result in negative publicity and/or the customer's purchase of B or C items depends on the availability of the A items. Lost sales for B and C items are not as critical.

The difference in the penalties for shortages in A, B, and C items is reflected in the *shortage factor* (SF). The shortage factor is an index applied to the selling price to reflect the magnitude of the damage of a lost sale. For example, shortages of core items may generate such negative customer reaction that customers begin to complain publicly about shortages. In those cases, the shortage factor may be as high as 200 to 300 percent.

Planning Parameters

We will use five key planning parameters to define the unique inventory management parameters for an item or enterprise:

- *Unit selling price* (USP)
- *Unit inventory value* (UIV)

- *Inventory carrying rate* (ICR)
- *Purchase order cost* (POC)
- *Setup cost* (SUC)

The USP for an item is the price paid by a customer for an item. The UIV for a purchased item is the price paid for the item; the UIV for a manufactured item is the cost of manufacturing the item.

The ICR is the percent of the UIV used to compute the ICC for an item. The ICR includes

- Opportunity cost of capital (the rate of return that could reasonably be achieved for each dollar not invested in inventory)
- Storage and material handling
- Loss due to obsolescence, damage, and/or pilferage
- Insurance and taxes

Inventory carrying rates vary widely across industries and countries. When we work in Latin American countries, the interest rates may be as much as 60 percent per year. As a result, the inventory carrying rate may be as high as 70 or 80 percent. When we work in Japan, where the interest rate is low, the inventory carrying rate is much lower, perhaps in the range of 5 to 15 percent. When we work in the Silicon Valley, where expectations for capital investments are upwards of 20 percent per year, the inventory carrying rate is normally around 40 percent. When we work in mature industries in the Midwest, inventory carrying rates are typically between 25 and 35 percent. Due to this wide variety of rates and conditions, each company should determine, maintain, and publish its own inventory carrying rate.

The POC is the cost of placing a purchase order from a vendor. Those costs include

- Order forms
- Postage
- Telecommunications
- Authorization
- Purchase order planning
- Purchase order entry time
- Purchase order processing time
- Purchase order inspection time
- Purchase order follow-up time
- Purchasing management
- Office space

- Office supplies
- Purchase order entry systems
- Tracking and expediting

The most expensive items on the list are the labor related items. Hence, automating purchase order processing typically yields significant labor cost reductions and productivity improvements. An example of a purchase order cost computation form is included as Figure 5-7. The example differentiates between domestic and international purchase orders. In this case, an international sourcing organization was used in planning and placing international purchase orders.

SUC is the cost to set up (prepare or changeover) a machine to make a production run for a particular item.

Financial Terms

We will use four key financial terms in discussing inventory management:

- *Average inventory value* (AIV)
- *Inventory carrying cost* (ICC)

FIGURE 5-7   **Purchase order cost computation.**
Source: LRI's Logistics Scoreboard

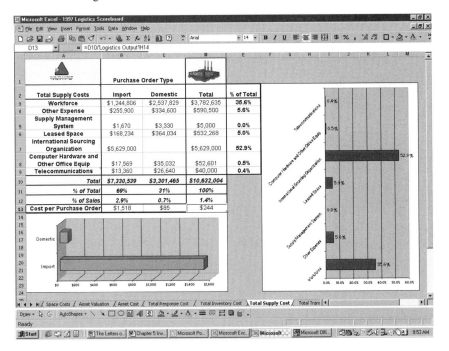

- *Lost sales cost* (LSC)
- *Total policy cost* (TPC)

AIV is the average value of the total inventory investment over the course of a year. It should be computed as the average of several on-hand inventory values measured at random times during the year. (The on-hand inventory value [or total inventory investment] at any point in time is the sum of the unit inventory values for all items.)

ICC is the annual cost of carrying (or holding) the AIV. It is computed by multiplying the AIV by the ICR.

$$ICC \;=\; AIV \;\times\; ICR$$

For example, if the AIV in a warehouse is $10,000,000 and the inventory carrying rate is 30 percent per year, then the ICC in the warehouse is

$$ICC \;=\; \$10,000,000 \times 30\%/\text{year} \;=\; \$3,000,000 \text{ per year.}$$

LSC is the revenue lost when we are not able to satisfy customer demand. The lost sales cost for an item is computed by multiplying the annual sales potential (that is, sales that would have occurred if all demand was satisfied) by the portion of sales that we were not able to satisfy by the shortage factor.

$$LSC \;=\; AD \;\times\; USP \;\times\; (1 - UFR) \;\times\; SF$$

In the equation, UFR stands for the *unit fill rate*, the percent of unit demand that is satisfactory from on-hand stock.

For example, if the *annual demand* (AD) for an item is 1,000 units, the unit selling price is $2.00; the UFR is 90 percent, and the shortage factor is 50 percent, then the LSC for the item is

$$LSC \;=\; 1{,}000 \text{ units/year} \times \$2.00/\text{unit} \times (1 - 0.9) \times 0.5 = \$100/\text{year}$$

The total lost sales cost is the sum of the lost sales costs for all the items.

The *inventory policy cost* (IPC) for an item is the sum of the inventory carrying and lost sales costs for the item.

$$IPC \;=\; ICC \;+\; LSC.$$

Example IPC computations for varying UFRs are provided in Figure 5-8.

Demand Terms

Every item has a unique set of demand characteristics. Some of those characteristics can be represented mathematically including

- *Annual demand* (AD)
- *Forecast annual demand* (FAD)

FIGURE 5-8   Inventory policy cost calculations.
Source: LRI's Fill Rate Planner

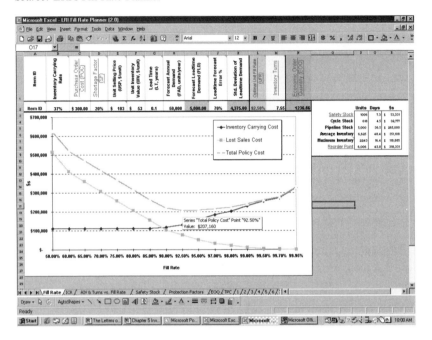

- *Lead time* (L)
- *Lead time demand* (LD)
- *Forecast lead time demand* (FLD)
- *Standard deviation of lead time demand* (SDLD)

The AD for an item is the number of units requested for an item during a year. The FAD is the forecasted (or expected) annual number of units requested by customers. The L for an item is the elapsed time from the placement of the replenishment order until the item is available to satisfy customer demand. Lead time demand is the historic number of units requested by customers during an L. The FLD is the forecasted (or expected) number of units that will be requested by customers during an L. The SDLD is a measure of the variability of the demand during an L. The greater the variability in L demand, the greater the need for safety stock to protect against large demand spikes during an L. Figure 5-9 illustrates key concepts in LD management.

Decision Variables

Throughout our study of inventory management, we will be working to identify optimal values for a variety of decision variables including

FIGURE 5-9   Lead time demand management concepts.

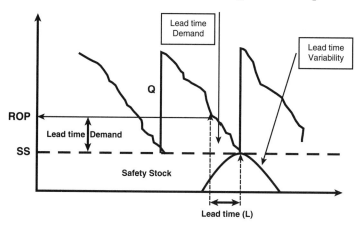

- *Economic order quantity* (EOQ)
- *Unit fill rate* (UFR)
- Optimal *safety stock* (SS) level
- *Reorder point* (ROP)
- *Order-up-to-level* (OUL)
- *Review time period* (RTP)

The EOQ is the number of units per replenishment order that minimizes the total cost of ordering and carrying the inventory associated with the order. The higher the order quantity, the greater the inventory level. However, the higher the order quantity, the fewer times we will need to order and the lower the resulting ordering cost. The formula to compute the EOQ is as follows:

$$EOQ = [(2 \times FAD \times POC)/(UNI \times ICR)]^{1/2}$$

The UFR for an item is the portion of the total number of units requested by customers that we have available to provide to the customer. As discussed previously, the higher the UFR, the lower the lost sales cost. However, the higher the UFR, the greater the inventory required to provide it, and the greater the resulting inventory carrying cost. The optimal UFR is found at the point that minimizes the total policy cost (sum of lost sales and inventory carrying cost) associated with various fill rates. An example of fill rate optimization is illustrated in Figure 5-10. The example is from an analysis of B items in the service parts industry for a European distribution center. The optimal unit fill rate in this case is 92.5 percent.

FIGURE 5-10   **Fill rate optimization.**
Source: LRI's Fill Rate Planner

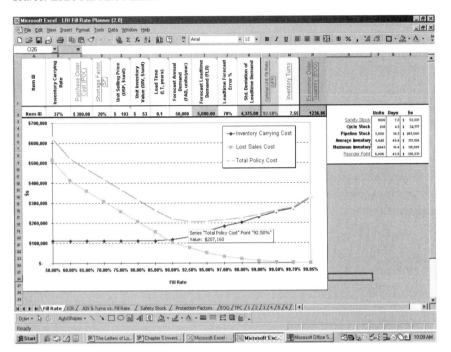

The literal definition of SS is the amount of inventory on-hand when a replenishment arrives (see Figure 5-11). The average SS is the average on-hand inventory at the end of several replenishment cycles.

Safety stock is required to support promised levels of inventory availability when the demand during an L or the length of an L are variable. For example, if a replenishment is delayed or if the demand during an L is much greater than normal, SS is in place to fulfill demand until the replenishment arrives or to satisfy some portion of the excess demand. There would be no need for SS if we knew exactly what quantity the customers wanted, when they wanted it, and exactly when a replenishment would arrive. To the extent there is uncertainty in any of those three variables, we need SS to provide anything better than a 50 percent inventory availability.

The ROP is the inventory level at which a replenishment order is placed. The ROP is typically set at the LD plus the safety stock.

$$ROP = LD + SS$$

FIGURE 5-11   Safety stock dynamics.

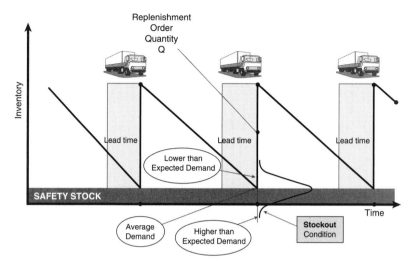

FIGURE 5-12   Inventory dynamics with OULs.

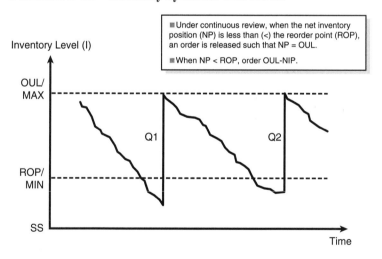

The OUL is the level of inventory a replenishment quantity should yield when it is placed. Figure 5-12 illustrates the workings of a typical inventory program utilizing OULs. The main differential between the use of OULs and EOQs is that order sizes vary in an OUL program. We will discuss inventory control policies that utilize OULs in detail in the section on inventory control policies.

FIGURE 5-13   **Inventory dynamics with RTPs.**

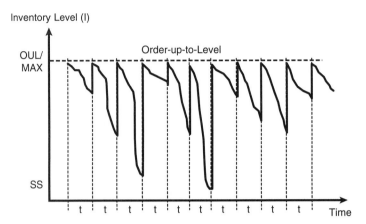

Up until now, we have assumed that inventory levels are under continuous review. It may be less expensive to review inventory levels at fixed periods. The time between inventory reviews is called the RTP. Figure 5-13 illustrates the typical workings of an inventory program with RTPs. The longer the RTP, the lower the administrative costs of the inventory policy. However, the longer the RTP, the greater the likelihood of stockouts.

5.2   INVENTORY ACTIVITY PROFILING

The main purpose of inventory activity profiling is to reveal inventory shortages and excesses at major points in the supply chain in the units of measure and buckets that can be acted upon. The revelations in turn suggest courses of action for increasing availability in under-served segments and reducing inventory levels where excesses have accrued. We will consider some example profiles and recommended courses of action in the following.

Figure 5-14 is an ABC Inventory Synchronization Profile. It illustrates the percent of inventory value tied up in A items, B items, and C items as compared to the corresponding percent of sales in those categories and the management strategy. The example is a typical finding where A items are understocked and C item inventory is excessive. In most cases, this is a reflection of a poor forecasting process and/or a lack of discipline in purging slow moving inventory.

Figure 5-15 is an example ABC days-on-hand inventory profile. The profile illustrates the average days-on-hand of inventory in ABC item categories. Days-on-hand reporting is often more effective than percentages or turns

FIGURE 5-14   Inventory synchronization profile.

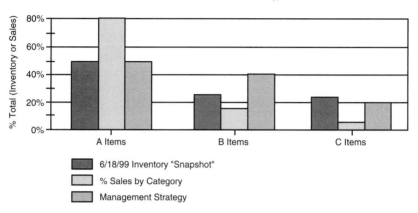

FIGURE 5-15   ABC days-on-hand inventory profile.

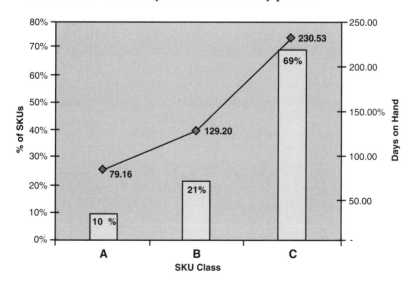

because of the mental comparison that is easily made between days-on-hand and typical item lead times. The example in Figure 5-15 is typical, where C items may have nearly a year or sometimes many more days-on-hand. In the example, nearly 70 percent of the items have an average of 230 days-on-hand (more than 6 months worth of supply). Depending on the type of business (this was a retail business), this often represents a dramatic opportunity for inventory reduction through item elimination and/or outsourcing the supply of those items.

Figure 5-16 is an ABC inventory turns profile that also categorizes items by domestic and international sourcing and *cross-dock* (XD) versus traditional warehouse (WHC) flow patterns. This profile helped to identify the surprising result that domestically sourced merchandise and internationally sourced merchandise were turning at nearly the same rate, even though international vendors were located literally half-way around the world. As our practice analysis revealed, the international vendors were linked into an EDI-based consolidation program managed by a large trading company. Domestic vendors were managed with pencil and paper and with little to no automated purchase order management. A simple spreadsheet-based tool was developed to help double the turns of domestic A items and increase service levels.

Figure 5-17 is an example of an ABC inventory valuation analysis. It is a little like drilling for oil, in that the analysis helps reveal where the pockets of excess inventory investment have accumulated. The analysis considers A, B, and C SKUs, purchased domestically and internationally, cross-docked or moved through the warehouse. This analysis helps reveal the most significant opportunities for reducing inventory investments.

FIGURE 5-16   **ABC inventory turns analysis.**

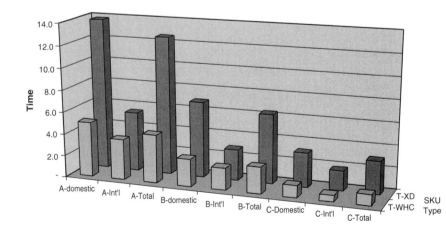

FIGURE 5-17   ABC inventory valuation analysis.

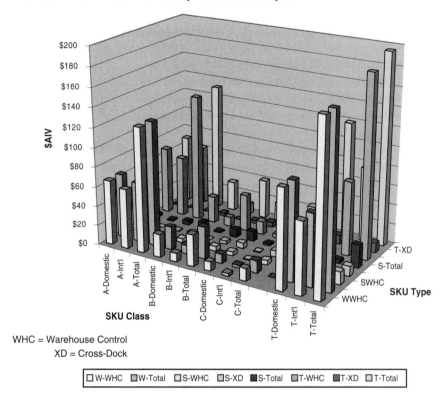

WHC = Warehouse Control
XD = Cross-Dock

☐ W-WHC   ■ W-Total   ☐ S-WHC   ☐ S-XD   ■ S-Total   ☐ T-WHC   ■ T-XD   ☐ T-Total

5.3   INVENTORY PERFORMANCE MEASUREMENT

The key financial indicators for inventory performance are the average inventory investment and the associated inventory carrying cost. The key productivity indicators of inventory performance are inventory turns and the number of items managed by an inventory planner. The key quality indicators of inventory performance are forecast accuracy and fill rates.

These measures should be available at the SKU, family, country, and business unit level in real-time. The inventory management organization should be held accountable for performance in each of these interdependent indicators, with their evaluation based on their ability to meet predefined goals for performance in each area. Each of these metrics are defined in detail in the following.

Inventory Investment

The average inventory investment is computed as the average over time of the sum of the inventory values for individual items. The *average inventory value* AIV of an item at any particular time is the product of its *average inventory level* (AIL) and its *unit inventory value* (UIV).

To improve cash flow, some companies are particularly concerned about their average inventory investment. The projected average inventory investment as a function of alternative customer service levels is illustrated in Figure 5-18. The illustration is derived from LRI's fill rate planner. Tools like this can be used to assess the inventory investment required to protect a specified fill rate or to established a target fill rate associated with maximum acceptable inventory investment levels.

Inventory Carrying Cost

Inventory carrying cost (ICC) is the product of the AIV and the *inventory-carrying rate* (ICR). The ICR includes the cost of investing in inventory, storing and handling, obsolescence, taxes, insurance, and shrinkage (due to damage and/or pilferage).

$$ICC = ICR \times AIV$$

Inventory Turns

Inventory is one of the essential logistics resources. Just as we are concerned with the productivity and utilization of people, space, and vehicles, we are even more concerned with the productivity of inventory. The productivity of inventory is typically measured as the *inventory turnover rate* (ITR). The ITR is simply expressed as the ratio of *annual dollar sales* (at cost, ADS) to the AIV.

$$ITR = ADS / AIV$$

Forecasting Accuracy

Improving forecast accuracy begins with measuring it. Options for measures of forecast accuracy include the *algebraic deviation* (ALD), *mean absolute deviation* (MAD), *percent forecast error* (PFE), and the *standard deviation of forecast demand* (SDFD).

The AD for any period *t*, is the arithmetic difference between *actual demand* (D) and *forecasted demand* (F) during that period. It could be positive or negative.

$$ALD_t = D_t - F_t$$

FIGURE 5-18   Average inventory value, inventory turns, and customer
service levels.

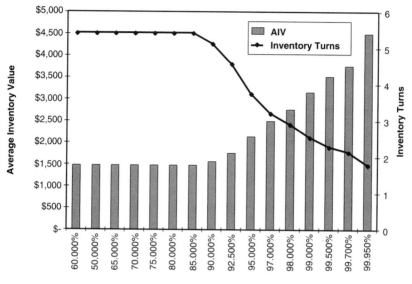

Customer Service Level Level Measured as Unit Fill Rate

The MAD of forecast errors over several (n) periods is the average of
the absolute value of the ALDs over those n periods.

$$MAD = \sum_{t=1}^{n} (|ALD_t|)/n$$

The PFE$_t$ in any one period is the ratio of the absolut e deviation to the
actual demand expressed in percentage terms.

$$PFE_t = |ALD_t| / D_t$$

For other inventory planning computations, the most helpful measure of
forecast accuracy is the standard deviation of forecast errors. When forecast
errors are normally distributed, the SDFD can be estimated as

$$SDFD = 1.25 \times MAD$$

World-class forecast accuracy measurements include all three types of
forecast accuracy at the SKU, family, and business unit level in absolute and
statistical terms. Some benchmarks for forecasting accuracy are provided in
Figure 5-19.

FIGURE 5-19   Benchmarks for SKU forecast accuracy.
Source: Smith, B.T., Focus Forecasting, BookCrafters, Fredicksberg, Virginia, 1997.

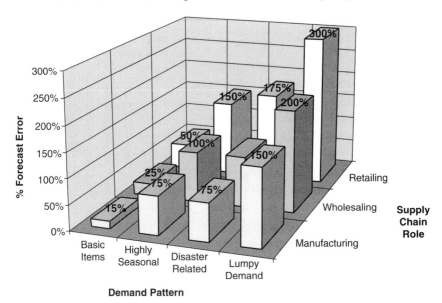

Note that the law of large numbers is vividly illustrated. The accuracy for basic items (those that experience the most frequent demand) is much better than the accuracy for seasonal and slow-moving items, and the accuracy for manufacturers is much better than for retailers because the demand for a single SKU is concentrated at manufacturing and diluted at the retail level. For example, Nike's demand forecast for a particular shoe is more accurate than that for a single retailer of that shoe because all of the demand for that shoe is experienced by Nike and the single retailer only experiences the demand that its customers require.

Customer Service Levels and Fill Rates

In the context of inventory management, customer service levels indicate the overall inventory availability, typically measured as the *first-time-fill-rate* (FTFR). As the target FTFR is increased, the overall inventory level, investment, and carrying cost increases, while LSC are reduced. The sum of the two related costs—inventory carrying and lost sales— is the inventory policy cost. The least-cost FTFR should be targeted for each item and/or family of items. These calculations were explained and illustrated in Section 5.1, "Inventory Fundamentals and Notations."

5.4   FORECASTING

Several years ago, I had a heated debate with the chief technology officer of a large sporting goods company over the value of forecasting. He argued that his company shouldn't even mess with forecasting because the forecast will be wrong. He was right on one point. The forecast will be wrong. (Forecasting has been likened to driving a car blindfolded while taking directions from someone in the back who is looking in the rearview mirror.) There is only one source of perfect future information and He doesn't work for most inventory organizations.

The chief technology officer was way off on the other point. We should mess with forecasting. In fact, we should master it. The reason is that we would like to know how far wrong we are and plan accordingly. We would also like to be closer to right than we used to be and closer to right than the competition. That is the game in forecasting, to improve and to be more accurate than the competition. To throw up our hands at the process is decision-making suicide because most major corporate and logistics decisions are based on the forecast including

- Capital investments
- Marketing campaigns
- Service level planning
- Warehouse sizing
- Staffing plans
- Manufacturing expansions
- Carrier negotiations
- Transportation network designs
- Supplier negotiations

Despite the debates in logistics academic journals, the major source of inaccurate forecasting is not insufficiently sophisticated forecasting models. Even ERP systems have a suite of forecasting algorithms that when used properly are adequate for most major organizations. Hence, we will not teach or review forecasting algorithms here. Forecasting algorithms are taught effectively in a variety of textbooks.[1] Instead, we will focus our attention on the process of forecasting, which is the source of most forecasting errors and interpretations. We will consider first the sources of most forecasting mistakes and then a set of principles for making the forecasting process as accurate as possible.

[1] Silver, E.A. and R. Peterson, *Decision Systems for Inventory Management and Production Planning*, John Wiley, New York, New York, 1985.

The major sources of inaccurate forecasting are

* Denial
* Bias
* Ignorance
* Supply chain ripple effects

Denial is prevalent in forecasting because rarely is anyone in organization held accountable for the accuracy of the forecast. As a result, the organization is in "denial" in regards to the inaccuracy of the forecast. Denial occurs when we assume forecast accuracy is improving when we are not even measuring it and when we are doing nothing to improve it.

Bias is introduced in forecasting when true demand is not recorded. Unsatisfied demand (resulting in balking, backorders, and/or substitutions) is rarely included in demand signals. Overstated demand (evidenced by cancelled orders and/or returns) is rarely recognized or eliminated from the demand patterns used to forecast future demand.

Bias is also introduced into forecasting when human nature and/or corporate culture unduly influences the forecasting process. For example, if the sales organization creates the forecast and the organization rewards optimism, then the forecast will typically overstate future demands. Or, if the organization rewards exceeding expectations, then the forecast will typically underestimate future demands. In either case, the other areas of the organization lose faith in the forecasting process, and each area of the enterprise begins to create its own version of the forecast. At that point, the forecasting process has failed.

Bias in a forecasting process can be detected, measured, and corrected. An example of a biased forecasting process is provided in Figure 5-20.

FIGURE 5-20   Forecast bias example.

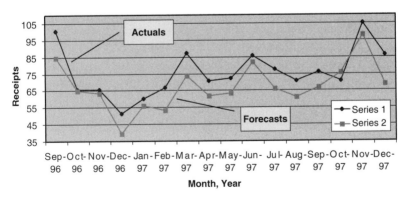

The figure illustrates the difference between forecasted and actual receiving quantities for a large distribution center. Note that the actual receiving volume exceeds the forecasted receiving volume in all but one month in a 16-month period and by nearly the same percentage difference. Because the budget for the DC was based on forecasted quantities, the DC always required excess overtime and off-site storage space. The analysis revealed a bias in the forecasting process, a culture that rewarded exceeding expectations, and the sandbagging (intentionally understating) of forecasted demand. A revised process was put into place to bring the forecasting process in line and to re-establish trust in the forecasting process.

Ignorance is introduced into the forecasting process when there is a lack of awareness of high-level industry and economic trends, key customer information, major promotional events and/or price shifts, and/or forecast accuracy indicators. Many organizations believe they are so unique that there is no high-level indicator that could predict their demand pattern. I have not been in an organization yet where there was not some high-level indicator of future demand.

We worked with a large organization that makes carpet backing for residences. The vice president of sales claimed that we were wasting our time searching out a high-level indicator of future demand. When we completed our analysis and found a 0.97 correlation between the re-sell of existing homes and the sales for carpet backing, the vice president was pleasantly dumbfounded. It's not always that easy, but it is nearly always a fruitful exercise to identify, capture, and incorporate the high-level influential indicators of demand patterns.

Supply chain ripple effects amplify forecast errors because retailers try to forecast consumer demand patterns; wholesalers try to forecast retailer demand patterns; manufacturers try to forecast wholesaler demand patterns; and suppliers try to forecast manufacturer demand patterns. As each organization creates a new forecast, which includes the error factor in the predecessor's forecast, the forecast error propagates exponentially across the supply chain.

The following forecasting principles are designed to attack the sources of forecast error described here.

Forecast Elimination

If possible, eliminate the need to forecast.

Because we know the forecast will be wrong, if we can eliminate the need to forecast (or guess), then we will essentially achieve 100 percent accuracy by not forecasting. The guesswork in forecasting can be eliminated when we

- Make/assemble/engineer-to-order.

- Use dependent demand data.
- Shorten vendor lead times.

In the make, assemble, build, and purchase-to-order logistics models, we wait until we receive a firm order from a customer until we make, assemble, build, or purchase what the customer requests. Dell Computer made this model famous; however, the model can be developed anywhere an assembly/manufacturing/replenishment operation is quick enough and the supply reliable enough to satisfy customer wait times.

Another way to eliminate the need to forecast is to use dependent demand data when it is available. For example, if we make bicycles, we know there are two wheels on each bike. If we forecast the independent demand for bicycles, the demand for wheels does not need to be independently generated; it is simply a $2\times$ multiple of the forecast for bicycles.

Finally, the need to forecast demand can be eliminated anytime vendor or manufacturing lead times are less than customer wait times. Here we see again the importance of aggressively reducing lead times throughout the supply chain.

Forecast Measurement

Measure and monitor forecasting accuracy.

It is very difficult to improve something that is not being measured. Yet many organizations still fail to measure their forecast accuracy even knowing how critical it is to the ability of the organization to make strategic and tactical decisions. Forecast accuracy should be measured for each SKU, category, commodity, location, region, customer class, and business unit. A variety of measures and benchmarks for forecast accuracy were defined in Section 5.3, "Inventory Performance Measures."

Forecast Accountability

Establish individual accountability for forecasting accuracy.

If no one is held accountable for the forecast accuracy, as is often the case, the accuracy level will reflect the lack of accountability. Some large U.S. corporations are creating dedicated forecasting organizations whose only evaluation criteria is the accuracy of the forecast. The bonuses, promotions, and evaluations of the personnel in the organization depend on improvements in forecast accuracy. The forecasting organization is often part of the logistics planning team described in Chapter 10, "Logistics Organization Design and Development."

True Demand Capture

Measure true demand at the point of consumption.

In shortage gaming (customer's lack of trust of the vendor's ability to stock product), customers often order more than they truly need to protect against shortages. In cases of unsatisfied demand, the unsatisfied demand (backorders, substitutes, and/or lost sales) often goes unreported and therefore is not incorporated into the forecasting process. In either case, the true demand is not captured and is often ignored in the forecasting process. Every attempt to adjust reported demand for instances of backorders, lost sales, and substitutes should be made.

Demand should also be captured as close to the point and time of consumption as possible. In retail, the point of consumption is at the scanner where the bar code on the unit is scanned at the point-of-sale. The point of consumption in healthcare is often in the hospital or operating room when a syringe or pack of bandages is scanned from a cart or cabinet into the hospital or operating room. In service parts, the point of consumption is wherever a machine is being repaired and the new part is placed on to the repaired machine. In either case, the data stemming from the point and time of consumption is the most accurate data to reflect true demand. Any further handling or consolidation of the pure point-of-consumption data may destroy the integrity of the data.

Forecast Sharing

Communicate and reconcile forecasts with supply chain partners.

One of the major causes of forecast inaccuracy is the ripple effect of demand forecasting in the supply chain. As retailers try to forecast consumer demand, and wholesalers try to forecast retail demand, and manufacturers try to forecast wholesale demand, and suppliers try to forecast manufacturer demand, the error rate in the forecast increases exponentially. To combat this effect, there should be information sharing of consumer demand throughout the supply chain so that each participant can plan accordingly.

When I teach this principle in class, I ask the students to consider a way to get five pianists to play the same song at the same time in the same tempo without being able to see each other. Invariably, the answer comes back that we should give each pianist the same sheet of music, a metronome to keep tempo, and a director that each pianist can follow to learn when to begin, how to correct his play in mid-song, and when to stop. In forecast sharing, we need to give each player a consumer demand forecast to work to, a forecast for each subsequent product movement between each link in the supply chain, and a fourth-party director and supporting software tool to collaborate the activities of the players during the supply chain operations. These principles are the basis for *collaborative planning, forecasting, and replenishment* (CPFR), which is described in Chapter 6, "Supply Management."

Event Calendaring

Establish and implement an event calendar to improve accuracy.

The demand for many products and/or the dramatic increase in demand for many products is often related to a special event. For example, most Coke product purchased in Mexico are purchased on Friday, which is payday in most areas in Mexico. Most large appliances in Rochester, New York, are purchased on bonus day at Kodak. Mother's Day is one of the busiest days for the telephone companies.

The timing of these special events is typically known well in advance of the event itself. The impact on demand of these events is easily predictable from the impact patterns in previous events. That said, a good forecasting system should have a built-in event calendar that automatically tracks and forecasts for these special events.

One of the best examples of this phenomenon we have worked with is in the healthcare industry (see Figure 5-21).

For many products, the manufacturer, wholesale distributor, and health-care provider each carry several weeks of inventory for the same item. For many of those products, the demand is tied directly to surgeries that are scheduled eight or more weeks in advance, which is more than the manufacturing lead-time for many items. Simply incorporating the surgery schedule in the forecasting and supply chain scheduling process permits the elimination of 30 to 40 percent of that inventory.

Outlier Recognition and Patter Recognition

Eliminate statistical outliers from future forecasting models.

Many demands are mistakes—requests for the wrong item or the wrong quantity. Outlier identification and pattern recognition can and should prevent those demands from entering the system. An outlier is a data point that lies so far outside the norm that it should be tested, called into question for reasonability, and handled differently from normal demand data points. An example outlier is the demand during July, 1995, in Figure 5-22.

Pattern recognition or outlier identification algorithms should be used to prevent the outlier from skewing the regular forecasting process and algo-

FIGURE 5-21   Supply chain scheduling in the healthcare supply chain.

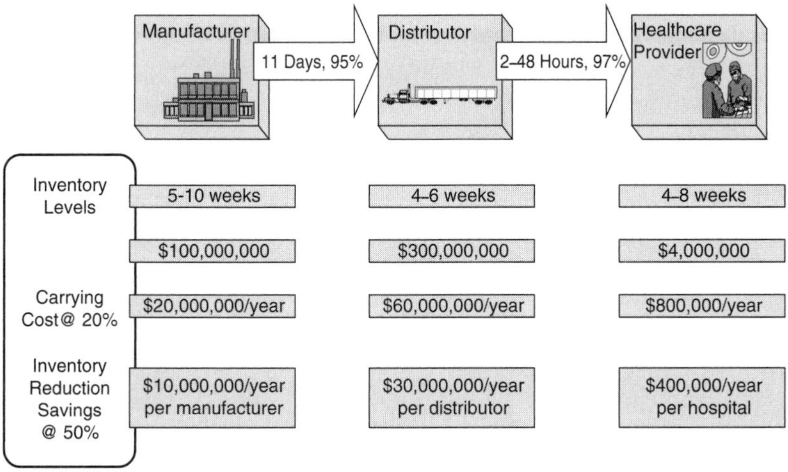

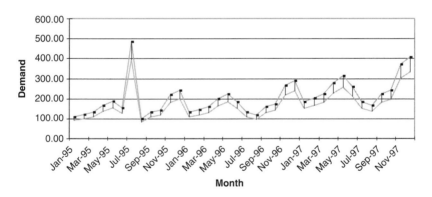

FIGURE 5-22   Outlier example.

rithms. (Pattern recognition algorithms are used by credit card companies to identify credit card theft when the card is used in types of stores to purchase amounts that deviate too far from the real owner's normal buying patterns.)

I came across an outlier and its effects when I was working with a roofing tile manufacturer in Florida a few years ago. As I toured their warehouses, I noticed that they were completely full. As I toured their manufacturing operations, I noticed the production lines were running at full capacity with no end in site. I asked the plant manager what their plan was for storing all the tiles. He had no answer. He explained that they were just following the production plan. Then it dawned on me that we were exactly one year down the road from hurricane Andrew, one of the most devastating on record. Can you imagine the impact of a hurricane on the demand for roofing tiles? Someone had not identified the hurricane demand as an outlier and the roofing tile manufacturer was running a production plan based on the impact of one of the most devastating hurricanes on record. That's an outlier that should have been eliminated.

High Reactivity

> *Design organization and control policies to insure quick reaction to forecast errors.*

Regardless of the forecast accuracy, the forecast will be wrong. Every effort should be made to respond quickly to the forecast errors that are the most costly in terms of excess inventory and/or lost customer service. Those errors should be prioritized and presented to the logistics planners for correction by the forecasting system. In those cases, orders can be expedited or delayed as required.

Top-Down, Bottom-Up Forecasting

> *Integrate and rationalize top-down and bottom-up forecasts with human intelligence.*

In almost every industry, leading and/or lagging economic and industry indicators can be used to help predict overall demand. In international business, the indicators should be incorporated from each country. Those-high level indicators should be used with the forecasted product mix to forecast SKU demand from the "top-down." Point-of-consumption data should also be used to generate SKU demand forecasts. The SKU forecasts should be used with the forecasted product mix to create category and business unit level forecasts, that is, from the "bottom-up." The "top-down" and "bottom-up" forecasts will no doubt differ to some degree and should be rationalized by a cross-functional forecasting planning team. *No forecasting system can replace the value of human judgment. The trick is to enable the system to manage the routine to enable human experts to focus on exceptional situations, corrections, and promotions.*

Best-Fit Forecasting

> *Choose the best forecasting model from among several competing options.*

Not all SKUs are made alike. Each item has its own unique demand pattern. Because some forecasting models work well for some demand patterns and other models work well for other patterns, a variety of forecasting models

FIGURE 5-23   Best-fit forecasting example.

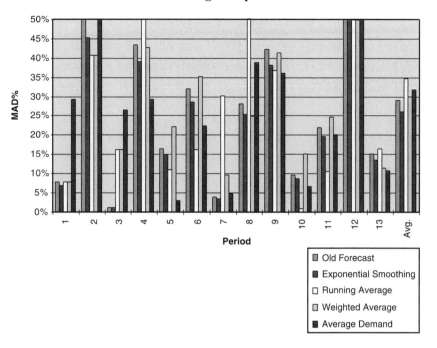

should be tested for each item (or demand pattern), and the model that works most accurately for each item should be utilized. This principle is sometimes referred to as *back-casting* because the models look back at historical demand and simulate the use of different forecasting techniques on historical data. An example back-casting analysis is provided in Figure 5-23.

Closed-Loop Forecasting

> *Develop and implement a repeatable, cross-functional, and measurable forecasting process.*

As I mentioned earlier, the problem with inaccurate forecasting rarely lies with the forecasting algorithm. In nearly every client situation I have worked in, the problem lies in the forecasting process. Closed-loop forecasting adopts the forecasting principles defined previously into the organizational discipline illustrated in Figure 5-24.

5.5   ORDER QUANTITY ENGINEERING

Efficient order quantities (EOQs) consider the *purchase order cost* (POC), the *annual demand rate* (AD), the *inventory carrying rate* (ICR), and u*nit inventory rate* (UIV). Large order quantities yield high inventory levels and

FIGURE 5-24   **Closed-loop forecasting.**

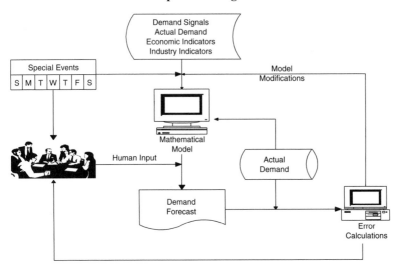

high inventory carrying costs but fewer orders and lower ordering costs. High ordering costs and demand rates suggest large order quantities. High ICRs and high unit inventory values suggest small order quantities. The tradeoffs are depicted graphically in Figure 5-25.

Mathematically, the EOQ is computed as follows:

$$EOQ = [(2 \times POC \times AD)/(ICR \times UIV)]^{1/2}$$

The formula does not consider opportunities for joint purchases or efficient handing units. The EOQ should be adjusted to consider quantity discounts, joint purchase opportunities; efficient handling units including full carton quantities, pallet layer quantities, full pallet quantities, full trailer load quantities; and the available storage capacity. These adjustments make the economic order quantity an *efficient logistics quantity* (ELQ).

The adjustment for the EOQ with quantity discounts is as follows:

$$EOQ = [(2 \times POC \times AD)/(ICR \times \{1 - d\} \times UIV)]^{1/2}$$

where d is the discounting rate (such as, 5 percent, 10 percent, 15 percent).

Many people argue that EOQ analysis is outdated. I argue that despite its deficiencies, an EOQ analysis should be completed as a part of any inventory strategy. First, the analysis suggests appropriate reordering intervals for all items. (The forecast annual demand divided by the EOQ is the optimal time between orders.) In addition, the analysis points out the importance of

FIGURE 5-25   Order quantity tradeoff curves.

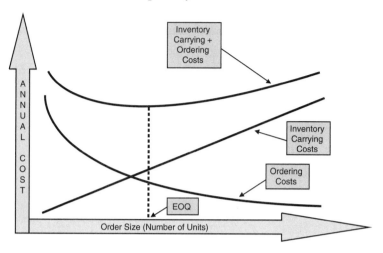

reducing the costs of placing purchase orders. The lower the purchase order cost, the more economical it becomes to order in small increments and the less inventory we will have in the system. The purchase order cost is typically dominated by the labor and paperwork costs of planning, negotiating, executing, and tracking purchase orders. The extent to which these functions can be automated via automated purchase order planning, e-procurement, online catalogs, online bidding, and online exchanges, is the extent to which inventory levels and lost sales costs may be reduced in the supply chain. The automation of these activities is addressed in Chapter 6.

In manufacturing, the purchase order cost corresponds to the setup cost of a machine or an entire production line. In manufacturing, large production runs are justified when the setup cost is high and the objective is to minimize the number and costs of setups. The tradeoff is the inventory that builds up as a result of the large production runs. The production run size that minimizes the total cost of setup and inventory carrying is the economic order (or run) quantity. An example economic run quantity calculation is provided in Figure 5-26. In that example, we were assisting a client with production planning for manufacturing rolls of carpet. At issue was the number of rolls to produce after the completion of a changeover of the machinery to a new type of carpet.

Note that in the example, the inventory carrying cost increases as the production run length increases and the setup cost declines accordingly. For the particular item in the example, the optimal run length is three rolls.

The analysis to determine the optimal run length is helpful; however, the most productive strategy for reducing total manufacturing costs is to

FIGURE 5-26   **Manufacturing run quantity analysis.**

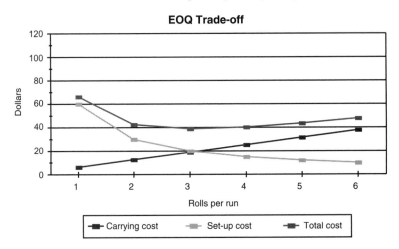

reduce the cost of setting up and/or changing over the machinery. The basic principles of setup time reduction are enumerated in the following:

- Focused factories
- Dedicated setup personnel
- Specialized tooling
- Point-of-use tooling
- Dedicated production lines
- Slow period scheduling
- Brand minimization
- Parallel tasking
- Optimal job scheduling
- Training and practice

The details, tips, techniques, and illustrative examples for these principles are available in many texts.[2]

5.6   FILL RATE PLANNING

Fill rate planning is the process of determining optimal service levels and inventory turns for each item. It is one of the most difficult planning decisions in all of logistics. The tradeoff between *inventory carrying costs* (ICCs) due to excess inventory and lost sales costs due to insufficient inven-

---

[2]Monden, Y., Toyota Production System, Institute of Industrial Engineers, Norcross, - Georgia, 1983.

tory is easy to state but difficult to model. Failure to work through the details of the modeling exercise leaves most of our clients on the inventory see-saw. We worked with the service parts organizations of one of the world's largest auto companies. They ride the inventory see-saw every quarter. When the dealerships receive complaints from customers due to out-of-stocks, the dealers send a scathing e-mail (with a copy to the vice president of sales) to the head of logistics demanding more inventory. The logistics manager typically responds by increasing the inventory allocations to the dealers. The next quarter, the CFO sees the excess inventory investments and sends the manager of logistics a scathing e-mail demanding that the inventory levels be reduced. The logistics manager responds by reducing the inventory allocations to the dealers, and so on.

The best way we have found to get off the see-saw is to model the effect of varying inventory and service levels on lost sales and inventory carrying cost. To assist our clients with this modeling and optimization effort, we developed a service level optimization tool called the fill rate planner. The tool (Figure 5-27) recommends the service and inventory level for each item that minimizes the sum total of inventory carrying and lost sales cost.

FIGURE 5-27   **Fill rate optimization tool.**
Source: LRI's Fill Rate Planner

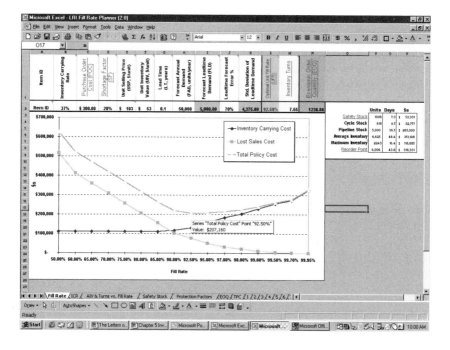

The tool takes into consideration the ICR, the *purchase order cost* (POC), the *shortage factor* (SF), UIV, *unit selling price* (USP), *lead time* (LT), *forecast annual demand* (FAD), and the forecast accuracy in computing the optimal *unit fill rate* (UFR*), optimal inventory levels for safety stock, cycle stock, and pipeline stock; optimal inventory turn rates, optimal order quantities, optimal reorder points, and optimal reorder time periods. The optimization is based on the minimization of the sum of ICCs and LSCs.

ICCs are estimated to be

- $ICC = ICR \times AIV$
- $AIV = AIL \times UIV$

- $AIL = SS + (EOQ/2) + \left(L \times \dfrac{AD}{365} \right)$

All other variables have been defined.
The lost sales cost is estimated to be

- $LSC = USP \times FAD \times (1 - UFR) \times SF$

The shortage factor is the portion of the unit sales price lost when a unit is not available (that is, when a unit is out of stock). The more critical the item, the greater the competition, and the more difficult the substitution, the higher the shortage factor. This is the only subjective factor in the analysis, and it is the stumbling block for most organizations working to determine optimal inventory targets. Most organizations argue that it is impossible to determine this shortage factor. My experience and research suggests that it is possible to determine a reasonable estimate of the shortage factor. In some situations, it is explicitly stated in a service contract. For example, one of our clients must pay their customer $200,000 per hour for every hour the customer's manufacturing line is shut down due to an out-of-stock condition. In other situations, we can know directionally what the percentage might be. I recently lived through one example.

I was on the faculty at Georgia Tech for several years. When I left to start LRI, I had to purchase a new computer. I wanted the newest, fastest, slickest laptop I could find. I remember finding a laptop made by the ABC computer company in a catalog that exceeded all of my expectations. I decided to order the computer. It cost $8,000 at that time.

After I gave the 1-800 customer service operator my credit card information, I asked when I should expect to receive the computer. The operator told me it would be 17 weeks. I was shocked. I remember telling the operator that I could go out of business in 17 weeks. I asked if there was anything I could do to expedite the delivery. She explained that if I let her debit my credit card immediately that I would go to the front of the line and receive the first computer in the shipment they were expecting the next week from the ABC company. I said that would be satisfactory. When the next week passed and I had not received the computer, I called the catalog company. I asked about the status of my order. The customer service representative explained that the ABC company was no longer quoting lead times. I was shocked again, first that the computer company could be out of stock on such a popular item and second that the catalog company had not called to inform me. I asked the representative if they had another computer with similar features. She directed me to page 24 in their catalog where I found a Toshiba Tecra 720 CDT. It had all the same features as the computer I had ordered and was $1,000 less, at $7,000. I asked when I could have the computer. She said I could have it the next day. I said, "Ship it!" I upgrade laptops nearly once each year and since the 720 CDT, I have owned the 740CDT, the 780 CDT, the Toshiba Portege 3100, Portege 3110, and I am typing this chapter on a Toshiba Tecra 8100.

How much did the ABC company lose because they were out of stock? They lost at least $8,000 in revenue plus the potential revenue they could have received had I had a good customer service experience. In that case, the shortage factor might be 200 or 300 percent, perhaps more. Now suppose the ABC company had called me directly, apologized for their stockout, and offered me their upgraded computer for the same price with a free extended warranty? They may have lost a little in the upgrade, but they would have picked that up many times over in potential future sales. These are the kinds of situations that must be considered in shortage factoring.

Fill rate can be expressed as the line, order, and/or UFR. In each case, the fill rate measures the ratio of satisfied to total demand. The UFR is the ratio of the total units shipped to the total units requested. The *line fill rate* (LFR) is the number of order lines completely satisfied to the total order lines. The *order fill rate* (OFR) is the ratio of the number of orders completely filled to the number of orders placed. In each case, the fill rate can be measured as the *first-time fill-rate* (FTFR), which assesses the fill rate upon initial demand. *Secondary fill rate* (SFR) is the fill rate achieved via substitutions and backorders. Unless stated otherwise, all references to fill rate here will be to FTFR.

5.7   INVENTORY CONTROL POLICY AND REPLENISHMENT DESIGN

As is the case in any type of system, there needs to be a reliable control policy for the operation of an inventory system. The choice of the control system depends on the complexity of the operating scenario, the number of items that need to be controlled, the number of locations where inventory may be housed, and the availability of timely information to support the inventory control policy. As we will see, simulation may be used to help choose the most effective inventory control policy.

We will consider here three types of inventory control policies:

- Distribution inventory control
- Manufacturing inventory control
- Situational inventory control

Distribution Inventory Control

There are nine popular distribution inventory control policies organized into three categories:

- Manual inventory control
  - *Two-Bin Systems* (2BS)
  - *Visual Review* (VR)
- Basic replenishment schemes
  - *Re-Order Point* (ROP) with *Economic Order Quantities* (EOQ) – ROP/EOQ
  - Re-Order Point (ROP) with *Order Up to Levels* (OUL) – ROP/OUL
  - *Review Time Period* (RTP) with Order Up to Levels (OUL) – RTP/OUL
  - Review Time Period with Re-Order Points and Order-Up-To-Levels – RTP/ROP/OUL
- Advanced control policies
  - *Joint Replenishment Programs* (JRP)
  - *Distribution Requirements Planning* (DRP)
  - *Continuous Replenishment Programs* (CRP)

We will consider the operation, advantages, disadvantages, and proper applications for each control policy.

Manual Inventory Control

The most common manual inventory control systems are two-bin systems and visual review.

Two-Bin Systems   In a 2BS, two, side-by-side locations are dedicated to an item. When the on-hand inventory in one location is depleted, an order large enough to fill the depleted location is placed, and the inventory in the other location begins to be withdrawn. This normally takes place with a manual visual review.

The 2BS is common in small manufacturing operations where a location may be a tote or pallet with component parts at an assembly station or in small warehouses where a location may be a lane in a flow rack or a compartment in a shelving unit.

The advantage of the 2BS is its simplicity. Many homes work on 2BSs for items ranging from potato chips to milk. The disadvantage is lack of reliability if the operators are not disciplined to monitor the inventory levels and/or if housekeeping obscures the inventory levels from the view of the operators.

Visual Review   Under VR, the on-hand inventory in each location is visually inspected and based on the inspector's judgment and/or using visual aids a replenishment order for an item may be placed. VR is common in small retail outlets and warehouses that lack the technology required to support automated inventory control policies.

As was the case with the 2BS, the advantage of visual inventory control is its simplicity. Most homes are managed with visual inventory control. The disadvantage is the lack of reliability if the workforce is undisciplined and/or if the housekeeping practices do not permit good sightlines for the products.

After the implementation of a large ERP system had blinded their inventory eyes and shutdown their inventory control programs, we recently recommended to one of our large Latin American retail clients that they relocate the buying staff from the fancy downtown offices to the warehouse so they could see the impact of their buying decisions on the occupancy, productivity, and safety of the warehouse operations. The initial resistance was fierce; however, the relocation yielded tremendous reductions in inventory and stockouts because the buying agents could see the impact of their decisions and reorder accordingly.

Basic Replenishment Schemes

There are four basic replenishment designs in use in industry: (ROP, EOQ), (ROP, OUL), (RTP, OUL), and (RTP, ROP, OUL).

(ROP, EOQ)   Under continuous review, the EOQ is ordered when the inventory position drops to or below the reorder point (see Figure 5-28). This is the simplest of the four basic inventory control policies. The ROP is typically set at the safety stock plus the forecasted lead time demand. One advantage is the use of the EOQ, which minimizes the sum of the ordering and inventory carrying costs. One disadvantage is the need to continuously review the inventory levels.

FIGURE 5-28   Reorder point with an EOQ.

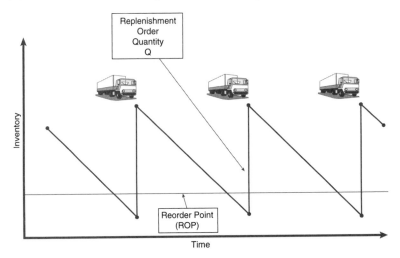

(ROP, OUL)   Under continuous review, a variable amount of inventory sufficient to bring the inventory position up to the OUL is ordered when the inventory position drops to or below the ROP (see Figure 5-29). The OUL is set to yield a target stockout probability.

(RTP, OUL)   Every RTP, a variable replenishment quantity is ordered to bring the inventory position up to the OUL (see Figure 5-30). One advantage is the periodic versus continuous consideration of inventory levels. The periods can be common for a variety of items and can be used in joint replenishment schemes. One disadvantage is the excess inventory that may be required to support this policy because inventory is ordered every period regardless of the inventory level. Another disadvantage is that lumpy or seasonal demand during a review period may lead to stockouts before the next review time period.

(RTP, ROP, OUL)   Every RTP, a variable replenishment quantity (OUL – I) is ordered to bring the inventory position up to the OUL *if* the inventory position is at or below the ROP (see Figure 5-31). This is generally the least costly of the four basic control policies; however, it is also the most difficult to understand and may lead to stockouts for those periods where the ending inventory is nearly at the ROP.

The advantages and disadvantages of the basic replenishment schemes are summarized in Table 5-2.

As described in the table, the most appropriate policy depends on the characteristics of the item it will be used for and the logistics conditions

FIGURE 5-29   Reorder point with a fixed OUL.

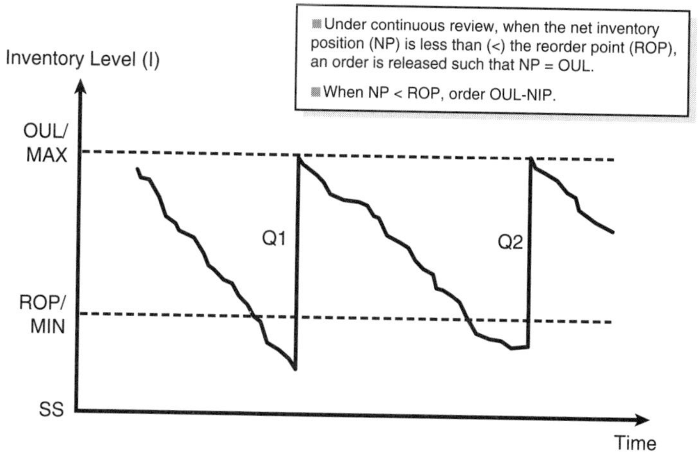

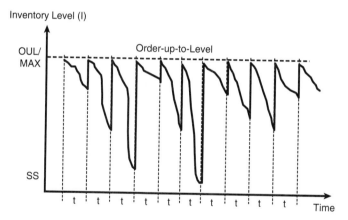

FIGURE 5-30   Review time period with OULs.

affecting the control policy. How then can we choose the best policy and the best configuration for each policy?

Control Policy Simulation

The best means we have found to choose the most appropriate policy parameters (that is, OUL, RTP, ROP, and EOQ) and to choose from among the potential policies is simulation. I have included some sample control policy simulation results in Figures 5-32 and 5-33.

Figure 5-32 is a simulation analysis we developed with a retail client who was trying to determine the optimal RTP (or days between store deliveries) and the optimal ROP for a RTP-ROP-OUL policy. The objective was to choose

FIGURE 5-31   Review time periods, ROPs, and OULs.

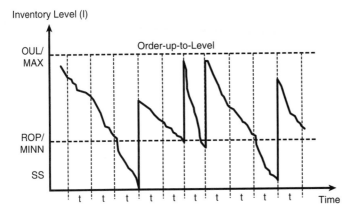

TABLE 5-2   Advantages and Disadvantages of Basic Replenishment Schemes

Control Policy	Advantages	Disadvantages	Notes
ROP/EOQ	Simple system. Fixed order quantity.	Can't cope with big swings.	EOQ computation may be unreliable.
ROP/OUL	Best ROP/OUL = best ROP/EOQ.	Heavy computational effort not justified except for A items.	Most popular policy but with arbitrary parameters.
RTP/OUL	Coordination of replenishment of related items. Regular opportunity to adjust the OUL.	Carrying costs are higher than in continuous review systems.	Good when demand pattern is changing regularly with time.
RTP/ROP/ OUL	Overall least cost control policy.	High computational effort. Difficult to understand.	Not justifiable for B or C items.

the set of control parameters (ROP, RTP, and OUL) with the lowest sum of inventory and replenishment costs that yielded a zero percent stockout using a historical demand data set. For next-day deliveries, a ROP of 4 days on-hand was the lowest inventory level that would yield zero percent stocks; for 2-day deliveries, 6 days on-hand; and for 3-day deliveries, 7 days on-hand.

Figure 5-33 is a simulation analysis, which determines the optimal OUL (expressed in days-of-supply) considering next-day, 2-day, and 3-day replen-

FIGURE 5-32   **Inventory control policy simulation results.**

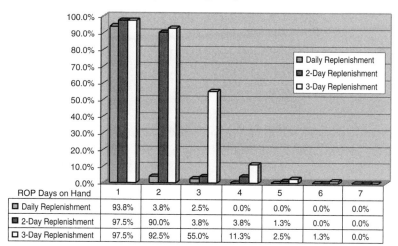

ROP Days on Hand	1	2	3	4	5	6	7
☐ Daily Replenishment	93.8%	3.8%	2.5%	0.0%	0.0%	0.0%	0.0%
■ 2-Day Replenishment	97.5%	90.0%	3.8%	3.8%	1.3%	0.0%	0.0%
☐ 3-Day Replenishment	97.5%	92.5%	55.0%	11.3%	2.5%	1.3%	0.0%

FIGURE 5-33   **Replenishment scheme simulation results.**

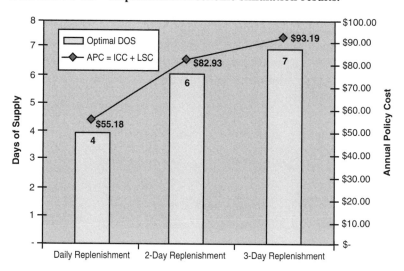

ishment schemes and the sum of inventory carrying and lost sales costs. The optimal policy under these conditions is next-day replenishment with 4 days-of-supply set as the OUL.

Advanced Inventory Control Policies

The advanced inventory control policies defined here are

- Joint, coordinated replenishments
- *Distribution requirements planning* (DRP)
- Continuous replenishment

Joint, Coordinated Replenishments

To leverage the cost of ordering, joint, coordinated purchases should be arranged for those items with common economic time supplies. (The *economic time supply* [ETS] is the optimal time between replenishments based on the EOQ for the item. The ETS is expressed in years as the EOQ divided by the FAD. (The ETS is expressed in days by multiplying the ETS in years by the number of business days per year.) Based on the ETS profiles, fixed cycle replenishment schedules should be established with each vendor. A dedicated volume should be scheduled on the cycle with forecasted purchase orders converted to firm POs at the latest possible date. To take advantage of handling and transportation economies, order quantities should round up or down to case, layer, pallet, and/or container quantities.

An example coordinated, joint replenishment scheme for a large food wholesaler is depicted in Figure 5-34. The figure depicts the sales per week as a percent of a full truckload and the current ratio of the shipping weeks to the receiving weeks for 30 SKUs with common economic time supplies (in this case weekly). The coordinated replenishment scheme assigns the SKUs into truckloads to minimize the number of required truckloads.

FIGURE 5-34   Joint replenishment program example.

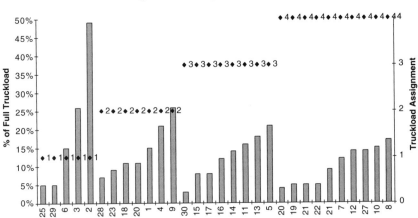

Distribution Requirements Planning (DRP)

Distribution Requirements Planning (DRP) is a methodology for forecasting, calculating, and summarizing shipping requirements between locations in a distribution network. (This description is not meant to be a detailed description of the computations in DRP.[3]) DRP treats distribution hierarchies like bills-of-material in computing requirements.

An example DRP requirements calculation is illustrated in Figure 5-35. The figure illustrates a three-level distribution network with a factory shipping to two regional distribution centers, each regional distribution center shipping to two local distribution centers, and each local distribution center shipping to two, three, or four customers. The DRP calculation simply estimates the shipping requirements for each node in the network as the sum of the shipping requirements for each node one-level downstream that the node serves. For example, in Figure 5-35, the shipping requirements for DC I are the sum of the shipping requirements for the four customers it services (4+2+3+5 = 14); the shipping requirements for regional DC A are the sum of the shipping requirements for the two local DCs it services (14+12 = 26); and the shipping requirements for the factory are the sum of the shipping requirements for the two regional DCs it services (26+18 = 44). The factory shipping requirements are then fed as end requirements into the factory's MRP algorithms.

FIGURE 5-35   **Distribution requirements planning example.**

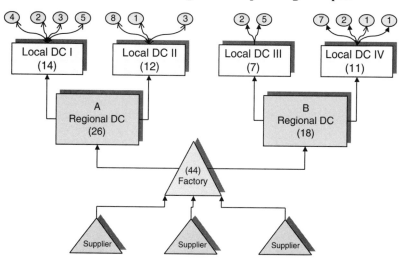

---

[3] Smith, B.T., *Focus Forecasting and DRP*, Vantage Press, New York, New York, 1991.

Continuous Replenishment

According to the ECR Report, continuous replenishment is "the practice of partnering between distribution channel members that changes the traditional replenishment process from distributor-generated purchase orders, usually based on EOQs, to the replenishment of products based on actual and fore-casted demand." Figure 5-36 illustrates the principles of continuous replenishment in action for a supply chain including a retail store, wholesale distributor, and supplier.

Retail store inventories are maintained perpetually, meaning that *point-of-sale* (POS) data is used in conjunction with cycle counting to insure 100 percent inventory accuracy at the store level. Under perpetual inventory, the retail store inventory is calculated continually as follows:

- $I_{i,t} = I_{i,t-1} + R_{i,t} - POS_{i,t}$
- $I_{i,t}$ = On-hand inventory for item i at the end of period t
- $R_{i,t}$ = Receipts for item i during period t
- $POS_{i,t}$ = Sales for item i during period t

At the cutoff time for each ordering or RTP (we will assume here that each store receives daily deliveries under true continuous retail replenishment), an order is placed with the distributor for any item for which

- $I_{i,t} \leq ROP_i$.
- ROP_i = Reorder point for item i

FIGURE 5-36   **Continuous replenishment program concept.**

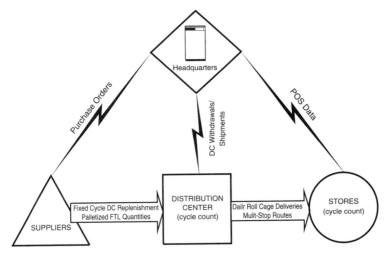

- The size of the order for item I, $Q_{i,t} = OUL_i - I_{i,t}$.
- $OUL_{i,t}$ = Order-up-to-Level for item i in period t

The OUL is computed as a function of desired service levels, material handling efficiencies, and ordering costs.

At the wholesale level, the daily shipping requirements for each item for each customer are summarized and planned into multi-stop deliveries for each store the wholesale location services. The inventory levels at the wholesale level are also maintained perpetually with cycle counting and warehouse withdrawal data. The inventory level for an item i at the end of any period t at the wholesale level is computed as

- $I_{i,t} = I_{i,t-1} + R_{i,t} - W_{i,t}$

where

- $R_{i,t}$ = Receipts for item i during period t
- $W_{i,t}$ = Withdrawals (or shipments) for item i during period t

As was the case at the retail level, an order is placed with a supplier for an item when the inventory level reaches or dips below the ROP for the item. In the most advanced inventory control systems, the forecasted retail and wholesale replenishment orders are calculated, collaborated, and communicated in advance.

Best practices in replenishment schemes combine the best features of these policies with considerations for joint purchasing, efficient handling increments, and capacity constraints.

5.8   INVENTORY DEPLOYMENT
Inventory deployment is the assignment and allocation of inventory to levels and/or facilities in a logistics network (see Figure 5-37). World-class practices in inventory deployment incorporate

- Optimal positioning
- Dynamic redeployment
- Postponement
- Four-wall inventory management
- Global inventory visibility

Optimal Inventory Positioning
In the simplest deployment scheme, all inventory is housed in a single, central distribution center. Though the least inventory cost option, the single DC deployment model is usually inadequate to meet rapid response time

FIGURE 5-37   Three-level deployment model.

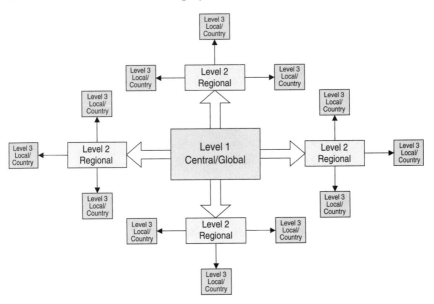

requirements. (We have one client that must deliver parts to a global client base within 2 hours of receiving an order. That is physically impossible from a single DC.) Hence, inventory must often be deployed in locations (regional and local) closer to customer locations. The most difficult challenge is to determine the amount and timing of the deployment.

A compromise and often optimal deployment scheme is to deploy A items all the way to level 3, B items to level 2, and hold C items centrally at level 1. A items are the most critical to the customer and must be delivered quickly to support a segmented customer service policy. In addition, A items are frequently delivered and the transportation cost to deliver them from a central DC is often prohibitive. C items are the least critical to the customer and the inventory investment required to forecast and position C items locally is often prohibitive.

Dynamic Redeployment   Once a plan for inventory positioning has been planned and executed, changes in the business environment and/or item characteristics quickly obsolete the original plan. Good deployment systems constantly review the efficiency of the current deployment and recommend redeployment scenarios. The redeployments should rebalance inventory levels (matching overages and shortages) at the lowest possible transportation cost and with the least impact of stockouts in the network.

Postponement Another critical inventory deployment decision is the timing of the customization and positioning of inventory. This deployment decision is sometimes referred to as postponement. The premise of postponement is that inventory investments can be minimized by delaying decisions related to the configuration of an item in manufacturing (manufacturing postponement) or assembly (assembly postponement) and to the positioning of an item in distribution (distribution postponement). The opposite of postponement is speculation—manufacturing/assembly speculation and distribution speculation. Descriptions, examples, advantages, and disadvantages of the various postponement/speculation strategies are provided in Tables 5-3 and 5-4.

Four-Wall Inventory Management Four-wall inventory management is the management of inventory within the four walls of a warehouse or distribution center. The impact of inventory management within a warehouse or DC on overall inventory investments and total supply chain performance is oftentimes underestimated. This is especially the case in the face of SKU proliferation, smaller shipment sizes, lower margins for error, and shrinking order ship times.

TABLE 5-3   Manufacturing and Distribution Speculation and Postponement*

		Distribution	
		Speculation	Postponement
Manufacturing/Procurement	Speculation	*Full speculation* Products are made to a production forecast and pre-positioned in a distribution network. Ex. Campbell's Soup, Coke	*Distribution postponement* Products are made or purchased based on forecasted demand and held centrally for distribution. Ex. L.L. Bean, Lands' End Sears.com
	Postponement	*Manufacturing postponement* Products are engineered, made, and/or assembled after an order has been received at a variety of locations close to customers. Ex. Flower Shop, Subway	*Full postponement* Products are engineered, made, and/or assembled after an order has been received at a single location. Components may even be merged-in-transit. Ex. Dell Computer, MICRON

*Adapted from M.C. Cooper, Ohio State University

TABLE 5-4　Pros and Cons of Speculation and Postponement*

	Full Speculation	Manufacturing Postponement	Logistics Postponement	Full Postponement
Production costs	⇓	➚	⇓	➚
Inventory costs	⇑	➚	↙	⇓
Distribution costs	⇓	⇓	⇑	⇑
Customer service	⇑	➚	↙	⇓

* Adapted from M.C. Cooper, Ohio State University, Journal of Business Logistics, 1998

The most important disciplines of four-wall inventory management are

- ABC cycle counting
- Container and location tracking
- Real-time warehouse management systems

ABC Cycle Counting

The discipline of cycle counting requires counting a portion of the warehouse locations each day (in lieu of a single annual count of all locations known as a physical inventory). As a result, each item and location is counted once during a counting cycle. For example, if one percent of the items/locations are counted each day, then each item is counted every 100 days. The advantages of cycle counting include avoiding the massive disruption of operations inherent in annual physical inventory counts, obtaining discrepancy notifications closer to the time of occurrence so that corrective action is more likely to occur, and the ability to count different items/locations on different cycles. Some items, due to their value and/or velocity, are more critical to the overall inventory and shipping accuracy than are other items. Those A items should be counted more frequently than the other items. A cycle counting schedule based on the value and/or velocity of the items is called ABC cycle counting. A recent survey by KPMG revealed the following cycle counting frequencies among a variety of corporations (see Figure 5-38).

Container and Location Tracking

Container and location tracking simply requires that every container (tote, case, pallet, trailer, railcar, and so on) and every location (bin, half-bin, pallet opening, staging position, and so on) be automatically identified by bar code scanning or RF tagging. A variety of automatic identification tech-

FIGURE 5-38   **Cycle counting frequencies.**
Source: KPMG

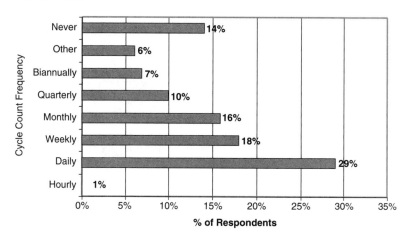

nologies are described and illustrated in Chapter 9, "Logistics and Supply Chain Management Systems," on logistics information systems. These new-fashioned technologies are current generation means of implementing the old-fashion practice of having a place for everything and keeping everything in its place.

Real-Time Warehouse Management Systems

Real-time warehouse management systems are required to support container and location tracking. Due to intensified cross-docking, value-added activities and shrinking order cycle times, batch warehouse management systems cannot keep pace with inventory movements in the 21st century warehouse. Warehouse management systems are described in Chapter 9 on logistics information systems.

Global Inventory Visibility

Our human nature is to lack trust in the things we can't see. (The greatest example I know of is the test of salvation, which requires an expression of faith in God whom we can't see but whose work is real.) Wherever there are places we can't "see" inventory in the supply chain (called supply chain blindspots), we tend to order excess to cover our lack of trust. Some customers place the same order multiple times if they are not notified of a delivery date or a status on the order. Some players in the supply chain inflate order sizes to cover "unforeseen" circumstances that may occur in the "blindspots" or "black holes" in the supply chain.

The only way I know around this phenomena is to provide true global inventory visibility by item, by order, by location, and in-transit. This capability is sometimes referred to as the glass pipeline. The best example of this glass pipeline capability in the logistics world is most likely the *Total Asset Visibility* (TAV) program within the U.S. Army. The program was developed to enable a commanding officer located on a battlefield anywhere in the world to know within real-time what assets are in his control in close proximity and their specific location within a container. A picture of the RF tag and automated manifest used to support the TAV program are provided in Figure 5-39.

5.9 INVENTORY MANAGEMENT SYSTEMS
As evidenced by the length of this chapter, the functionality of an *inventory management system* (IMS) must be reliable and substantial. A partial list of IMS requirements is provided in the following:

- Inventory activity profiling
  - ABC days-on-hand profile
  - ABC turns profile
  - ABC inventory valuation analysis
  - ABC demand variability analysis
- Inventory performance measurement
  - Inventory investment and carrying cost analysis
  - Inventory turns and days-on-hand analysis
  - Planner productivity and performance monitoring
  - Forecasting accuracy
  - Unit, line, and order fill rates

FIGURE 5-39   **RF tag for container tracking and optical memory card for automated manifesting.**
Source: U.S. Armed Services

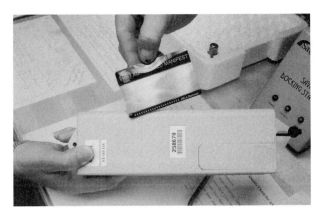

- Forecasting
  - Best-fit forecasting
  - Top-down and bottom-up forecasting
  - Outlier and pattern recognition
- Order quantity engineering
  - Economic order quantity analysis
  - Efficient logistics quantity adjustments
- Service level optimization
  - Safety stock calculations and recommendations
  - Optimal turn and fill rate recommendations
- Inventory control systems
  - Re-order points, order-up-to-levels, and fixed cycle replenishment
  - Inventory control policy simulation
  - Joint replenishment
  - Continuous replenishment
  - Distribution requirements planning
- Inventory deployment
  - Deployment optimization
  - Dynamic redeployment
  - Container and item tracking
  - Global inventory visibility

The role of an IMS, links with other logistics information systems, and prominent IMS vendors are described more fully in Chapter 9.

5.10   INVENTORY ORGANIZATION DESIGN AND DEVELOPMENT

Because inventory investment and availability is so critical to the overall success of a logistics-oriented enterprise, the organization of the inventory management activity is crucial to the success of the organization as a whole. Within the inventory management activity, we recommend the following organizational techniques. The techniques are designed to assist the enterprise with increasing inventory turns and service levels at the same time.

Dedicated Forecasting Organization

If forecasting is carried out in anything other than a dedicated forecasting organization, the forecast will carry some inherent biases. For example, if the forecast is developed in the sales organization, the forecast will be biased upward if the sales culture rewards optimism, or biased downward if the culture rewards exceeding expectations. Knowing these inherent biases, the other parts of the organization — manufacturing, warehousing, transportation, and so on—begin to create their own forecasts, adjusted in their favor. All of sudden, there is no real forecast, just a variety of interpretations of projected sales adjusted in each party's favor. This is a result of human nature and individuals following the organization's spoken or unspoken system of metrics. We can borrow an analogy from music, where to get many instruments playing together in concert; all of the musicians need to be working from the same sheet of music and under the direction of a single director.

We typically recommend that an individual or group of individuals be dedicated to the forecasting process. Their evaluation is based solely on the accuracy of the forecast at all levels. That forecast is produced and shared at all levels in the organization and in all relevant units of measure.

Certification in Inventory Management Principles
The tradeoffs in inventory management are many, varied, and oftentimes counterintuitive. The interdependencies and analytics involved in forecasting, lost sales computations, order quantity engineering, safety stock calculations, reorder points, combined replenishments, and so on, have left many of the best logistics organizations in a supply chain quandary. The level of understanding of the tradeoffs and analysis imbedded in these critical inventory management decisions cannot be underestimated. Yet, many of the largest inventory management organizations in the United States are staffed with individuals who have not been formally trained in the science of inventory management.

We recommend that individuals in key inventory management roles be certified in inventory decision science through organizations like APICS or The Logistics Institute at Georgia Tech.

Integration with All Other Logistics Activities
The decisions made by individuals working in customer service, procurement, manufacturing, transportation, and warehousing all impact inventory investments and availability. Operating in isolation, those individuals and teams cannot possibly maximize the effectiveness of the inventory that is available to the enterprise. Those individuals and teams should operate with a common purpose and plan toward utilizing the inventory investment. That common purpose and plan should be established in shared meetings, metrics, and systems that give visibility and urgency to the inventory performance of the enterprise.

Evaluations Based on Performance to Target Fill Rates and Turn Objectives
Because there is a dual objective in inventory management— maximize service levels and minimize inventory investment—the individuals responsible for managing inventory should have individual evaluations based on the service level and inventory investment performance of the items under their management.

C H A P T E R

SUPPLY MANAGEMENT

> "The foolish ones took their lamps but did not take any oil with them. The wise, however, took oil in jars along with their lamps."
>
> *Matthew 25:3-4*

D URING THE LAST **20 YEARS,** I have led more than 300 logistics seminars and conference programs. In all that time, I have had only one situation where students were literally willing to fight over an issue. It occurred when I was teaching about procurement policy in a supply chain strategy class. One of the students was the head of procurement for one of the large auto companies. In the prior month, one of his company's assembly lines was shut down for a couple of days because of an interruption in the supply of car seats. As it would happen, another student in the class had custom ordered a car from that company that was supposed to be produced during those same days in the same factory where the shutdown occurred. Evidently, the student needed the new car to impress a friend or business associate. In anger and in retaliation over not receiving his car on the day it was promised, he decided to try to humiliate the head of procurement from the auto company by loudly elaborating on the procurement deficiencies of the auto company. The procurement chief was quick to defend himself and his organization. When the disgruntled customer started to speak again, I worked to politely calm their nerves. When he and the procurement chief continued to debate under the tone of my lecture, I finally had to ask them to either step outside or dismiss themselves from the seminar. Can you imagine a high-noon draw over a car seat?

Supply is an important topic. It can be an emotional topic. The stakes are high. Disruptions can be expensive. One of our clients must pay a large chip manufacturer more than $200,000 per hour for any interruption they cause due to lack of supply. A recent study showed a 9 to 10 percent decline in share price on the day following announcements of supply disruptions.

Supply is the process of acquiring (through purchase or manufacture) inventory to satisfy the inventory requirements developed in the inventory master plan. In our logistics master planning methodology, supply master planning (see Figure 6-1) follows inventory master planning because we need the inventory availability schedule, fill rate requirements, and deployment plan as requirements for the supply plan. Supply master planning precedes transportation master planning because the number and location of all inbound locations is not fixed until all sourcing decisions have been made.

6.1 FUNDAMENTALS OF SUPPLY

Supply master planning (see Figure 6-2) is the organized program of (1) compiling and analyzing supply activity profiles, (2) establishing and monitoring supply performance measures, (3) implementing world-class supply practices, (4) designing a supply management system, and (5) developing a supply organization.

The objective of supply master planning is to identify the supply measures, practices, and systems that will minimize the total supply cost while meeting the inventory availability schedule determined in inventory master planning. We will be focusing primarily on the procurement side of supply logistics, or inbound logistics.

6.2 SUPPLY ACTIVITY PROFILING

In profiling supply activity, we compile and analyze supply and supplier activity to build a database for decision making throughout the supply master planning program. Done properly, the profiling process should yield the design and population of a supply activity data warehouse. Ideally, the *logistics information system* (LIS) should maintain a repository of historic purchase orders and a supplier master file in a data warehouse equipped with data-mining tools to discover and illustrate patterns in supply activity.

The principle components of a supply activity profile are the *supplier activity profile* (SAP), *item purchasing activity profile* (IPAP), *supplier-item activity profile* (SIAP), and purchase order profile. These are essentially the customer activity profiles viewed from the opposite side of the table.

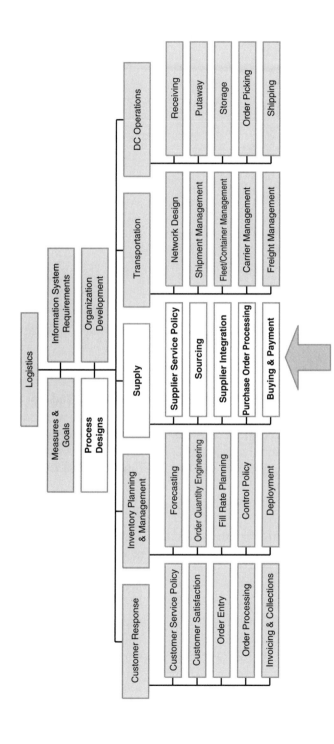

FIGURE 6-1 Supply in the logistics framework.

FIGURE 6-2   Supply master planning methodology.

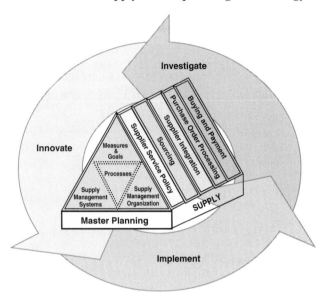

Supplier Activity Profile
In supplier activity profiling, the LIS should compute, monitor, and report purchasing activity by supplier and supplier location in dollars, cases, pieces, weight, volume, frequency, orders, lines, and deliveries, creating and maintaining rankings, and supplier segments (ABC). The SAP can and should be used in vendor negotiations and to reveal opportunities for supplier rationalization.

Item Purchasing Activity Profile
In item purchasing activity profiling the LIS should compute, monitor, and report line item purchasing activity in dollars, pieces, cases, pallets, cube, weight, and lines.

Supplier-Item Purchase Activity Profile
In supplier-SKU activity profiling, the LIS should compute, monitor, and report the purchasing activity in dollars, cases, cube, and weight in nine purchasing segments: AA, AB, AC, BA, BB, BC, CA, CB, and CC (supplier class or SKU class). As was the case in customer response, this joint distribution will be used in creating a segmented supplier service policy and a segmented inbound logistics strategy.

Purchase Order Profile

In purchase order profiling, the LIS should compute, monitor, and illustrate the distribution of lines, cases, weight, and cube per purchase orders.

6.3   SUPPLY PERFORMANCE MEASUREMENT

As we have explained throughout, it is important to hold each logistics activity accountable to business measurements that align the execution and planning of the activity with the other logistics activities and motivate highly competitive performance. Doing so requires a set of financial, productivity, quality, and response-time metrics. Here we review the related indicators in supply management. These indicators are a mix of metrics for monitoring the performance of our internal supply organization and the performance or our suppliers. The supplier metrics should be a foundation for a supplier selection and negotiation program.

Supply Financial Indicators

The four key supply financial indicators are

* *Total supply cost* (TSC)
* *Purchase order cost* (POC)
* *Supplier return on inventory* (SROI)
* *Supplier total logistics cost* (STLC)

Total Supply Cost (TSC)   The TSC includes all the costs related to supply planning, supplier management, and procurement execution. Those costs include related personnel costs, telecommunications, office space, and computer hardware and software dedicated to the supply process. An example computation of the total supply cost is provided in Figure 6-3.

Purchase Order Cost (POC)   The cost per purchase order is a critical element in supply planning, affecting the size of order quantities and related inventories. The most familiar affect is in the *economic order quantity* (EOQ) where the greater the POC, the greater EOQ, and the greater the resulting average inventory levels. One of the keys to reducing inventory levels then is to dramatically reduce the cost per purchase order.

The overall cost per purchase order can be computed simply by dividing the TSC by the number of purchase orders placed. Ideally, the POC should be computed, maintained, and monitored for each vendor and purchase order type. The individual elements of the POC include the staff, space, communications, supplies, and overhead cost to plan, negotiate, check, execute, track, and pay a purchase order.

FIGURE 6-3   Total supply cost calculation.
Source: Logistics Scoreboard

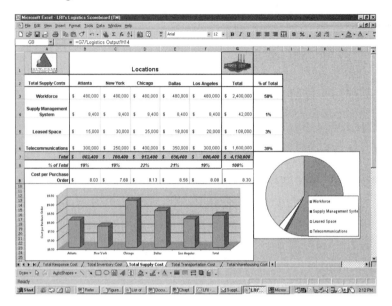

Supplier Return on Inventory (SROI)   The SROI is computed as the total profit on SKUs provided by that vendor divided by the average inventory value for that vendor. It is an effective indicator of the efficiency of logistics transactions executed with that supplier. The LIS should compute, monitor, and report the return on inventory for each vendor, providing rankings and segments accordingly.

Total Acquisition Cost (TAC)   The TAC of an item (sometimes referred to as total ownership cost or total logistics cost) for each supplier includes the cost of the item and the cost of purchase order placement, float, inventory carrying, lost sales, transportation, warehousing, and international logistics fees. Since the terms of payment, unit cost, logistics capabilities, and locations infrastructure vary widely by supplier, the TACs can vary greatly for the same SKU. Hence, the TAC is a critical metric upon which to base sourcing decisions.

Because many of the costs included in TAC are typically either ignored or hidden, and because the unit cost is the most readily available indicator and has historically been used as the sole basis for supplier selection, computing the total acquisition cost for the supply and SKU base is normally an eye-opening experience. An example TAC analysis comparing international and domestic sourcing options is provided in Figure 6-4.

FIGURE 6-4 Total acquisition cost analysis.
Source: LRI's Sourcing Optimizer

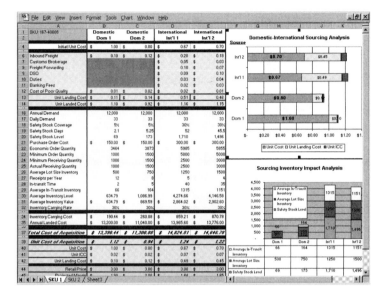

Supply Management Productivity

Supply management productivity indicators are used primarily to monitor and motivate buyer performance. The most popular supply productivity measures for the organization and for each buyer/planner are the following:

- Number of SKUs managed
- Number of suppliers managed
- Dollar amounts of purchasing managed
- Number of purchase orders launched per person-hour
- Inventory turns versus target
- Fill rate performance versus target

The inverse of the purchase orders per person-hour is the person-hours per purchase order, an indicator of the human work content per person-order. Because labor is typically the most expensive element of purchase order cost and because the overall availability of labor is shrinking, continuing to reduce the person-hours per purchase order is a critical success factor in supply management. In fact, many of the world-class supply practices described here are aimed primarily at reducing the human work content and related propensity of errors in the communication of order quantities requirements up and down the supply chain.

Supply Quality

Four helpful indicators of supply quality are

* *Perfect purchase order percentage* (PPOP)
* *Vendor fill rate* (VFR)
* *Supplier satisfaction index* (SSI)
* Matching rate of receipts and purchase orders

The PPOP is the percentage of all purchase orders that are delivered perfectly. A perfect purchase order arrives on time, without damage, and with perfect documentation at the right location with each line item request completely satisfied with the correct item in the correct quantity. This indicator should be closely monitored for each vendor and vendor location. It is not unusual to find perfect PO percentages below 50 percent.

The VFR measures the percentage of demand satisfied by a vendor. It can and should be measured as order fill, line fill, and unit fill.

The SSI is an overall indicator of a supplier's performance, incorporating a variety of factors typically including the elements of the perfect order percentage along with less quantifiable factors such as general responsiveness, honesty, and service attitude.

The matching rate of receipts and purchase orders records the percentage of receiving lines that match the delivery timing and quantities specified on the purchase order.

Supply Cycle Times

Purchase order cycle time (POCT) and *purchase order cycle time variability* (POCTV) are the principle indicators of supply cycle time performance for each vendor and vendor location.

6.4   SUPPLIER SERVICE POLICY (SSP)

A SSP is a set of guidelines for choosing suppliers, monitoring supplier performance, and designing inbound logistics programs. The SSP should include

* Supplier logistics certification criteria and monitoring to established targets
* Supplier classification based on logistics performance and activity levels
* Nonconformance penalty programs
* Segmented inbound logistics strategies

Supplier Certification Criteria

A key step in supply master planning is the creation of a set of supplier logistics certification criteria, a set of performance measures, logistics capabilities, and other business requirements that must be met or exceeded that qualify a supplier to participate in our supply base. The logistics information system should compute, monitor, and report supplier performance to these predetermined supplier certification criteria such as on-time delivery, fill rate, delivery quality, documentation, unitization, labeling, packaging, and PPOP.

Nonconformance Penalties

An important follow-up to the creation of supplier certification criteria is the design of rewards and penalties for extraordinary performance or nonconformance to established criteria. Typical rewards are high-profile vendor recognition, long-term contracts, and sole sourcing. Typical penalties include fines for specific violations of the certification criteria, sourcing reductions, and/or rejected receipts. The LIS should support and automate a program of chargebacks for nonconformance to stated criteria according to published nonconformance charges.

One of our retail clients inspects each receipt, takes a digital picture of each nonconformance, invoices the supplier for each violation based on its published penalty charge, and includes the digital picture with the nonconformance invoice. Another organization classifies their vendors into "white hat" and "black hat" categories based on their historic delivery quality. Black hat vendors are charged $20 per hour for every hour spent in receiving inspection. The most severe nonconformance penalty program I am aware of is a client who charges each vendor twice the retail value of all the contents of an inbound truckload if there is ANY nonconformance in the entire truckload.

Supplier Classification

Based on performance to established targets and inbound logistics volumes, suppliers should be classified into three or four segments. One large retailer classifies suppliers as red light (100 percent receiving inspection), yellow light (50 percent receiving inspection), and green light (5 percent receiving inspection). The LIS should continually rank and classify suppliers based on their performance to certification standards. A template for segmenting vendors and items for the purposes of inbound logistics planning is provided in Figure 6-5.

FIGURE 6-5   **Supplier-item classification.**

		Supplier Classification		
		A	B	C
Item Classification	A	A Items from A Suppliers	A Items from B Suppliers	A Items from C Suppliers
	B	B Items from A Suppliers	B Items from B Suppliers	B Items from C Suppliers
	C	C Items from A Suppliers	C Items from B Suppliers	C Items from C Suppliers

Segmented Inbound Logistics

The performance and activity classification of suppliers should be used in conjunction with the SKU inbound activity classification to segment the inbound logistics activity into nine or more segments. As a minimum, specific inbound strategies should be developed for A items inbound from A suppliers, A items inbound from B suppliers, and so on, to C items inbound from C suppliers. This segmentation will suggest an initial rationalization of the supply base and a streamlining of alternative logistics programs for specific inbound flows.

The logistics information system should support a segmented logistics policy with logistics strategies developed uniquely for ABC × ABC supplier-SKU segments. An example appears in Figure 6-6. The figure presents an inbound logistics strategy developed for a recent client. Suppliers are classified by size and performance into A, B, C, and D categories. Seven commodities and A, B, C, and D classes of items based on unit sales and item popularity have been specified. For each cross-section of suppliers and items, an optimal inbound logistics strategy is recommended based on

FIGURE 6-6   **Inbound logistics strategy and stratification.**

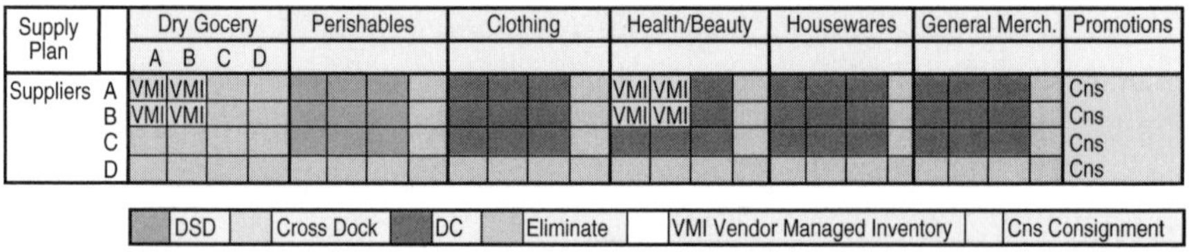

improvements in customer service and logistics cost reductions. The optional strategies include

- *Vendor managed inventories* (VMI) for stable, popular items coming from reliable suppliers
- *Cross-docking* for time-sensitive products
- *Traditional warehousing* and delivery for slow-moving products and commodities
- *Consignment inventory* for promotional items
- *Outsourcing* to wholesalers for the slowest moving items in all categories

6.5 SOURCING

World-class sourcing practices include

- Make-buy analysis
- Total acquisition cost analysis
- Global sourcing
- Ongoing supply base rationalization and consolidation
- Primary-secondary sourcing
- Electronic bid-based sourcing

Make-Buy Analysis

The first sourcing decision for each item is whether to make it or buy it. The decision should take into account a long-term business strategy, core competencies, the capabilities of optional supply sources, total ownership cost, and quality implications associated with internal versus external sourcing. Internal sources should be held accountable to the same supplier certification criteria established in the supplier service policy.

A common supplier sourcing review involves outsourcing component supply. An example is illustrated in Figure 6-7. The results presented in the figure are from an assessment of the cost per vehicle advantage related to component outsourcing among the Big Three auto makers. In this assessment, Chrysler maintains a $660 per vehicle cost advantage over General Motors and a $220 per vehicle cost advantage over Ford due to outsourcing major components.

Outsourcing benefits are not always this significant and there can be some loss of quality and customer service in outsourcing. Nonetheless, the benefits are potentially large enough to nearly always warrant a consideration of external vendors.

FIGURE 6-7   Outsourcing benefits for Big-3 automotive companies.
Source: Business Week

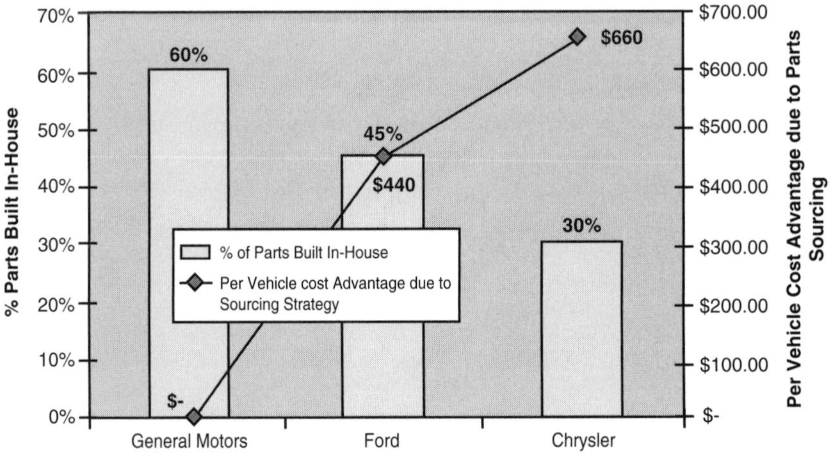

Once all the items for internal sourcing have been identified, those items should be optimally scheduled and assigned to specific sourcing locations. The emphasis of the remainder of this section is on externally sourced items.

Total Acquisition Cost (TAC) Analysis

A variety of factors should be used in selecting an external supplier. However, one of the most important is the *total acquisition cost* (TAC). TAC analysis goes well beyond traditional unit purchase cost considerations to include the cost of inbound transportation, inventory carrying, lost sales, warehousing, international logistics fees, and the cost of poor quality. The TAC should be computed and compared for each item for all sourcing alternatives. TAC analysis is especially important when considering global sourcing alternatives where a low unit purchase cost may be offered but is more than offset by high transportation, lost sales, inventory carrying, and international logistics costs. An example TAC analysis comparing domestic and international sources for apparel is presented in Figure 6-8. In addition to the total logistics/acquisition cost, the analysis incorporates gross margin, associated inventory turns, and an estimate of return on inventory.

Global Sourcing

Limited domestic labor availability, high domestic labor costs, domestic demand for a great variety of unique products, global communication

FIGURE 6-8   Total acquisition cost analysis.

License Plate	Total Logistics Cost	Annual Turn	COG Received	GM ROI	Gross Margin	Average Inventory Value
Domestic Scenarios						
1st Break	$25,577	8.23	45.5%	934%	$26,354.15	$2,820.69
2nd Break	$21,977	7.34	39.5%	1,090%	$29,929.30	$2,744.98
3rd Break	$21,007	6.43	37.8%	1,032%	$30,983.85	$3,002.88
4th Break	$19,494	6.03	35.0%	1,098%	$32,482.13	$2,958.31
Current Buy-Domestic	*$22,177*	*4.31*	*39.5%*	*650%*	*$30,364.55*	*$4,670.60*
International Scenarios						
1st Break	$20,105	2.86	30.6%	613%	$32,651.86	$5,324.13
2nd Break	$19,564	1.88	28.9%	444%	$33,960.09	$7,649.83
3rd Break			0.8%			
4th Break			0.8%			
Current Buy-International			0.8%			
Crossdock Scenarios						
Domestic Crossdock	$27,879	12.51	47.5%	1,227%	$23,759.51	$1,936.00
Crossdock Buy-Dom Cross			0.0%			
International Crossdock			0.8%			
Current Buy-Intl Cross			0.8%			

systems availability, low trade barriers, increasing sophistication and capability of international suppliers, and developing pockets of production expertise unique to specific world regions have led to the need for all corporations to create global sourcing strategies. Global sourcing strategies have paid big dividends for a number of U.S. corporations. Nike, with 100 percent global sourcing, is probably the best U.S. example. Unfortunately, many U.S. companies have swung the pendulum too far toward global sourcing, overlooking the benefits of domestic sourcing including shorter in-transit times, lower transportation costs, lower inventory levels, and rapid and reliable communications. A balanced sourcing strategy employing an optimal mix of global and domestic sources based on the total acquisition cost, global business strategy, and high-level sourcing policies should be in place.

On-Going Supply Base Rationalization and Consolidation   The objective in supply base rationalization and consolidation is to minimize the number of suppliers while satisfying all the quality and cost objectives of the sourcing policy. Fortunately, those goals—minimizing the number of suppliers, improving supply quality, and reducing the total acquisition cost—go hand in hand. Raising quality standards automatically disqualifies many suppliers. Increasing the volumes contracted with the smaller supplier base should also yield unit purchase price reductions. In addition, long- and short-term logistics initiatives aimed at enhancing customer service and reducing total logistics cost are much easier to implement with a few, highly-integrated, and highly-capable suppliers than with a large mix of loosely integrated, inconsistently capable suppliers.

Supply base rationalization and consolidation should be an ongoing, cross-functional practice supported by updated supplier performance metrics provided by the logistics information system.

Sole and Primary Sourcing   Supply base rationalization will naturally lead to sole or primary and secondary sources for most items. Sole sourcing is feasible when the sole source has the capacity, commitment, and proven track record to earn the trust required in sole sourcing. Even in the case of sole sourcing, a contingency plan should always be in place in case of unexpected shifts in the business environment, ownership changes, and/or acts of God. In primary-secondary sourcing, a primary source is used as long as they are available to meet requirements and have continued to meet or exceed supplier performance targets. If there is some slippage in a particular primary supplier's performance, demand can be shifted to the secondary supplier in proportion to the degree of slippage.

Electronic Bid-Based Sourcing   For commodity items, new specialty items, or for special customer requests, electronic bid-based sourcing (see Figure 6-9) may be used to streamline the bidding process among several suppliers. An example is the General Electric Information System, which permits buyers to post their requirements and specifications on an electronic

FIGURE 6-9   **Electronic bid-based sourcing.**

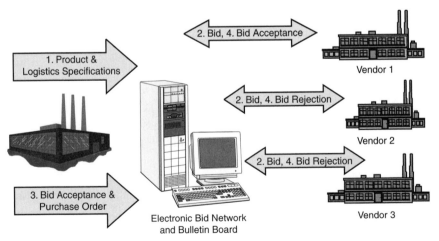

bulletin board. Prequalified, potential suppliers may post their proposal to the request on the secured bulletin board. The system eliminates paperwork, reduces negotiating time, and yields lower total acquisition costs than traditional bidding processes. Another example is the U.S. government, which has migrated to electronic, paperless procurement. We will address paperless procurement in more detail in the section on purchase order processing.

Contingency Sourcing Plans   Regardless of the specific sourcing policy, there should always be a contingency sourcing plan in place in the event of natural disasters or major shifts in the business environment. (In case you haven't noticed, the number and variety of those interruptions to "normal life" is increasing rapidly.)

6.6   SUPPLIER INTEGRATION AND RELATIONSHIP MANAGEMENT
The supplier base is really an extension of the enterprise. As such, supplier relationships (face-to-face, telecommunications, or the Internet) need to be developed as aggressively and strategically as customer relationships. The reliability, predictability, and value added in links with suppliers serve as the foundation for the ability to serve customers reliably, predictably, and with increasing value. Wal-Mart's supplier relationships (though criticized as heavy-handed in many circles) are the foundation of their business success. Dell Computer and Harley-Davidson's on-site supplier community serve as the foundation for their successes in logistics. These relationships have been developed through a formal *supplier relationship management* (SRM) program. SRM programs include annual conferences where logistics trends in all organizations are shared, upcoming business initiatives that will impact the supplier community are presented, and agreements are reached for future logistics standards and capabilities.

Supplier integration and excellence in SRM are difficult to measure, but they are easily recognized by the presence or absence of the following practices:

- Supplier partnerships
- *Vendor managed inventory* (VMI)
- Forecast sharing
- Supply chain collaboration, optimization, scheduling, and simulation
- Prereceiving
- Standard, economic-handling increments
- Supply chain exchanges

Supplier Partnerships

Supplier partnerships are the ultimate expression of supplier integration—implying sharing in profits and losses stemming from changes in the material, information, or cash flows between two organizations. A good example is the recent program initiated between some major grocery retailers and *Procter and Gamble* (P&G). P&G customers were given product discounts from implementing standard guidelines for receiving dock operations, allowing P&G trucks and carriers to unload faster.

Supplier partnerships require ongoing, regular, and ad-hoc meetings focused on streamlining and standardizing products, information, and cash flows between the two parties. Supplier partner meetings should also be a forum for sharing business plans and demand projections.

Supplier partners may represent between 5 percent and 20 percent of the supply base, and 50 percent to 80 percent of the inbound product volume. They are typically the most loyal and logistically sophisticated subset of suppliers. Suppliers can and should be classified as partners, strategic allies, or commodity providers based on the degree of partnering and information sharing (see Figure 6-10).

Vendor Managed Inventory (VMI)

Some supplier relationships have evolved to the point of permitting the supplier (or vendor) to manage customer inventory levels. VMI programs

FIGURE 6-10   **Classification of supplier relationships.**
Source: KPMG

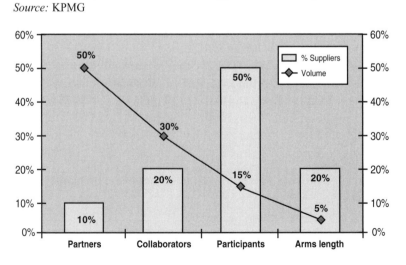

require the supplier to maintain inventory visibility, place replenishment orders (with themselves) on behalf of the customer, and achieve agreed-upon customer service levels. As a result, VMI programs require a high degree of trust between the parties and extensive logistics capabilities on both sides. There have been a variety of successful and disastrous VMI initiatives.

Three of the most successful VMI programs are the BOSE JIT II program, where suppliers monitor component inventory levels from offices inside the BOSE speaker factory; Harley-Davidson's supplier city; and Dell Computer's on-site supplier program. In each case, the initial concerns were the "fox in the chicken coop" syndrome. However, in each case, the foxes learned that the best way to keep their good standing in the chicken coop was not to eat the chickens, but to coddle and protect them.

Demand Information Sharing

An absolute necessity in supplier integration is true demand information sharing. Demand information could be point-of-consumption data, future demand period forecasts, existing orders, and/or future growth plans. Without this sharing, the supplier is left guessing as to the amount and timing of future demand. Since most reputable suppliers err on the side of providing enough inventory for the worst case, excess inventory is built up at every point where guessing occurs. Demand information sharing eliminates the guesswork in supply chain and inventory planning. Any time this information is not shared, the supplier must create a forecast of our forecast, significantly proliferating the forecast error and leading to excessive inventory or shortages in the chain.

Supplier Visibility

Just as suppliers need visibility into our inventory levels to execute vendor-managed inventory programs, we need visibility into our supply partner's inventory, production schedule, and production capacity to permit supply chain scheduling and optimization. Demand information sharing and supplier visibility are two essential elements that build trust between supply partners and form the foundation of supplier integration. Our human nature only trusts what we can see. For some reason, we don't trust what we can't see. As a result, any blind spots in the supply chain become seedbeds for excess inventory buildups to cover worst-case scenarios.

A variety of Web-based tools are available in the marketplace today that permit total supply chain visibility. One example from SupplyPoint.com is provided in Figure 6-11.

FIGURE 6-11   Web-based supply chain visibility.
Source: SupplyPoint.com

Total number of customer order summary records in each status. See order Values

By Request Date

Status	<= -1 Day <= 12/3/98	Today 12/4/98	1 Day 12/5/98	2 Days 12/6/98	3 Days 12/7/98	1 Week 12/8/98 - 12/13/98	2 Weeks 12/14/98 - 12/20/98	3 Weeks 12/21/98 - 12/27/98	4 Weeks 12/28/98 - 1/3/99	5 Weeks 1/4/99 - 1/10/99	6 Weeks 1/11/99 - 1/17/99	>= 7 Weeks >= 1/18/99	Totals
Incomp Entry						1						12	13
No PromiseDt													
Need MRP Qts	0	1			3	1		1	13	0	101	120	
Scheduled									2	13	27	192	225
Shortages	9	1	1	1	2	3	10	15	5				47
Clear	3	1			1		1	1					7
Kitting	4		1			3	4	3		1		3	19
Mfg Shorl	4	1			1	4	3	3	5				21
In Mfg	8	1				2	4	3	3	1	1	1	31
Ship Hold						6		10	1				17
In FGI	2								2		1	22	28
Partial Ship	4					1		2		1			9
Full Shipped													
Totals	37	4	3	1	4	15	31	24	31	29	32	339	553

Supply Chain Collaboration, Scheduling, Optimization, and Simulation

Just like a factory's optimal production schedule minimizes the total production and inventory carrying costs, given labor and material availability, manufacturing and storage capacities, and demand requirements, an optimal supply chain schedule minimizes the total cost to consumption. This includes inventory carrying, transportation, warehousing, and lost sales, given the supply chain's production, transportation, warehousing capacity, and inventory requirements at every node in the logistics network. In some supply chains, a fourth party (see Figure 6-12) is used to produce the optimal schedule, and each major player (supplier, customer, and carrier) shares true demand and capacity information with this fourth party who is responsible for producing an optimal supply chain design and operating schedule. This schedule includes retail receiving hours, warehouse shipping and receiving schedules, transportation schedules, and production schedules.

One fallacy in supply chain scheduling is that all scheduling should be pull-based. Study after study has revealed that a mix of pull- and push-based scheduling techniques characterize supply chain optimization. Tools such as the IBM supply chain simulator and the growing list of supply chain planning tools are required to identify the appropriate mix and links for pull- and push-based scheduling.

FIGURE 6-12   Supply chain collaboration, scheduling, and optimization.

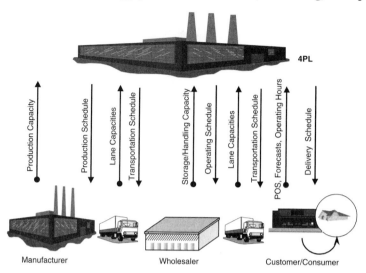

Prereceiving

A more practical manifestation of supplier integration is prereceiving, which is preclearing receipts from vendors based on receiving certification and historic performance in a variety of delivery quality measures. Bar code license plates on all inbound unit loads, advance shipment notifications, low to near-zero in-transit damage, and high purchase order to receiving quantity match percentages are typical requirements for prereceiving.

Standard, Economic Handling Increments

Another practical manifestation of supplier integration is the use of standard, economic handling units inbound from the supplier. Ideally, products should flow in full case (with broken case customer demand), layer, full pallet (with full case customer demand), and/or full truckload quantities in standard case, pallet, and truckload configurations to minimize transportation and warehousing costs and cycle times.

Paperless Information Exchange

A paperless, electronic, real-time information exchange is a key enabler of supplier integration. Forecasts, automatic replenishments, *manufacturing resource planning* (MRP) requirements transmitted as purchase orders, electronic funds transfers, and advance shipment notifications should all flow through electronic links between supplier and customer. The Internet, intranets, EDI, and even fax (a poor man's EDI) can, have, and should be used to reduce the possible friction of information exchanges between supplier and customer.

Thousands of organizations participate in supply chain exchanges today. Functionality in those exchanges, such as BuildNet in the construction industry, Rossettanet in the computer industry, and NonStopPharmaceuticals in the pharmaceuticals industry, includes e-procurement, inventory auctions, *electronic funds transfer* (EFT), electronic bidding for product and transportation services, forecast sharing, and supply chain visibility. A conceptual drawing of a supply chain exchange is provided in Figure 6-13.

6.7　PURCHASE ORDER PROCESSING

World-class purchase order processing is world-class customer order processing applied in reverse. The same practices and systems described in Chapter 4, "Customer Response Principles and Systems," work in reverse here. Three worth repeating are

FIGURE 6-13　Supply chain exchange.

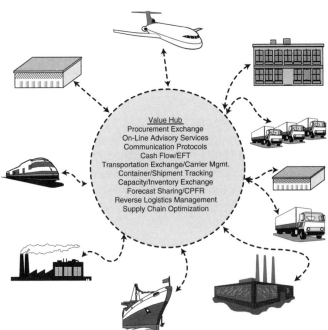

- E-procurement
- Perpetual PO status visibility
- Proactive supplier exception reporting

E-Procurement

Purchase orders should be placed electronically and automatically for those items not requiring buyer or supplier review. Purchase order costs can be cut in half and/or virtually eliminated utilizing e-procurement applications such as online catalogs, automatic purchase order recommendations, online and automatic vendor negations, and tendering.

As stated previously, the Internet, intranets, EDI, and even fax are popular platforms for electronic purchase orders (see Figure 6-14). Product availability, inventory commitments, and transportation arrival times should also be reported in real-time via e-procurement systems.

Perpetual PO Status Visibility

The status of all purchase orders (in process, in verification, in manufacturing, in picking, in packing, awaiting parts, loading, in transit, and so on) should be updated and visible at all times.

Proactive Supplier Exception Reporting

In addition to providing perpetual PO status visibility, suppliers should proactively report any exceptions to order commitments made at the time of order entry.

FIGURE 6-14   **Purchase order communication media.**
Source: Supplier Selection and Management Report

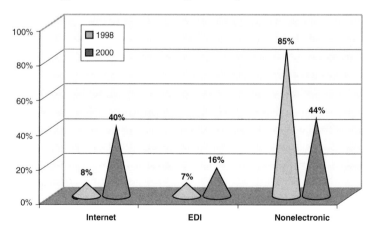

I witnessed a recent example at a client site where one aisle of the automated storage/retrieval system was down due to a part failure for nearly 24 hours. Our client proactively called and posted electronically expected delivery times for each line item request that was delayed for every customer awaiting a line-item shipment.

6.8 BUYING AND PAYMENT
World-class practices in buying and payment include

*   Central buying—local delivery
*   Buying partnerships
*   Consignment inventory
*   Electronic funds transfer

Central Buying, Local Delivery
All purchasing requirements should be estimated in advance and consolidated across all divisions and departments. This practice permits the organization to wield as much negotiating leverage as possible with each supplier, yielding the lowest possible unit purchase cost.

Once negotiated, each division and/or department should have local authority to direct deliveries to their particular location and control purchases under an authorized purchasing budget. This approach meets the two-fold objective of low unit purchase cost and excellent service to local operations.

One recent client in the chemical industry brought together all of their business units, which utilized rail transportation in a common negotiation with the railroads. In so doing, they brought together more than three times the negotiating leverage than any single business unit had been able to negotiate with previously. The associated freight savings nearly paid for the new, common transportation management system implemented across all business units.

Buying Partnerships
Another means of wielding increased negotiating leverage with suppliers is to partner with other organizations using common commodity purchases. Another example in the transportation industry is the buying partnership between two large, non-competing food manufacturers companies who jointly negotiate for transportation services in all countries they operate in. Another large client with a substantial private fleet joined forces with another large private fleet operator to purchase truck trailers and cabs. The

International Grocers Alliance (IGA) is another example, bringing together thousands of independent grocery stores worldwide to cooperatively negotiate with large food manufacturers.

Consignment Inventory
One objective in buying and payment is to negotiate the most favorable payment terms. Some of the most favorable terms imaginable are incorporated into consignment inventory programs in which payment for supplier inventory is not released until goods have been sold at the customer location. Delayed payment terms can yield significant positive float for the organization. Some large retailers with tremendous buying clout can and have successfully negotiated, implemented, and maintained consignment inventory programs.

Electronic Funds Transfer (EFT)
World-class buying and payment practices also include *electronic funds transfer* (e-cash) programs. The logistics information system should facilitate consignment inventory programs with electronic payment on consumption initiated at the point of sale. Electronic procurement and debit cards are means of EFT for small purchasing transactions.

6.9   SUPPLY MANAGEMENT SYSTEMS
The world-class practices described here impact the design requirements for supply management systems. In summary, the supply management system should support the following:

- Supply activity profiling, reporting, data warehousing, data mining, pattern recognition, and graphical presentation
- Supply organization and supplier performance reporting
- Supplier service policy design, implementation, and maintenance
- Supply chain collaboration, optimization, and simulation
- Electronic, real-time links for demand information sharing, purchase order submittal, forecast sharing, funds transfer, purchase order status, advance shipment notifications, automatic replenishments, and inventory visibility
- Consolidated purchasing requirements
- Electronic bidding and negotiating
- Total acquisition cost analysis
- Purchase order tracking

6.10   SUPPLY ORGANIZATION DESIGN AND DEVELOPMENT

The customer response organization is responsible for developing and executing a *customer service policy* (CSP). The inventory management organization is responsible for establishing inventory targets throughout the supply chain that satisfy the CSP yet minimize overall inventory investments. The supply organization is responsible for acquiring the inventory that meets target inventory levels established in the inventory plan, within the response time requirements of the CSP, at the required quality levels, and at the lowest possible total acquisition cost. That acquisition cost should include the unit cost paid to the supplier (or manufacturing cost transferred internally), transportation costs, importing costs, and related inventory carrying costs.

The supply organization is often pulled in at least two competing directions. The supply organization is encouraged by the finance organization to reduce unit purchasing costs and at the same time is encouraged by the logistics organization to reduce cycle times and increase fill rates. Since the supply base that yields the lowest unit purchase cost is most likely the supply base that will offer the longest lead times and lowest fill rates, the supply organization is caught between a rock and a hard place. Making the supply organization part of a total logistics organization incorporating customer response (setting customer service policy), inventory planning and management (setting inventory targets and deployment plans), transportation (planning and coordinating inbound transportation), and warehousing (planning and managing warehouse operations) is part of the solution. In that structure, the role of the supply organization is to develop and negotiate with a supply base that will yield the lowest cost to consumption and provide the quality and service levels specified in the customer and supplier service policies.

Within the supply organization, it is often helpful to establish commodity teams that specialize in the nuances of particular commodities, and to develop buyer-planners responsible for supplier management and inventory planning for a particular set of SKUs. Since their decisions and actions have a tremendous impact on total logistics cost and overall customer service, buyers and planners should be APICS-certified and/or have advanced training in the principles of logistics, inventory planning, and procurement.

C H A P T E R

TRANSPORTATION AND DISTRIBUTION MANAGEMENT

"You and these people who come to you will only wear yourselves out. The work is too heavy for you; you cannot handle it alone."

Exodus 18:18

RANSPORTATION IS THE MOST expensive logistics activity, representing over 40 percent of most corporations' logistics expense (see Figure 7-1) and over $400 billion in annual expenses in the United States alone. Global transportation expenditures exceed $2 trillion annually (Michigan State University). With smaller, more frequent orders, increasing international trade and global logistics, rising fuel charges, labor shortages, decreased carrier competition due to carrier mergers and acquisitions, and increased union penetration in the labor market, transportation expenses are rising disproportionately and rapidly versus other logistics costs. These cost increases are reflected in the recent increases in U.S. logistics costs to GNP ratios. Reducing transportation costs while maintaining/improving customer service levels, and leveraging private and third-party transportation systems is the focus of this chapter.

FIGURE 7-1   Transportation expenses as a percentage of total
logistics expenses.
Source: Bob Delaney, Cass Logistics

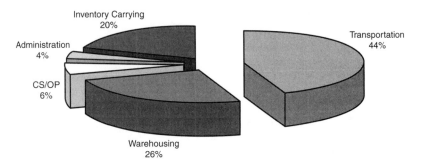

The growth of the transportation industry can be traced in large part to the early 1980s when transportation was deregulated in the United States and when personal computers were mainstreamed into U.S. homes and offices. Transportation deregulation yielded more flexible and more rapid service offerings from most carriers, allowing U.S. companies to begin *substituting transportation for inventory.* (The same service level could be achieved with fewer inventory holding points more distant from the customer base. In 1996, U.S. corporations spent 2.2 times on transportation what they spent on inventory carrying costs, compared with 1.4 in 1980 [see Figure 7-2].)

In addition, the rapid adoption of personal computing in the 1980s put supply chain information and analysis tools in the hands of logistics managers, permitting them to see and seize opportunities to substitute information for inventory (such as for improved forecasts, transportation schedules, scheduled receipts, and so on).

As evidenced by the dramatic reduction in the ratio of U.S. logistics costs to GNP from 14 to 10 percent during 1980 to 1996 (see Figure 7-3) and the success of the merge-in-transit logistics model (which is build upon the substitutionary premise), the strategy of substituting transportation and information for inventory has yielded big productivity dividends. However, very recent increases in logistics cost ratios, reduced competitiveness among carriers, overburdened transportation infrastructures, and environmental concerns suggest we may have reached the limit at which the substitution can continue.

We will address the means of deciding the proper tradeoffs between inventory carrying, transportation, and warehousing as we work through the major decision points in transportation master planning.

FIGURE 7-2   U.S. transportation costs versus inventory carrying cost
ratios, 1960 to 1996.
Source: Adapted from Bob Delaney, Cass Logistics

FIGURE 7-3   U.S. total logistics costs versus GNP, 1960 to 1996.
Source: Adapted from Bob Delaney, Cass Logistics

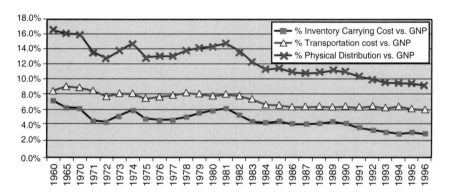

7.1   TRANSPORTATION OPTIMIZATION

The overall goal in transportation should be to connect sourcing locations
with customers at the lowest possible transportation cost within the constraints of the customer service policy. To do so, we need to know the customers that will be served (customer response master plan), the response
time and other time constraints that they must be served within (customer
response master plan), the sourcing location (supply master plan), and the
volumes of material movement (inventory master plan). As a result, we
present transportation as the fourth element in the logistics framework (see
Figure 7-4).

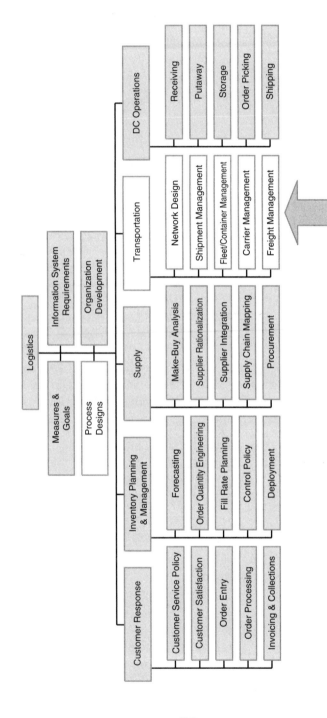

FIGURE 7-4   Transportation in the logistics framework.

172

As we address each individual topic in transportation, our persistent goal will be the optimal selection, deployment, and utilization of transportation resources: transportation optimization. The highest level transportation optimization equation can be expressed as follows:

Minimize: *Total Transportation Costs* (TTC)

Subject to: *Customer Service Policy* (CSP) Requirements

The total transportation costs include

- Freight
- Fleet
- Fuel
- Maintenance
- Labor
- Insurance
- Loading/unloading
- Insurance
- Demurrage/detention
- Taxes/tolls
- International fees

The transportation solution dramatically affects inventory carrying and warehousing costs, each of which must be incorporated in the objective function to the degree in which they are impacted by the transportation solution.

The optimal transportation solution must also satisfy the requirements set forth in the CSP, including

- Response time requirements (arrive before)
- Time windows (arrive after/depart before)
- Volume requirements (cube or weight delivered between each origin and destination)
- Frequency requirements (shipments per time period)
- Minimal damage in route

At the same time, the optimal transportation solution must not exceed the following:

- Lane capacities (cube, weight, travel speed, or frequency restrictions between origins and destinations)
- Vehicle capacities (cube, weight, or operating hour restrictions per vehicle)

- Container capacities (cube, weight, balance, or dimensional restrictions per container)
- Workforce capacities (restrictions on consecutive operating hours or lifting)
- Workload imbalances (restrictions on workload imbalances amongst transportation professionals)

We will use subsets of these objectives and constraints in many areas of transportation planning, including logistics network design, shipment planning, mode and carrier selection, and freight-rate negotiating. Hence, these costs and constraints must be accurately modeled as a precursor to developing an optimal transportation solution, regardless of the degree of sophistication of the decision support software.

7.2   TRANSPORTATION FUNDAMENTALS

The long history of transportation has left us with some somewhat confusing terminology. Before we launch into this chapter on transportation problem-solving, we need to make sure everyone is up to speed with common transportation terms.

One of the best ways I have found to explain transportation terminology is to describe the basics of a transportation transaction. In a basic and typical transportation transaction, a *shipper* pays a *carrier* to transport *cargo* from an *origin* to a *destination* where the *consignee* receives the cargo. The payment made to the carrier is called a *freight payment* and the document describing and contracting the movement of the goods is called a *bill of lading*. The carrier could be an express/parcel carrier (UPS, Fedex, USPS), a *less-than-truckload* (LTL) trucking company (Yellow Freight, Overnite, Roadway), a *full-truckload* (TL) trucking company (Schneider, JB Hunt, Werner), an ocean liner (Maersk Lines, Evergreen, American President Lines), a railroad (CSX, Norfolk-Southern, Union-Pacific), or an air carrier/integrator (Emery, DHL, BAX Global). The carrier may also be the shipper or consignee operating a private fleet.

Cargo is housed in a *container* (trailer, railcar, or ocean container) for transportation and is moved by a *vehicle* with motive power (tractor, locomotive, airplane, or ocean vessel). Cargo is moved to, from, and between various logistics facilities (warehouses, terminals, distribution centers, and ports). The arrangement and location of the logistics facilities is called the *transportation network*. A *shipment* is one or more orders traveling together.

The logistics of transportation (Figure 7-5) include

- Transportation network design
- Shipment management
- Container/fleet management
- Carrier management
- Freight management

Transportation master planning (see Figure 7-6) leads corporations to an optimal transportation solution for their supply chain, addressing the five activities in the logistics of transportation. In turn, the methodology addresses

- Transportation activity profiling and data mining (Section 7.3)
- Transportation performance measures (Section 7.4)
- Logistics network design (Section 7.5)
- Shipment planning and management (Section 7.6)
- Fleet, container, and yard management (Section 7.7)
- Carrier management (Section 7.8)
- Freight and document management (Section 7.9)
- Transportation management systems (Section 7.10)
- Transportation organization design and development (Section 7.11)

7.3 TRANSPORTATION ACTIVITY PROFILING AND DATA MINING

The underlying *transportation activity profile* (TAP) must be accurate, thorough, and representative of current and future transportation activity to yield reliable transportation solutions. Fortunately, the underlying transportation activity database is essentially the same for each transportation decision. The transportation activity database (or transportation data warehouse) should specify the following information between each origin and destination pair in the network (see Figure 7-7):

- Shipment frequencies
- Cube-per-shipment distributions
- Weight-per-shipment distributions
- Value-per-shipment distributions
- Shipment classifications
- Origin-destination time windows
- In-transit time requirements
- Mode and carrier availability and capacities
- Transportation rates

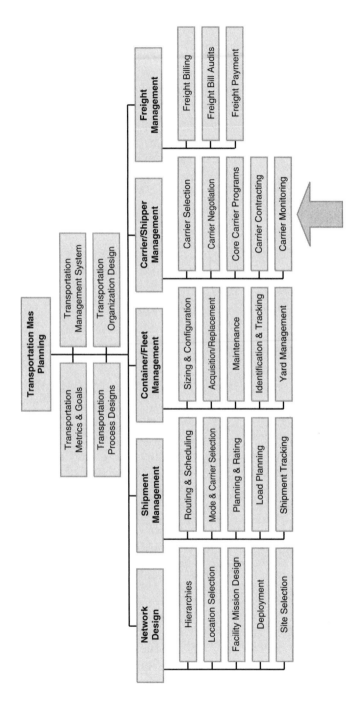

FIGURE 7-5 Transportation decision tree.

FIGURE 7-6   Transportation master planning.

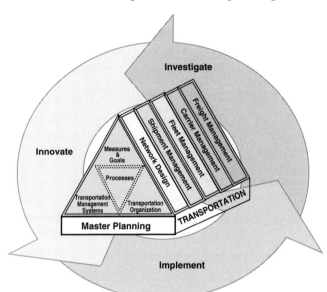

FIGURE 7-7   Origin-destination transportation activity profile.

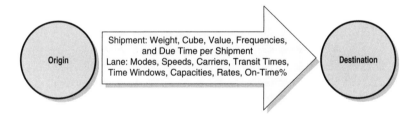

- Carrier on-time performance statistics
- Claims and loss rates
- Average and deviant travel times and speeds
- Distances

Figures 7-8, 7-9, and 7-10 are examples of transportation activity profiling in action in a variety of client settings.

Figure 7-8 is a TAP taken from a recent chemical industry client relying heavily on rail and truck shipping. The profiles specify for three commodities (and in total) the value per shipment, value per order, shipments per order, freight paid per order, freight paid per shipment, weight per order, weight per shipment, miles per shipment, ton-miles per shipment, and

FIGURE 7-8   Multicommodity transportation activity profile from the chemical industry.

T&D Profile	Unit of Measure	Commodities			TOTAL
		Feedstock	Intermediate	Polymers	
Shipment Value	$'s per shipment	$ 64,726	$ 55,247	$ 44,911	$ 52,256
Order Value	$'s per order	$ 21,670	$ 56,964	$ 39,950	$ 44,753
Shipments per Order	Shipments	$ 0.33	$ 1.03	$ 0.89	$ 0.86
Freight per Order	$s	$ 613	$ 1,746	$ 2,790	$ 1,896
Freight per Shipment	$s	$ 1,831	$ 1,693	$ 3,136	$ 2,214
Weight per Order	Tons per order	40	101	56	74
Weight per Shipment	Tons per shipment	118	98	62	87
Miles per Shipment	Miles	1118	352	724	538
Ton-Miles per Shipment	Ton-miles	333,430,396	700,831,839	569,911,228	1,656,240,498
Ton-Miles per Order	Ton-miles	111,630,742	722,606,699	506,968,093	1,418,425,240

FIGURE 7-9   International transportation activity profile in international health and beauty aids.

	Revenue $000s	Freight $000s	Weight 000 lbs.	Cases	Shipments	Freight/ Revenue
Japan	$ 17,680	$ 413	284	12,390	15	2.33%
Taiwan	$ 8,295	$ 104	232	9,210	17	1.25%
Hong Kong	$ 1,375	$ 16	42	1,670	9	1.17%
Australia	$ 883	$ 36	30	1,335	9	4.12%
New Zealand	$ 395	$ 11	11	511	6	2.81%
Malaysia	$ 1	$ 1	0	3	1	56.25%
Asia-Pacific	**$ 28,630**	**$ 581**	**599**	**25,118**	**57**	2.03%
Canada	$ 1,234	$ 45	49	2,756	8	3.61%
Mexico	$ 226	$ 8	10	344	3	3.65%
U.S.	$ 16,705	$ 446	-	-	-	2.67%
NAFTA	**$ 18,164**	**$ 499**	**59**	**3,100**	**11**	2.74%
Netherlands	$ 1	$ 4	13	366	2	387.50%
Europe	**$ 1**	**$ 4**	**13**	**366**	**2**	387.50%
Guatemala	$ 2	$ 2	3	105	1	108.33%
Latin America	**$ 2**	**$ 2**	**3**	**105**	**1**	108.33%
OVERALL	**$ 46,796**	**$ 1,085**	**673**	**28,690**	**71**	2.32%

ton-miles per order. The profile revealed an opportunity to improve the routing of feedstock shipments to reduce the disproportionately high travel distance per shipment.

Figure 7-9 is a TAP taken from a recent client project in the international health and beauty aids industry. The profile specifies for U.S. shipments to a variety of foreign countries the total sales, freight paid, weight shipped, cases shipped, number of shipments, and freight as a portion of sales. The profile helps to identify opportunities for freight savings in those

Number of Trips

TYPE	% of Carriers	% Trips
A	21.7%	80.0%
B	30.4%	15.0%
C	47.8%	5.0%

Carrier Name	Number of Trips	%	Cumulative %	Class
Transp. Propio	7725	45.6%	45.6%	A
Transportista 6	2328	13.7%	59.3%	A
Transportista 2	2169	12.8%	72.1%	A
Transportista 11	683	4.0%	76.2%	A
Transportista 4	455	2.7%	78.8%	A
Transportista 8	453	2.7%	81.5%	B
Transportista7	416	2.5%	84.0%	B
Transportista 16	341	2.0%	86.0%	B
Transportista 9	326	1.9%	87.9%	B
Transportista 24	317	1.9%	89.8%	B
Transportista 23	303	1.8%	91.6%	B
Transportista 13	298	1.8%	93.3%	B
Transportista 3	287	1.7%	95.0%	C
Transportista 17	235	1.4%	96.4%	C
Transportista 25	181	1.1%	97.5%	C
Transportista 12	141	0.8%	98.3%	C
Transportista 10	112	0.7%	99.0%	C
Transportista 28	78	0.5%	99.4%	C
Transportista 19	41	0.2%	99.7%	C
Transportista 26	20	0.1%	99.8%	C
Transportista 27	16	0.1%	99.9%	C
Transportista 20	12	0.1%	100.0%	C
Transportista 14	7	0.0%	100.0%	C

Cube Movement

TYPE	% of Carriers	% Trips
A	17.4%	80.0%
B	34.8%	15.0%
C	47.8%	5.0%

Carrier Name	Cubic Meters	%	Cumulative %	Class
Transp. Propio	140,013.2	39.5%	39.5%	A
Transportista 6	66,841.4	18.8%	58.3%	A
Transportista 2	54,512.6	15.4%	73.7%	A
Transportista 11	13,260.4	3.7%	77.4%	A
Transportista 7	11,066.5	3.1%	80.6%	B
Transportista 9	9,935.5	2.8%	83.4%	B
Transportista 13	8,400.1	2.4%	85.7%	B
Transportista 17	8,232.7	2.3%	88.1%	B
Transportista 8	7,335.0	2.1%	90.1%	B
Transportista 4	6,444.8	1.8%	91.9%	B
Transportista 24	5,076.4	1.4%	93.4%	B
Transportista 16	4,900.3	1.4%	94.8%	B
Transportista 23	4,716.6	1.3%	96.1%	C
Transportista 3	4,343.7	1.2%	97.3%	C
Transportista 25	2,798.2	0.8%	98.1%	C
Transportista 12	2,467.8	0.7%	98.8%	C
Transportista 10	1,913.7	0.5%	99.3%	C
Transportista 28	1,232.7	0.3%	99.7%	C
Transportista 26	333.8	0.1%	99.8%	C
Transportista 20	234.5	0.1%	99.8%	C
Transportista 19	229.5	0.1%	99.9%	C
Transportista 27	216.0	0.1%	100.0%	C
Transportista 14	129.0	0.0%	100.0%	C

FIGURE 7-10 Carrier activity profile.

countries in which the freight-to-sales ratio is excessively high compared to the norm, and the profile might identify countries in which the logistics costs to serve the country outweigh the revenue potential.

Figure 7-10 is a carrier activity profile developed for the largest retailer in Central America. The profile provides ABC classifications of carriers based on the number of loads and total cube. This profile is helpful in carrier negotiations and in developing a core carrier program built by giving fewer carriers increasing volumes.

Unfortunately, the transportation function is not very high on the MIS totem pole for requests for data or reports. That's the bad news. The good news is that the sources of this information are fairly limited and include shipment manifests, customer master files, supplier master files, and carrier master files. (For detailed logistics network design or routing, geocode mapping data may be required to pinpoint the location of specific origins and destinations.) The good news is also that this same information will be used in many logistics planning decisions, including transportation performance measures and goals, logistics hierarchy design, DC location analysis, site selection, vehicle routing and scheduling, consolidation analysis, third-party proposal evaluation, shipment planning, load planning, mode and carrier selection, fleet sizing, fleet configuration, carrier performance monitoring, and freight rate negotiation among others. Hence, the financial return on information in transportation is overwhelmingly compelling.

To assist our clients with transportation and logistics activity profiling, we recently developed a logistics data mining tool called the Logistics Oracle. The tool permits real-time functionality, drag-and-drop, graphical analysis, and an exploration of logistics and transportation data. An example analysis is illustrated in Figure 7-11. The screen shot illustrates a year-to-year analysis of units transported on regular, emergency, and backorders, via air and truck, to distribution centers in California, Illinois, Nebraska, Oregon, and Texas from a manufacturing plant in St. Louis, Missouri. The four-way analysis was executed in less than three seconds from more than 400,000 records. The Logistics Oracle data mining tool works from transportation transaction data fed into a transportation data warehouse directly from the transportation management system. We will address transportation management systems design in more detail later.

7.4 TRANSPORTATION PERFORMANCE MEASURES

As explained many times, a logistics measurement system should hold the logistics manager accountable in four categories of measures: finance, productivity, quality, and response time. Transportation performance measures

FIGURE 7-11 Transportation data mining.

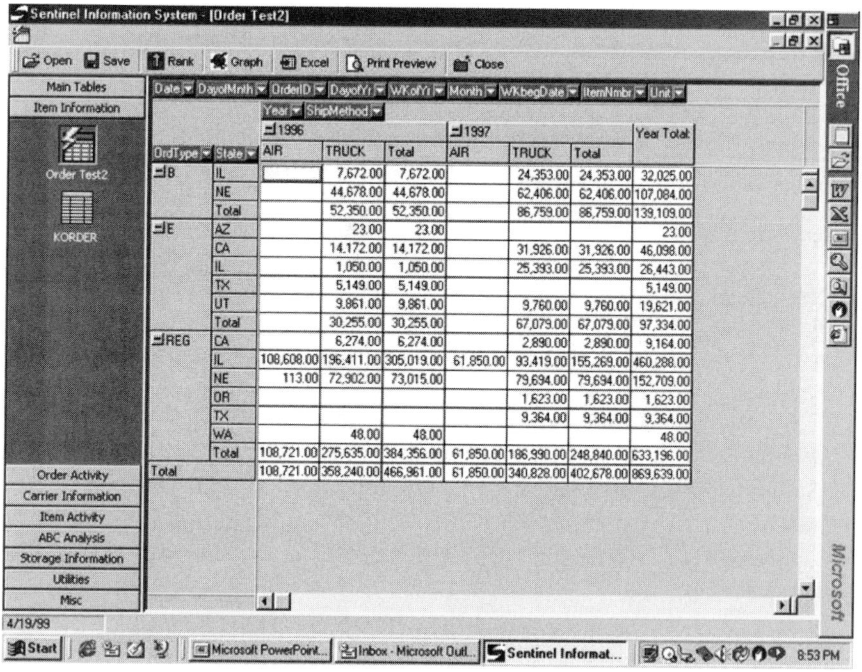

OrdType	State	1996 AIR	1996 TRUCK	1996 Total	1997 AIR	1997 TRUCK	1997 Total	Year Total
B	IL		7,672.00	7,672.00		24,353.00	24,353.00	32,025.00
	NE		44,678.00	44,678.00		62,406.00	62,406.00	107,084.00
	Total		52,350.00	52,350.00		86,759.00	86,759.00	139,109.00
E	AZ		23.00	23.00				23.00
	CA		14,172.00	14,172.00		31,926.00	31,926.00	46,098.00
	IL		1,050.00	1,050.00		25,393.00	25,393.00	26,443.00
	TX		5,149.00	5,149.00				5,149.00
	UT		9,861.00	9,861.00		9,760.00	9,760.00	19,621.00
	Total		30,255.00	30,255.00		67,079.00	67,079.00	97,334.00
REG	CA		6,274.00	6,274.00		2,890.00	2,890.00	9,164.00
	IL	108,608.00	196,411.00	305,019.00	61,850.00	93,419.00	155,269.00	460,288.00
	NE	113.00	72,902.00	73,015.00		79,694.00	79,694.00	152,709.00
	OR					1,623.00	1,623.00	1,623.00
	TX					9,364.00	9,364.00	9,364.00
	WA		48.00	48.00				48.00
	Total	108,721.00	275,635.00	384,356.00	61,850.00	186,990.00	248,840.00	633,196.00
Total		108,721.00	358,240.00	466,961.00	61,850.00	340,828.00	402,678.00	869,639.00

in those four categories as well as their use in transportation performance benchmarking and project justification are explained in this section.

Financial Metrics

Transportation financial metrics should include total transportation costs and related ratios, as well as economic values for fleet assets.

Total Transportation Costs and Cost Ratios A detailed estimate of total transportation cost incorporates the following expense and capital elements in Table 7-1.

Figure 7-12 depicts a transportation cost analysis in the grocery industry reflecting inbound and outbound freight, staffing (including drivers, supervisors, planners, managers, and maintenance technicians), fleet ownership costs, transportation management system capital and expense costs, land and building ownership costs for terminals and maintenance facilities, and leased space costs for offices. The analysis was used in a category management program to estimate the logistics cost and related profitability of each category.

Transportation Asset Economic Value Analysis Private fleet operators often underestimate the capital consumption and economic value generation

TABLE 7-1   Transportation Expense and Capital Cost Listing

Expense	Capital
• Freight, inbound and outbound	• Fleet ownership costs
• Driver/operator wages and benefits	• Terminal ownership costs
• Planner/manager wages and benefits	• Officespace ownership costs
• Fleet leasing	• Maintenance facility ownership costs
• Terminal leasing	• Transportation management systems software ownership costs
• Office lease and utilities	• Transportation computing infrastructure ownership costs
• EDI/VAN and telecommunications fees	• Transportation infrastructure ownership costs (ports, bridges, and so on)
• Maintenance	
• Third-party transportation fees	
• Fuel	
• Customs brokerage and freight forwarding fees	
• Security	
• Packaging materials	

FIGURE 7-12   Transportation cost analysis for grocer's inbound and outbound operations.

Total T& D Costs	Locations					TOTALS
	DG/GM	Frozen	Produce	Meat/Diary	HBA	
Inbound	$ 1,300,000	$ 1,300,000	$ 1,000,000	$ 1,000,000	$ 800,000	$ 5,400,000
Outbound	$ 1,500,000	$ 1,500,000	$ 1,800,000	$ 1,800,000	$ 1,500,000	$ 8,400,000
Staffing	$ 5,000	$ 5,000	$ 6,500	$ 6,500	$ 8,000	$ 30,500
Fleet	$ 150,000	$ 150,000	$ 300,000	$ 300,000	$ 120,000	$ 750,000
TMS	$ 10,500	$ 10,500	$ 12,000	$ 12,000	$ 10,000	$ 52,500
L&B	$ 100,000	$ 100,000	$ 100,000	$ 100,000	$ 100,000	$ 500,000
Space	$ 31,000	$ 31,000	$ 60,000	$ 60,000	$ 47,000	$ 160,000
Total	*$ 2,965,500*	*$ 2,827,000*	*$ 3,118,500*	*$ 3,462,000*	*$ 2,438,000*	*$ 14,633,000*
Cost/Case	$ 0.074	$ 0.514	$ 0.312	$ 0.204	$ 0.488	$ 0.189
Cost/CF	$ 0.094	$ 0.231	$ 0.092	$ 0.152	$ 0.695	$ 0.141
Cost/Lb.	$ 0.004	$ 0.042	$ 0.011	$ 0.009	$ 0.054	$ 0.009

potential of the fleet. Many of our manufacturing clients who also operate a private fleet overlook the financial implications of fleet ownership because they are typically so focused on the manufacturing assets and because their accounting models are not typically configured to monitor the financial performance of transportation assets. For example, one of our manufacturing clients is also one of the largest private fleet owner-operators in the world. Their financial indicators for manufacturing line performance and utilization are the most comprehensive I have ever witnessed. Yet few, if any, indicators are reported on the financial performance or utilization of any of their more than 10,000 delivery vehicles.

To help monitor the capital consumption and value creation potential of logistics assets, we developed a logistics financial performance indicator coined *logistics value added* (LVA). LVA is based on Stern-Stewart's trademarked indicator, *economic value added* (EVA). The EVA of a corporation is computed as the difference between after-tax profit and cost of capital ownership:

$$EVA = (1 - t) \times (R - E) - CI \times CCR$$

- t = Tax rate (percent/year)
- R = Revenue ($/year)
- E = Expense ($/year)
- CI = Capital investment ($)
- CCR = Capital carrying rate (percent/year)

The LVA of a logistics asset is computed as the difference between the asset's profitability (generated revenue less associated expenses) and cost of ownership for the asset. The computation highlights the financial viability of specific logistics assets and can be used in determining when or if to replace, eliminate, lease, or acquire logistics assets. The following example is a LVA analysis for a rail car in one of the nation's largest rail fleets (see Figure 7-13). This particular vehicle is a drain on the wealth of the corporation because its profitability is eclipsed by its ownership costs. (The lease costs in the example refer to lease costs paid on space used in maintaining the rail cars.)

Productivity Metrics
Transportation productivity metrics fall in two categories: transportation asset productivity and transportation operator productivity.

Transportation Asset Productivity and Utilization The two main categories of transportation assets are containers and vehicles. *Containers*

FIGURE 7-13   Rail car logistics value added.[1]

Parameters		
Asset Carrying Cost		32%
Rail Car Value	$	25,000
Rail Car Revenue	$	11,429
Rail Car Operating Expenses		
Leasing	$	2,400
Maintenance	$	1,200
Cleaning	$	1,020
Insurance	$	25
Taxes	$	750
Registration	$	2,000
Total Operating Expenses	$	7,395
Rail Car EVA		
Rail Car Operating Profit	$	4,034
Rail Car Capital Expenses	$	8,000
Rail Car EVA	$	(3,966)

include over-the-road containers, ocean containers, air containers, and so on. The utilization of a container must incorporate the weight and cube utilization since container capacity is restricted in both dimensions. *Container utilization* (CU) is computed as

- CU = Max {Cube utilization, Weight utilization}
- Cube utilization = Occupied cube/(Length × width × height)
- Weight utilization = Load weight/Container weight capacity

For a load weighing 35,000 pounds and occupying 2,720 cubic feet in a container with a weight capacity of 44,000 pounds and a length, width, and height of 40 feet, 8.5 feet, and 9 feet, the CU is

- Cube utilization = 2,720 ft³/(40' × 8.5' × 9') = 2,720 ft³/ 3,060 ft³ = 89%
- Weight utilization = 35,000 lbs./44,000 lbs. = 79.5%
- CU = Max {89%, 79.5%} = 89%

Transportation vehicles (trucks, airplanes, locomotives, and ocean vessels) consume *vehicle operating hours* (VOH), *vehicle available hours* (VAH), and capital investment. The desired outputs for a vehicle include the number of deliveries, pounds delivered, cube delivered, dollars delivered,

[1]Lease costs refer to space leased for maintenance facilities, not the vehicle.

miles traveled, and/or ton-miles delivered. Some helpful output to consumption ratios are

- Vehicle utilization = Operating hours/Available hours
- Vehicle yield = Delivered value/Vehicle investment cost
- Deliveries per operating hour
- Ton-miles delivered per vehicle
- Ton-miles per operating hour
- Cube-pounds per mile
- Delivered cube per operating hour
- Delivered pounds per operating hour

Transportation Operator Productivity   The metrics for transportation operator productivity do not differ that greatly from vehicle productivity because each vehicle is manned by an operator. The most common bases for assessing transportation operator productivity are the number of stops, miles traveled, dollars delivered, cases delivered, pounds delivered, or pallets delivered per person-hour.

Quality Metrics

Transportation quality and reliability are just as important, if not more important, than cycle time. A shipment delivered quickly to the wrong location or with damage is of no use to the shipper or the shipper's customer. A carrier with an average delivery time of 48 hours who always delivers in 48 hours may be preferred over one with an average of 24 hours if the latter delivers in less than 24 hours a majority of the time, but occasionally delivers in 96 hours.

We need just as comprehensive a set of indicators for the delivery quality of our private fleet or carrier base as we do for speed or productivity. We like to recommend the following set of transportation quality indicators to our clients as a starting point in transportation quality management:

- **Claims-free shipment percentage**   The percentage of shipments without claims for each driver or carrier on each lane at each location.
- **Damage-free shipment percentage**   The percentage of shipments without damage for each driver or carrier on each lane at each location.
- **Distance between accidents**   The miles or kilometers between accidents for each driver, carrier, and lane.
- ***On-time arrival percentage*** **(OTAP)**   The percentage of shipments that arrive on-time for each driver, carrier, and lane.

- *On-time departure percentage* (OTDP)   The percentage of loads that depart on-time for each driver, carrier, and lane.
- *Perfect delivery percentage* (PDP)   Similar to the perfect order percentage concept for logistics as a whole, the PDP assesses the percentage of shipments delivered without defects, including damage, documentation, arrival time, arrival location, loss, accidents, and claims of any kind for each delivery, driver, lane, and carrier.
- *Perfect Route Percentage* (PRP)   The percentage of routes or trips without an imperfect delivery.

Cycle Time Metrics

Our society is fascinated with time management. (We all have all there is, yet we never seem to have enough.) The transportation industry is no different. As evidenced by the proliferation of dot.coms offering to recover service failure guarantees, time is literally money in the transportation industry. Quicker transit, loading, and unloading times translate into greater asset utilization, which translates into greater leveraging of the corporation's capital.

Cycle time metrics are the most natural indicators of transportation performance. (Perhaps it dates back to the days when we used to bug our parents incessantly from the back seat of the car on long trips asking how long it would take to get there.) Some of the most popular cycle time indicators for transportation include

- *In-transit time* (ITT)   Point-to-point in-transit times by driver, carrier, lane, and location.
- **In-transit time variability**   Point-to-point in-transit time variability by driver, carrier, land, and location.
- **Vehicle load/unload time**   Vehicle loading and unloading times at each pickup/delivery location by driver, carrier, lane, and location.
- **Detention time**   Time spent waiting for loading or unloading at a pickup/delivery location due to dock congestion and/or delays caused by the shipper or consignee.
- **Delayed in traffic time**   The time spent idling or at reduced speed due to traffic congestion for each driver, carrier, lane, and pickup/delivery location.

An example cycle time analysis completed for a recent client with a large fleet of rail cars is illustrated in Figure 7-14.

It is not uncommon in cycle time analyses to learn that a large percentage of the operating time of any vehicle is spent waiting or in delays. For example, an analysis conducted by the Refrigerated Drivers Association revealed that 64 percent of nondriving time was spent waiting to load or unload the vehicle at the shipper's or consignee's dock (see Figure 7-15). I was struck by this same phenomenon at the Panama Canal where ships may wait for days on end at the entrance to the canal on the Pacific or Atlantic side for an opportunity to traverse the canal.

FIGURE 7-14   Rich Rail car fleet cycle time analysis.

FIGURE 7-15   National Refrigerated Driver's survey of nondriving time.

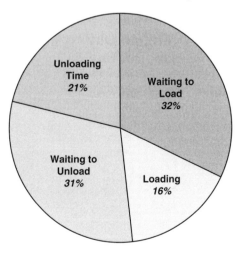

The worldwide transportation infrastructure and the interface points within it were not designed to support the volume or activity or the pace of change currently experienced in the transportation industry. Hence, an effective transportation cycle time analysis should examine each component of the cycle time in an attempt to reveal bottlenecks and potential opportunities for improvement.

As the worldwide transportation infrastructure is stretched even closer to its limits, on-time arrivals and departures may become even more elusive. Some evidence of this effect is the declining on-time arrival percentage in LTL transportation in the United States (see Figure 7-16).

7.5   LOGISTICS NETWORK DESIGN

For each commodity, the logistics network design specifies

- Number of *levels* of distribution in the network
- *Number* of distribution facilities
- *Location and mission* of each distribution facility
- *Assignment* of supplier and customer locations to each distribution facility
- *Deployment* of inventory in the network

The optimal network design minimizes the total of inventory carrying, warehousing, and transportation costs while satisfying customer response time requirements. The network is often optimized by identifying the fewest number of distribution facilities that will meet customer response time

FIGURE 7-16   **Sample LTL on-time arrival rates.**
Source: Logistics Management

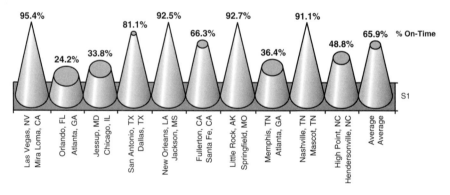

requirements. This is true because each new facility in the network requires additional inventory and fixed facility costs.

An example tradeoff of inventory carrying costs and transportation costs is illustrated in Figure 7-17. Because each new facility requires additional supporting inventory, the inventory carrying cost increases as the number of facilities in the network increases. However, because the distribution points are increasingly closer to the customer base, the transportation costs decline as the number of facilities increases.

Any network optimization analysis also needs to consider the impact of the network design on customer service. Specifically, the average and worst-case response time increases as the number of distribution facilities are reduced. An example cost and service tradeoff analysis is illustrated in Figure 7-18. The optimal solution is the minimum total cost network solution that meets the required response time.

Because each corporation's vendor and customer base are unique, so too is its optimal distribution network. To search out the optimal network design, we typically recommend a 10-step logistics network design program:

1. *Assess and evaluate the current network performance.* We need a baseline to compare network redesign opportunities against. Hence, an assessment of the transportation, inventory carrying, and warehousing costs, as well as response times offered to each location in the current network, must be documented.

FIGURE 7-17   **Distribution network cost tradeoff analysis.**

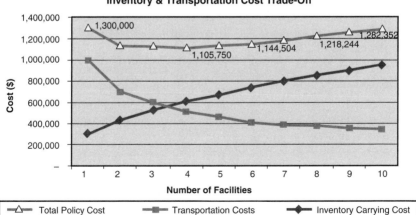

FIGURE 7-18   Cost-service tradeoff curves in logistics network analysis.

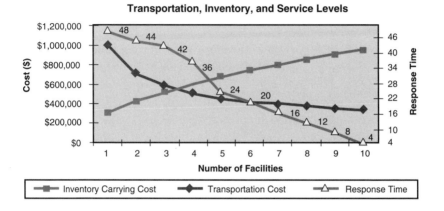

2. *Design and populate the network optimization database.* One of the most difficult and time-consuming steps in network optimization is the collection, purification, and rationalization of the underlying database of parameters, cost computations, and constraints. At a minimum, the database should specify geocoded locations and modal travel speeds along each leg connecting pickup, delivery, and distribution locations; fixed and variable warehousing, inventory carrying and transportation costs; response time requirements for each delivery point (and time windows if specified); product availability at each source and product demand at each delivery point; and any fixed locations' throughput and storage constraints. This process may take from a few weeks to a few months to complete, depending on the number and variety of pickup/delivery points, commodities, transportation modes, and alternative flow paths.

3. *Create network design alternatives.* This is the step in the network design process that requires the most creativity and experience. A logistics modeling tool can only give back an answer as good as the scenarios it is given to consider. Most decision support tools are really only useful for evaluating scenarios, not generating them. I'm sure you are familiar with the expression, "garbage in, garbage out." Well, if we only consider inefficient scenarios, we will only choose the best inefficient scenario. Our challenge is to evaluate current logistics paradigms and brainstorm as many clever scenarios as possible. That will require considering new logistics flow patterns for each commodity, including *direct shipping, cross docking, consignment inventory, inbound and outbound consolidation*, and *merge-in-transit* schemes. This step may require a pre-modeling analysis, such as the analysis we recently conducted with one client to help them determine for each item the optimal supply flow: international versus domestic, warehouse controlled, or cross docking (see Figure 7-19).

4. *Develop network optimization model.* The next step is to formalize the network optimization model, expressing the network operating scenarios mathematically into the form of a mathematical program. The mathematical program should include an objective function (typically to minimize the total logistics costs associated with the design) and a set of constraints (typically focused on the response time and demand requirements of the customer locations). (We will not treat the formalities of the math programming formulations of a logistics network optimization model here. A variety of excellent articles have been written on the mathematical solutions to logistics

FIGURE 7-19   **Flow optimization analysis.**

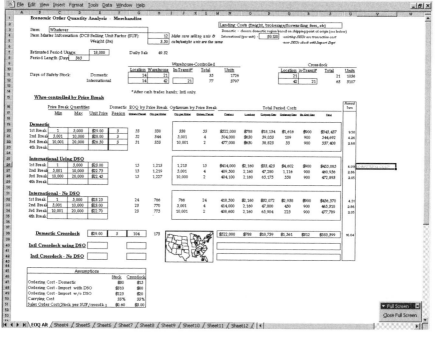

network problems[2]). The design team should develop the model to the level of mathematical sophistication they are capable of, to enhance their understanding of the tradeoffs involved, and to enable them to select wisely from amongst the available network optimization software tools.

5. *Select a network optimization tool.* Because there are so many potential solutions and scenarios to consider and so many interdependencies among the constraints and objectives in network optimization, most Fortune-1000-sized network optimizations require the use of a network optimization tool. The tools automate the calculations, evaluate multiple solutions quickly, graphically present scenario evaluations, and provide a user-friendly front-end for network modeling. A variety of network optimization tools are available in the marketplace (see Figure 7-20). The tools should be selected based on their modeling capabilities, presentation of results, and usability.

6. *Implement network model in selected tool.* The next step is to populate the selected tool's database, modeling forms, graphic interfaces, and evaluation forms with the data, scenarios, objectives, and constraints. This sounds easy, but takes a while to get used to.

FIGURE 7-20   **Network optimization tools.**
Source: Napolitano

Model	Price	Company
ASSIGN	$15,000/year	Herb Davis Co.
CAPS Logistics Toolkit	$60,000 to $80,000	Baan
LOCATE	Service Fee	CSC Consulting
LOPTIS	$12,000 license	KETRON
MIMI	$200,000 license, 15%/year maintenance	Chesapeake Decision Sciences
NETWORK	$12,000/year	Ron Ballou
OPTISITE	Service Fee	Micro Analytics
PHYDIAS	$25,000+	Bender Mgmt.
SAILS	$9,000 to $14,000/year	INSIGHT
SITELINK	$65,000	CGR International
SLIM/2000	$50,000	J.F. Shapiro

[2]Napolitano, M., *Using Modeling to Solve Warehousing Problems: A Collection of Decision-Making Tools for Warehousing Planning and Design*, Gross & Associates, Warehousing Education & Research Council, Chicago, Illinois, 1998.

Though most of the models are "Windowseque," some of the aftertaste of hard-coded simplex algorithms and "green-screen" motifs still remain. We usually recommend that our clients participate in the training sessions offered by most of the companies offering network optimization tools and/or retain the services of one of the company's trainers.

7. *Evaluate alternative network designs.* Each scenario should be evaluated on the basis of cost, service, and capital utilization. Most of the tools permit an online graphical comparison of alternative scenarios. The summaries normally allow executives to quickly decide from among alternative network designs since the cost and service tradeoffs are quantified and presented graphically. An example evaluation for locating an East Coast distribution center(s) is provided in Figure 7-21.

8. *"Practicalize" recommended network structure.* Sometimes the modeling tools suggest obscure and impractical locations for distribution facilities. I remember during one consulting assignment, a tool recommended Airville, Pennsylvania as the site for a major distribution center. Nothing against Airville, but with limited interstate access and a population less than 1,000, the recommendation was impractical. Suggesting a larger city in close proximity was an easy adjustment to make, but was necessary to maintain the credibility of the design team's recommendations.

9. *Compute reconfiguration cost-benefit.* No matter how good the new network design may be, the benefits, as compared to the baseline, may not be sufficient to offset the cost of reconfiguring the existing network. Those costs include the cost of relocating personnel, severance, relocating inventory, opening and closing costs, and the potential disruption to customer service. An example network reconfiguration cost-benefit analysis is presented in Figure 7-22.

10. *Make go/no-go decision.* At this point, we've done our homework and presented management with the best analysis we can provide. We can make a recommendation, but the ultimate decision ultimately rests with the highest level executives in the corporation. I've seen many network modeling analyses ignored in the final decisions made by a CEO or COO. They go with their experience, intuition, gut feeling, or political influence of one aspect of the organization over another. That is executive prerogative. That's OK. The objective of the modeling effort is to present management with the best representation of logistics cost and service tradeoffs associated with

ERO Service Level Study
Five Quarters Ending FY98

DEPOT	% local source	Total Transit Cost in K $	Inventory Level White Oak RSL OF $1.6M and Boston at $2.5m in '98 (after $500K ramp)	Annual Carrying Cost at 42% includes 17% cost of capital in K $	Total Annual Cost Transit + carrying costs in K $	Admin. time in hrs.	Min. transit time in hrs.	Avg. transit time in hrs.	Max. transit time in hrs.	ERO Max. Total Hours	Boston Area Customers	White Oak Max. Total Hours	Weighted Avg. Hrs. for Customers within 100 mile radius	Weighted Avg. Hrs. for Customers outside of 100 mile radius
											Service Level Statistics			
Assumptions--->														
Boston	15%	$1,369	$2.0	$840	$2,209	1		3.56			1.18	4.7	1.4	5.75
Boston	100%	$2,461	$4.1	$1,722	$4,183	1	0	3.56	11.3	12.3	1.18	4.7	1.4	5.75
Dulles	100%	$1,925	$4.1	$1,722	$3,647	1	0.2	6.14	9.2	10.2	4.23	2.5	1.7	4.48
Philadelphia Specifically: Airville, PA	100%	$2,405	$4.1	$1,722	$4,127	1	0.2	3.18	8.1	9.1	2.76	2.1	2.1	4.25
Boston & Dulles	100%	$1,910	$5.0	$2,100	$4,010	1	0.2	2.52	9.2	10.2	1.18	2.5	B 1.38 D 1.66	B n/a D 4.54
None	0%	$1,177	$3.0	$1,260	$2,437	1	7.8	11.78	13.5	14.5	13.31	12.1	n/a	11.78

CONCLUSIONS:
• The best cost and service level combination is in Dulles, Virginia at $3.6M in total costs with weighted average delivery times within one shift.
• The cost of supporting ERO customers with "one shift or less" service levels is $1.2M per year (Dulles $3.6 less Milpitas $2.4M).
• Maxium delivery time is 2 hours shorter in dulles than Boston (10.2 Vs. 12.3).
• Having 2 depots in ERO costs $400K per year and buys us 3 hours of cycle time for customers within 100 miles of Boston (1.38 Vs. 4.48 hrs.).
   Note: this analysis does not include Boston to Non-ERO customer demand which accounts for 33% of L/I demand. Example IBM Burlington.

FIGURE 7-21   Logistics network evaluation.

194

FIGURE 7-22   Cost-benefit analysis for a network reconfiguration.
Source: Adapted from Napolitano

Scenario	Existing	A	B	C	D
DC Locations	New York, San Jose, St. Louis, Dallas	New York	New York, San Jose	New York, San Jose, St. Louis	New York, San Jose, St. Louis, Dallas, Orlando
Warehousing Costs	$ 3,607	$ 2,605	$ 2,917	$ 3,060	$ 3,882
Inventory Carrying Costs	$ 2,504	$ 2,009	$ 2,167	$ 2,388	$ 2,755
Inbound Transportation	$ 376	$ 225	$ 338	$ 343	$ 407
Outbound Transportation	$ 2,550	$ 5,151	$ 3,615	$ 2,719	$ 2,498
Total	**$ 9,037**	**$ 9,990**	**$ 9,037**	**$ 8,510**	**$ 9,542**
Savings vs. Existing	$ –	$ (953)	$ –	$ 527	$ (505)
Cost to Reconfigure	–	$ 3,401	$ 1,498	$ 454	$ 1,996
Payback Period (Years)		(0.28)	–	0.85	(0.25)
% 2-Day Delivery Coverage	**98%**	**85%**	**92%**	**96%**	**99%**

network design decisions. The stakes are high. So high that we have one client who recomputes their network optimization every day based on the new day's impact on future demand forecasts. When the cost-benefit analysis suggests it's time to move, they move. A network of third-party logistics facilities on one-year contracts permits them this flexibility.

7.6   SHIPMENT PLANNING AND MANAGEMENT

We define a *shipment* simply as a collection of orders that travel together. Here we will use the terms load and shipment interchangeably.

Shipment planning (see Figure 7-23) is the process of choosing shipment frequencies and deciding for each shipment the orders which should be assigned to the shipment, mode of transport, appropriate carrier, route, and shipping schedule. *Shipment management* includes the assignment of shipments to containers and the tracking of the shipment in process. We will cover in turn the practices of (1) planning shipment frequencies, (2) choosing modes and carriers, (3) routing and scheduling individual shipments, (4) planning loads, (5) rating potential shipments, and (6) tracking outbound shipments.

Shipment Frequency Planning

Shipping frequencies are a primary determining factor in total transportation costs, inventory carrying costs, transportation administration costs, and customer satisfaction. If we ship less material more frequently (see Figure 7-24), the following will be achieved:

- Overall in-transit, lot-quantity, and safety stock inventory levels and costs are reduced because there is typically less inventory in-transit at

FIGURE 7-23   Shipment planning process.

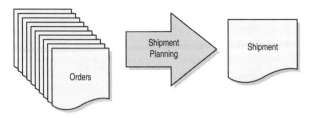

FIGURE 7-24   The impact of shipping frequency on logistics costs and performance.

	Inventory Carrying Costs			Transportation Costs		
Shipping Frequency	In-Transit	Lot Size	Safety Stock	Freight Costs	Administration Costs	Customer Satisfaction
More Often	↓	↓	↓	↑	↑	↑
Less Often	↑	↑	↑	↓	↓	↓

any one time, the recipient is receiving smaller lot quantities, and there are more opportunities to react to shifts in demand or supply streams.

- Transportation administration costs are greater because we have to incur the one-time expense of setting up a shipment for its accompanying paperwork and loading more often.
- Transportation costs are typically higher since we are moving smaller volumes per shipment and not benefiting from transportation discounts associated with large loads.
- Customer satisfaction is enhanced since customers are receiving goods more reliably more often.

Figure 7-25 illustrates the results of a recent shipping frequency analysis. In the engagement, we were assessing for a global manufacturer/distributor of health and beauty aids the frequency of shipments and the portion of product shipped by air or ocean. (The mode of transportation, like the shipping frequency, has a major impact on logistics cost and service.) Air, as compared to ocean shipping, has much higher freight charges ($5\times$ to $10\times$), much less in-transit inventory, and much shorter cycle times.

In the analysis, we considered 16 shipping scenarios represented by (x,y) pairs where x represents the percent shipping by air and y the number of shipments per month. We considered 1 percent, 3 percent, 5 percent, and 10 percent shipping via air, and 9, 4, 2, and 1 shipments per month to each

FIGURE 7-25   Shipping frequency analysis.

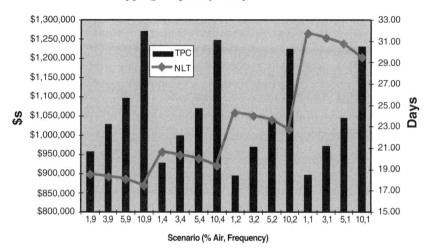

Scenario (% Air, Frequency)

country in the Asia-Pacific. The analysis compares the total logistics cost (inventory carrying and transportation) of each scenario with the door-to-door delivery cycle times experienced by the countries in the Asia-Pacific. Since the customers in the Asia-Pacific were not willing for their lead times to exceed 24 days, the recommended solution was the scenario yielding the lowest total logistics cost with net lead times less than 24 days. In this case, that shipment solution was to ship 1 percent via air four times per month.

The current air shipping percentage was close to 10 percent with shipments made eight or nine times per month. The high air shipping percentage and shipment frequency was due primarily to an inadequate advance planning capability and insufficient communication links between the U.S. and Far East. The study revealed an opportunity for over $350,000 annual savings by implementing and automating the practices required to implement a (1,4) shipping solution.

Mode and Carrier Selection

A transportation mode and carrier must be selected for each shipment. The decision impacts transportation and inventory carrying costs, in-transit times, delivery reliability, and overall customer service. The cube, weight, value, commodity, and chemical composition of each individual order and group of orders assigned together in a shipment all affect the selection of the proper mode and carrier.

The ideal mode selection best matches the requirements of the shipment with the characteristics of the chosen transportation mode. The general cost and logistics characteristics for each transportation mode are compared in Figures 7-26 and 7-27. The overall objective in mode selection is to choose the mode that minimizes the total logistics cost associated with the shipment while satisfying the due date requirements for the shipment. An example mode and carrier selection is illustrated in Figure 7-28. The example compares two air with two ocean carriers incorporating the impact of mode and carrier selection decisions on in-transit inventory, safety-stock inventory, cycle inventory, freight costs, and delivery cycle times.

The logistics information system should automatically select the mode and carrier that minimizes transportation costs while meeting due date requirements for each shipment in real-time.

Routing and Scheduling

Most of us are familiar with vehicle routing and scheduling problems from personal experience: bus routes, taxi routes, paper routes, traveling salesman problems, and even the neighborhood ice cream truck follows a route. Most of us have tried to plan efficient routes for vacation trips or errand runs. We are familiar with the challenges of planning to minimize left-hand turns, avoiding pockets of traffic congestion, visiting the locations in a logical sequence, such as making the grocery store the last stop so the ice cream won't melt on the way home, and working all of this against a deadline of getting home in time to cook supper or catch the end of a ballgame. (I even have routing software installed in my new car!)

The same challenges crop up in industrial settings, where efficient versus inefficient routing can save millions of dollars in fuel, labor, and capital

FIGURE 7-26   **Transportation mode factor analysis: 1=Very low, 2=Low, 3=Average, 4=High, 5=Very high**

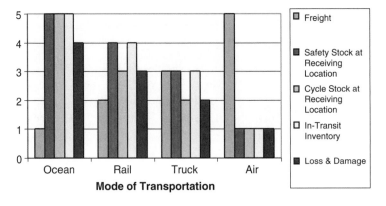

FIGURE 7-27   Transportation mode comparison factors.

	Road	Rail	Air	Marine	Pipeline
Cost/ton-mile	medium	low/medium	high	low/very low	very low
Speed (mph)	0–60	0–50	0–600	0–20	0–5
Frequency	very good	good	good	limited	continuous
Accesibility	extensive network	limited network	limited network	restricted network	dedicated network
Security	good	average	above average	poor	good
Key Advantages	mix of vehicle types, direct door-to-door	handling heavy loads, can carry trucks	lower inventory levels	cost	continous
Limitations	loading dimensions	inoperable with other modes	weight, weather	small packages, high stock levels	all but liquid
Reliability	very good	good	very good	limited	very good

FIGURE 7-28   Mode and carrier selection analysis.[3]

Parameters				
Product Cost	950			
ICR	20%			
	Air Carrier 1	Air Carrier 2	Ocean Carrier 1	Ocean Carrier 2
Annual Forecasted Demand	23,000	23,000	23,000	23,000
Transit Times Door-To-Door	7	7	28	35
Average In-Transit Inventory in Pipeline	441	441	1,764	2,205
Frequency of Shipment Arrival	7	7	7	28
Shipment Quantity	441	441	441	1,764
Average Cycle Stock Inventory at Logistics Center	221	221	221	882
Average Safety Stock Required at Logistics Center When Replenished by Air/Ocean Carrier	885	885	1769	1978
Total Inventory In-Transit + Logistics Center (SS+CS) in Units	1,546	1,546	3,754	5,066
Total Inventory In-Transit + Logistics Center (SS+CS) at Cost	$ 1,468,946	$ 1,468,946	$ 3,566,454	$ 4,812,445
Inventory Carrying Cost	$ 293,789	$ 293,789	$ 713,291	$ 962,489
Freight Cost Door-to-Door ($/unit)	55	52	13	11
Total Freight Cost Per Year	$ 1,265,000	$ 1,196,000	$ 299,000	$ 253,000
Total Logistics Cost per Mode/Carrier	$ 1,558,789	$ 1,489,789	$ 1,012,291	$ 1,215,489

[3]M.J. Liberatore and T. Miller, "A Decision Support Approach for Transport Carrier and Mode Selection," *Journal of Business Logistics*, Vol. 16, No. 2 (1995): 85–114.

expenditures and significantly enhance customer service. Formally, the routing problem can be expressed as a mathematical program. The objective could be to minimize the

- Total route costs (fuel, labor, and equipment)
- Number of routes (to minimize the number of required vehicles and/or personnel)
- Total distance traveled
- Total route time

The constraints include

- Customer response time requirements and time windows (specified times at which the vehicle must arrive after and depart before)
- Route balancing (so that no one vehicle or driver has a disproportionate share of the work)
- Maximum route times (for example, limiting the driving time of a truck driver or the flight time of a pilot)
- Vehicle capacities (limiting the amount of material assigned to a vehicle by the vehicle's weight and cubic capacity)
- Start-stop points (insuring that the vehicles start and stop at designated locations such as a home depot)
- Transportation infrastructure constraints (rates of speed and transportation volumes along lanes may not exceed specified thresholds)

Routing problems are computationally some of the most difficult encountered in mathematics. In fact, they are one of a class of problems that is not solvable to optimality in a less than infinite time. As a result, we normally employ one or more heuristics in solving a routing problem. Those heuristics are utilized in the background of the major routing software packages available on the market. A variety of excellent articles have been published on the mathematics of vehicle routing.[4]

An example routing solution developed by the CAPS Logistics Toolkit is illustrated in Figure 7-29.

Ideally, the routing solutions should be developed automatically and manually adjusted for anomalies. In addition, the capability to dynamically reroute a vehicle should be incorporated in the chosen routing solution.

[4]Napolitano, M.

FIGURE 7-29   Vehicle routing solution.

Source: CAPS Logistics Toolkit

Parameters		
Product Cost	$	950.00
ICR		20%

	Air Carrier 1	Air Carrier 2	Ocean Carrier 1	Ocean Carrier 2
Annual Forecasted Demand	23,000	23,000	23,000	23,000
Transit Times Door-To-Door	7	7	28	35
Average In-Transit Inventory in Pipeline	441	441	1,764	2,205
Frequency of Shipment Arrival	7	7	7	28
Shipment Quantity	441	441	441	1,764
Average Cycle Stock Inventory at Logistics Center	221	221	221	882
Average Safety Stock Required at Logistics Center When Replenished by Air/Ocean Carrier	885	885	1769	1978
Total Inventory In-Transit + Logistics Center (SS+CS) in Units	1,546	1,546	3,754	5,066
Total Inventory In-Transit + Logistics Center (SS+CS) at Cost	$ 1,468,946	$ 1,468,946	$ 3,566,454	$ 4,812,445
Inventory Carrying Cost	$ 293,789	$ 293,789	$ 713,291	$ 962,489
Freight Cost Door-to-Door ($/unit)	$ 55.00	$ 52.00	$ 13.00	$ 11.00
Total Freight Cost Per Year	$ 1,265,000	$ 1,196,000	$ 299,000	$ 253,000

Total Logistics Cost per Mode/Carrier				
	$ 1,558,789	$ 1,489,789	$ 1,012,291	$ 1,215,489

Backhauling and Continuous Moves

Good routing solutions also incorporate *backhauling*, the practice of inter-leaving pickups and deposits on a single route to maximize the vehicle utilization. The practice of backhauling is illustrated in Figure 7-30.

Some of the most advanced routing solutions identify *continuous move* programs, which essentially keep each vehicle in operation continually, moving between pickup and deposit locations throughout a country or region, much like a taxi cab. An example of continuous move solutions is depicted in Figure 7-31.

Vehicle Scheduling

Scheduling is an even more difficult problem than routing because it involves precedent relationships and time windows in addition to routing. An example routing and scheduling solution is depicted in Figure 7-32.

Advanced scheduling solutions should also avoid hub times, those times when major transportation hubs are clogged. For me personally, it's like avoiding the Atlanta airport on Sunday night or Friday afternoon. The likelihood of my flight being delayed in those conditions is much higher

FIGURE 7-30   **Deadheading versus backhauling.**

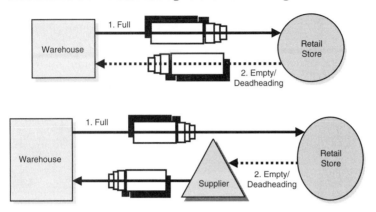

FIGURE 7-31   **Continuous moves solution.**
Source: CAPS Logistics

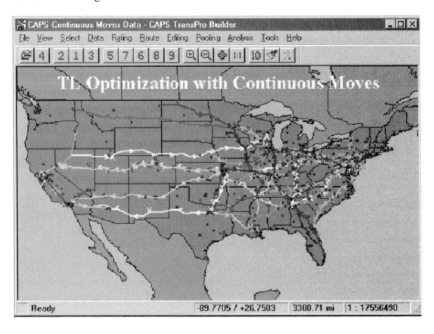

than if I fly Tuesday through Thursday. In addition, a scheduling solution should take into consideration and coordinate with the arrival and departure schedules of any third-party carriers being utilized in the scheduling program. Several hours or days may be eliminated from the overall transportation cycle time by coordinating internal transportation schedules with that of the major carriers when they are being utilized in the solution.

FIGURE 7-32   Vehicle routing and scheduling solution.
Source: CAPS Logistics

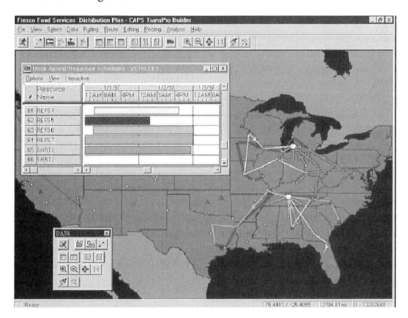

Inbound/Outbound Consolidation

Scheduling requirements are becoming increasingly more complex as more and more consignees consolidate and schedule inbound deliveries. Intelligent transportation management systems should reveal and suggest opportunities for inbound and outbound consolidation.

An example inbound consolidation program for a major retailer in the United States bringing goods in from the Asia-Pacific is illustrated in Figure 7-33. Inbound consolidation programs yield lower transportation rates over a large portion of the length of the major transportation segment, often building LTL loads in full truckloads in over-the-road transport and LCL loads into full-container loads in ocean or air shipping.

Outbound consolidation, or pooling, is another means of achieving freight savings. The practice is sometimes referred to as zone skipping in parcel shipping since full-container loads of parcels bound for destinations that are several USPS, UPS, or FEDEX zones away are shipped directly to those zones, skipping the transit through the zones along the way and avoiding the associated high transport rates. The consolidated loads are typically shipped directly to a sorting center or hub for the parcel handler of choice. Deconsolidation and loading for local delivery takes place at the hub. A major third-party logistics company in joint venture with a major material

FIGURE 7-33   Inbound consolidation program.

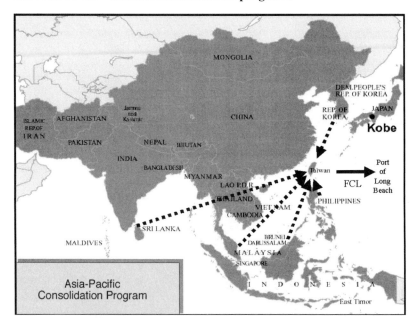

handling systems supplier recently developed an entire logistics infrastructure to support zone skipping practices and economies in the Internet catalog retailing industry.

Today's world-class routing and scheduling systems also maintain real-time links with traffic management and global positioning systems. Those links permit real-time rerouting around and between newly created points of traffic congestion. A new satellite-enabled email system called Truck-Mail was recently introduced by QualComm to permit continuous, online, electronic communications with a fleet of vehicles (see Figure 7-34). The system is a natural platform for dynamic routing and rerouting.

Load Planning and Management

The objective of load planning is to maximize the outbound container utilization while not exceeding the cubic or weight capacity restrictions of the container, loading in reverse order of the delivery locations for the load, and balancing the weight of the load across the floor of the container. The problem is complicated by many factors:

- The mix of product dimensions and weights
- Inconsistency in container dimensions and usability
- Double-faced loading capacity constraints for cube and weight

FIGURE 7-34 **Qualcomm's TruckMail on-board communication system.**

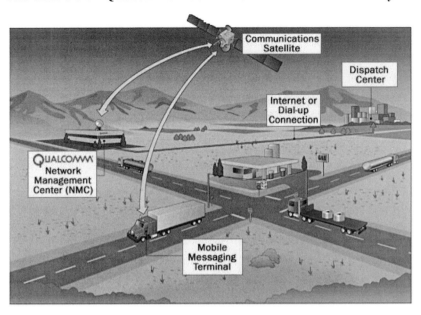

Because each container is limited by weight and cubic constraints, an ideal load plan comes as nearly as possible to maximizing both utilization factors.

In the face of these complexities, we typically recommend that our clients utilize an automated load planning tool. The tools accept as input the mix of case, pallet, weight, and other unit-load dimensions, as well as the dimensional and weight capacities for the assigned container. The tools then produce a near-optimal load plan. Example output from one of the tools is illustrated in Figure 7-35.

In some systems, not only should the load planning be automated, but also the loading activity itself. An increasing number of makes and models of automated loading devices are available today. One model for loading pallets of beverages outbound to the beverage wholesale marketplace in Japan is illustrated in Figure 7-36. The system enables the beverage manufacturer to load and unload trailers in less than 20 minutes, less than 10 percent of the typical load/unload time experienced in the industry.

Another type of automated truck loading system is illustrated in Figure 7-37. The system is utilized by KAO, the largest Japanese consumer products company. As opposed to using technology at the dock to automate loading and unloading, each trailer bed is equipped with an in-floor,

FIGURE 7-35   Optimized load plans.
Source: Astrokettle, Visual Load

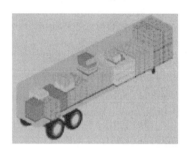
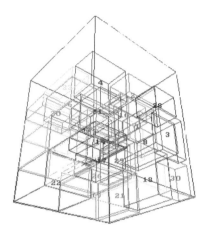

FIGURE 7-36   Automated truck loading system.

FIGURE 7-37   Automated trailer loading/unloading system.

powered-roller conveyor. Again, the system allows a load to be completely transferred from an inbound trailer into the DC in less than five minutes.

Shipment Rating

In addition to frequency planning, routing and scheduling, and load planning for each shipment, shipments must also be rated. *Rating* is the process of estimating the freight charge associated with any given shipment. Rating capability should be incorporated in the online *transportation management system* (TMS) and linked with the order entry system so that freight charges and estimated arrival times may be provided to the customer online and in real time. Increasingly, this functionality is available through online links with the carrier's Internet sites where their rate structures are continuously updated. If carriers are used, the online rating system must allocate promised volumes to preferred and contract carriers before searching for more attractive rates from alternative carriers.

Electronic shipment bidding (ESB) is a new rating practice and system. Via electronic shipment bidding, shippers post shipments (each with an origin, destination, weight, delivery time requirement, and classification) on an electronic bulletin board. Carriers may bid for shipments electronically by watching and capturing the shipments that are attractive for them. Bids are placed and accepted electronically.

A variety of transportation exchanges offer ESB and related services. An example ESB transaction screen is provided in Figure 7-38.

Shipment Tracking

The final issue that needs to be addressed in shipment planning and management is shipment tracking and visibility. This capability is critical in inventory management and customer response. In inventory management, we often order additional inventory to cover any blind-spot places where shipment visibility is lost. We lose faith in the system if we can't "see" the inventory. So, we lose trust and order more and more often than is really required. It's like our faith test in God; we are asked to have faith in what we hope for and can't see. It goes against our human nature, but is required for salvation.

Real-time shipment tracking and visibility is required to support excellent customer response since a large majority of customer service inquiries are related to shipment status requests. Ideally, we will be proactive in communicating with our customer's shipment status information through our real-time tracking capability. This capability can significantly reduce the workload for a customer service department.

FIGURE 7-38   Electronic shipment bidding.
Source: Transportation.com

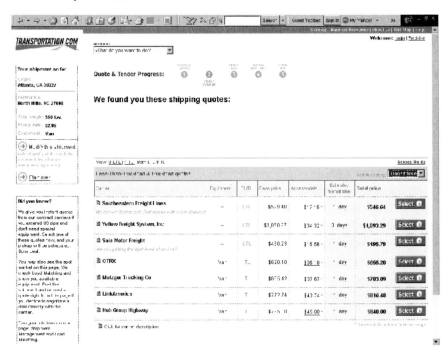

World-class shipment tracking and visibility begins before the shipment is released to the fleet or common carrier. The first time a customer places an order with us, we should be able to estimate a picking time, departure time, arrival time, and container assignment, and communicate that information via phone, fax, e-mail, and/or Internet during the communication. Any exceptions to that plan should be communicated to the customer proactively.

One of the best examples of exception reporting I've witnessed came during a recent visit to one of our clients in the valves and fittings business. During my visit, one of the aisles of the automated storage/retrieval system failed. As a result, nearly 15 percent of the customer orders for the day could not be completely satisfied. Our client called each of the affected customers and asked if they would prefer to have their order shipped partial or complete, incurred all the additional transportation charges for expediting and shipping partial, and called each as soon as the aisle was repaired to give them an updated arrival time for their shipment.

Maintaining real-time shipment visibility requires online EDI and/or Internet links with the fleet and/or carriers. It may also require the use of on-board communication systems and GPS to facilitate global shipment tracking of containers worldwide. That capability should be a primary carrier selection factor and requirement for an internal fleet management system. (Qualcomm's Truckmail system described earlier is an example.)

GE and IBM have recently developed systems to support global shipment tracking. GEIS and IBM Transconnect have built real-time shipment tracking links with most major carriers. Therefore, shippers need only to have links with either services to establish links with a large carrier base (see Figure 7-39).

7.7   FLEET, CONTAINER, AND YARD MANAGEMENT

If we decide to operate our own fleet, then our transportation management solution must address fleet, container, and yard management. Fleet, container, and yard management activities include the following:

- *Sizing and configuring* the fleet of vehicles and/or containers
- *Acquiring or replacing* individual vehicles and/or containers
- *Maintaining* vehicles and containers
- *Identifying and tracking* vehicles and containers
- *Planning and managing* docks, yards, and ports

We'll cover world-class practices and systems in each of those five activities in this section.

FIGURE 7-39   Online shipment tracking concept.

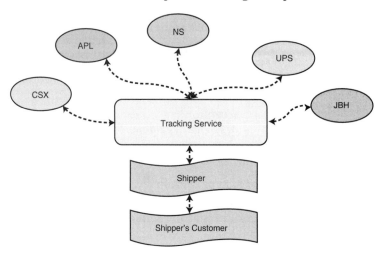

Fleet Sizing, Configuration, and Financing

The objective in fleet sizing is to employ through ownership, lease, and/or rental the fewest number of vehicles and containers possible to meet the hourly, daily, weekly, monthly, and annual shipping requirements. The decision is much like the decision of how much inventory to make available to customers. Increasing availability yields fewer lost sales, improved customer service, and higher inventory carrying costs. In fleet sizing, increased availability yields fewer lost sales, shorter customer cycle times, improved customer service, but higher fleet costs. The graph in Figure 7-40 illustrates the tradeoffs in play and suggests the optimal solution is the minimum fleet size, which satisfies a prespecified level of customer service during peak and average periods.

This same analysis should be performed for each type of vehicle or container chosen as a part of the fleet operations. These fleet sizing projections should be developed a few times during the year and at any time when a major shift in demand patterns occurs. In some cases, the cost of vehicle shortages can be estimated and a cost of shortage versus cost of ownership analysis can be made to determine the optimal fleet size.

The overall fleet requirements can be minimized by

- Utilizing standard and modular-sized cases, pallets, and transport containers
- Aggressively monitoring fleet utilization levels over each segment of the transportation network during each period of the year

FIGURE 7-40   Fleet sizing analysis.

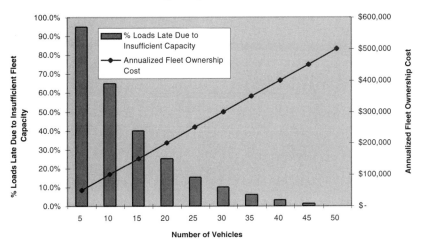

- Maintaining total fleet visibility, including loading times, unloading times, transit times, and maintenance times
- Choosing low-use periods to conduct routine maintenance
- Monitoring and charging for fleet detention by suppliers, customers, and/or carriers
- Utilizing alternative coverage means during super-peak periods to avoid carrying the burden of an oversized fleet

Fleet Acquisition and Replacement

Once the size of the fleet has been determined, the means of acquiring the fleet must be determined. A variety of acquisition options are available, including direct, private ownership, leasing, and dedicated contract carriage. The analysis to determine one method or a mix of methods of ownership should be made like any other major financial decision by considering the costs of ownership, the cost of capital, the impact on customer service, internal and external philosophies/reactions to outsourcing, and the competitive advantage or disadvantage of either method.

Figure 7-41 illustrates the terms of fleet capabilities acquisition in the food industry. Note that privately owned fleets still represent the majority of fleet activity in the food industry, as is common in many industries. The principle reason is the real or perceived customer service and internal control advantage offered by private fleets over and above contract carriage.

As with most other physical assets, the condition of the fleet deteriorates over time. Hence, elements of the fleet must nearly continuously be

FIGURE 7-41 Fleet terms of acquisition in the food industry.[5]

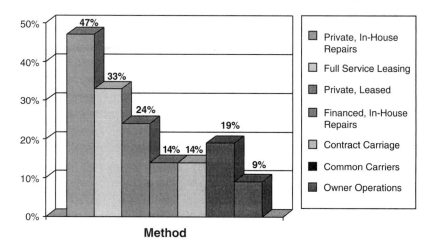

considered for replacement. Over the life of the asset, the condition of the asset continues to decline and the cost of maintenance continues to increase. At some point, projected maintenance costs exceed the annualized cost of replacing the asset. Figure 7-42 illustrates this phenomenon. The transportation management system should automatically track and report maintenance costs and projected maintenance costs for each transportation asset and recommend a replacement schedule for each vehicle and/or container.

Fleet Maintenance and Security

World-class fleet maintenance is one means of reducing the ownership cost of the fleet by delaying potential replacements and improving customer service through improved reliability. Because this document is not focused on fleet management as a discipline, but to a greater degree on transportation management, I suggest you consider references published by the National Private Truck Council as excellent resources for fleet maintenance advice.

Security is one of the world's fastest growing industries. Intensified global trade, broader and more frequent logistics partnering, increased information sharing in the logistics chain, and more use of third and fourth parties in supply chain activities make a seedbed for security violations. In addition to information security, fleet security programs have never been more important as a part of overall corporate security. The resources from the National Private Truck Council are excellent resources for the latest advances in fleet security.

[5]*1996 Food Service Transportation and Fleet Maintenance Report,* Food Distributors International. Washington, D.C.

FIGURE 7-42   **Transportation asset replacement analysis.**

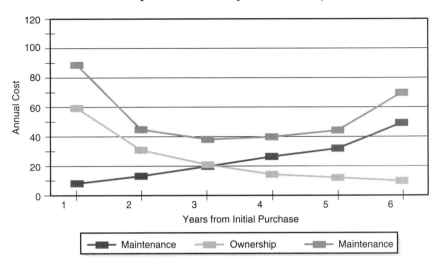

Vehicle/Container Identification, Tracking, and Communications

The ability to automatically identify, track, and communicate with stationary and in-transit vehicles and containers is a critical enabler in support of real-time shipment tracking. Fortunately, technology in this area is advancing faster than in any other area of transportation management. The advances have been motivated to a great extent by a mammoth failure in container/shipment tracking. That failure occurred in Operation Desert Storm as thousands of containers were placed and subsequently lost in the deserts of Kuwait.

To combat this, the U.S. Department of Defense began an aggressive campaign called Total Asset Visibility. One of the great advances stemming from that campaign was the use of bar coding, radio frequency communication, radio-frequency tags, and advanced global positioning systems for use in commercial transportation management. As long as each container has a bar code license plate, then bar code scanners can be used to automatically identify each container with handheld or automatic scanners.

Radio frequency communications can be used in conjunction with bar code scanning and then to relate any identified container with its contents, enclosed shipments, and location. Radio frequency tags in conjunction with tag readers or antennae are a step beyond bar codes since the tags are permanently implanted in the container, are far more durable than bar codes, can be read from or written to, and can be read and identified automatically with stationary antennae, which can read the tag or write to the tag as long as the tag is within a few hundred meters of the tag.

An example RF tag application is provided in Figure 7-43, where an over-the-road vehicle is automatically weighed and checked at an RF tag weigh station. RF tags are approximately the size of a button on a man's shirt and cost between $0.75 and $6.00.

The next advance in RF tag technology will most likely be the use of advanced global positioning systems and related satellites to provide real-time global tracking of every container equipped with the appropriate RF tag.

On-board vehicle communications have improved dramatically as well. The most recent advance is a system called TruckMail, developed by QualComm, which equips every cab with an on-board computer and perpetual, online e-mail via a special satellite link. The system is used by the driver to report the status and exceptions in his/her route and is used by headquarters to update route and delivery information online in real time.

Yard, Dock, and Port Management

Yard, dock, and port management is perhaps the most overlooked area in all of transportation management. Container yards, docks, and ports are typically the nodes in the transportation network with the least systems support, the least management sophistication, the least container tracking capabilities, the most crime, and the most frequent source of delays and cycle time variability. However, as the margin for error in all supply chain operations and communications is reduced still further, the container yards, docks, and

FIGURE 7-43   RF tag application.
Source: SpeedScale

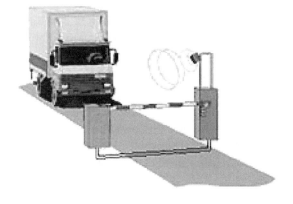

ports of the world will have to be transformed into hubs of real-time communications, value-added services, and on-time reliability.

Some world-class yard/dock/port management practices include

- Secured driver-load verification
- On-site, automatic driver routing
- Intelligent dock assignment
- Advanced crew and dock/berth scheduling
- Yard/dock/port staging location tracking and management

Secured Driver-Load Pickup Verification

As mentioned previously, transportation security is an integral and increasingly important link in overall corporate security. One of the most common transportation security violation scenarios is for a scab driver to pick up a load. Sapporo, a Japanese beverage company, combats this scheme by requiring drivers to identify themselves, their assigned vehicle, their assigned container, and their assigned loads with a smart card before the automated loading system would release the load to them (see Figure 7-44).

On-Site, Automatic Driver Routing

Another frustrating source of wasted time and capital in the yard/dock/port is the time spent by drivers on-site waiting for and looking for their assigned dock or berth. On-board communications and electronic maps have helped to some extent, but a recent innovation by Suntory has nearly eliminated the frustrations and inefficiencies. They devised a voice-activated system that identifies and verifies the driver by his/her voice print,

FIGURE 7-44 Smart card reader for driver-load-vehicle verification.

tells the driver in synthesized voice the assigned dock number, and enunciates the directions to the assigned dock. A picture of the system is provided in Figure 7-45.

Efficient Dock/Berth Assignment   Whether it is a load of pallets inbound to a warehouse from a supplier or a load of ocean containers due into port at the completion of an overseas journey, one objective in assigning the inbound vehicle to a dock/berth is to minimize the handling distance and time in unloading. Figure 7-46 illustrates the principle of efficient dock assignments in a warehouse in which the inbound vehicle is assigned to the open dock door nearest the centroid of the putaway locations of the pallets onboard the vehicle.

Advanced Crew and Dock/Berth Scheduling   Supply chain operations and activities are reaching higher degrees of synchronization around the world. Inbound and outbound operations are scheduled to tighter and tighter timelines. Eventually, docks, berths, and their associated loading/

FIGURE 7-45   **Voice-activated driver routing system.**

FIGURE 7-46   **Inbound dock assignment example.**

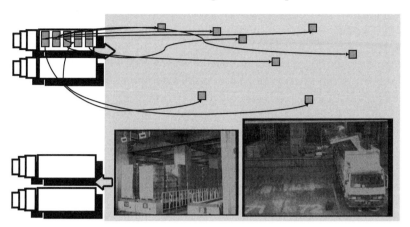

unloading crews will be scheduled in cargo operations with the same rigor and sophistication employed in passenger air transportation. Unfortunately, yard/dock/port management systems are severely underdeveloped in comparison with the requirements that are on the near horizon.

Yard/Dock/Port Staging Location Tracking and Management

A good simple rule of thumb for yard/dock/port staging location management is the old adage, "a place for everything and everything in its place." It is amazing to see container loads with values sometimes in excess of $10,000,000 haphazardly staged in unmarked locations without a container identification. However, you can walk inside a nearby warehouse and see a pallet of copy paper tagged with a bar code or RF tag, each case of which is perfectly labeled, and the entire load assigned to a neatly kept and perpetually tracked location identified by one or more bar code labels. The same disciplined rigor and degree of automation used to locate products in most warehouse operations needs to be extended outdoors where even larger quantities of even higher value are many times misplaced due to poor location marking and management.

7.8   CARRIER MANAGEMENT

I called out carrier management as a separate activity in transportation management for the purposes of framing the entire scope of transportation management. The core practices of carrier management, including carrier performance monitoring, carrier selection, carrier negotiations, and core carrier programs, have been addressed throughout this chapter.

7.9   FREIGHT AND DOCUMENT MANAGEMENT

The last of the five transportation management activities is freight and document management. Because over $500 billion is paid annually in freight bills in the United States alone, freight management and the associated activity of transportation document management is one of the most lucrative (if done properly) and expensive (if done poorly) aspects of transportation management.

Here we will cover world-class practices in negotiating, paying, and auditing freight and transportation document management.

Freight Rate Negotiations

Due to the rapid consolidation of the rail carriage industry, the Ocean Shipping Reform Act, intermodalism within and between trucking carriers, electronic shipment bidding, new transportation modes like the FastShip and CargoLifter, and the mainstreaming of time-definite deliveries, freight rate negotiations are not the three bids and a cloud of dust events they used to be. Today's negotiations require much more research and advance planning than at any time in the past. The preparation is nearly the same as that required in advance of an entire redesign of the transportation strategy. These preparations emphasize one more time the criticality of online transportation activity profiling and decisions support as a key capability in transportation management.

Shippers should come to the negotiating table ready with

- Historical and projected shipping volumes between each origin-destination pair
- Required delivery times and on-time reliability performance
- Required value-added services
- Guidelines for claims and conflict resolution
- Historical carrier performance records, volumes, and rates
- Required information systems support capability
- Preferred payment terms and rate structures
- Knowledge of the carrier's competitive position, market share, and underutilized capacity
- Knowledge of the carrier's current and future customer base
- Knowledge of recent or projected shifts in the carrier's organization structure
- Carrier hot buttons

Carriers should come prepared with exactly the same list substituting the words "available" for "required" and "shipper" for "carrier."

Despite all the e-uproar over online transportation booking and bidding, we recommend to our clients that they consolidate their transportation spending on a core group of reliable carriers. Core carrier programs usually yield lower transportation rates since a great volume of business is offered to fewer carriers and higher levels of customer service since a business partnership has been formed, as opposed to a single business transaction carried out between business strangers.

Freight Bill Payment

As I mentioned previously, over $500 billion in freight bills are paid in the United States alone. Some simple estimating reveals that on the order of five billion freight bills are paid each year in the United States. The cost of paying, processing, and auditing those bills was recently estimated to be in excess of $40 billion! Done inefficiently, just the process of paying freight bills can become a major cost center for any organization.

Three basic alternative procedures for freight bill payment exist: payment-on-invoice, positive pay, and outsourcing. In *pay-on-invoice,* the shipper waits for an invoice from a carrier, verifies it, and pays it directly. This procedure is fraught with mistakes and overbilling by carriers.

The mistakes and overbilling have given birth to an entire industry known as freight bill auditing, another potentially costly process for the organization to undertake. We found in one recent engagement that the organization was paying more than $25 just to pay a freight bill. A simple outsourcing analysis discovered one firm that would pay the same bill for $0.50 per bill. That was the simplest outsourcing study we have ever completed!

Another method of paying freight bills is a procedure sometimes referred to as *positive pay.* In the positive pay procedure, the shipper computes the freight bill associated with any shipment and releases funds to the carrier without an invoice. This procedure eliminates the need for the shipper to audit freight bills and the carrier's invoicing, but requires an earlier release of the shipper's funds and requires the shipper to maintain freight rates in their system. The procedure normally pays for itself quickly by the reduction in carrier overcharges in related paper handling.

The third freight bill payment technique is *outsourcing.* In outsourcing freight bill payments, a third-party bill payer is contracted on a per-transaction basis to provide a variety of services related to freight bill payments, including simply paying the bills, maintaining rates, auditing freight bills, analyzing freight bills, and helping the shipper to prepare for freight rate negotiations. One of the largest freight bill payment firms in the United States is NPC. They are the largest bill payer of any kind. One helpful service they provide is to scan, archive, summarize, and store each freight bill

FIGURE 7-47   **Electronic freight bill assessment tool.**
Source: NPC

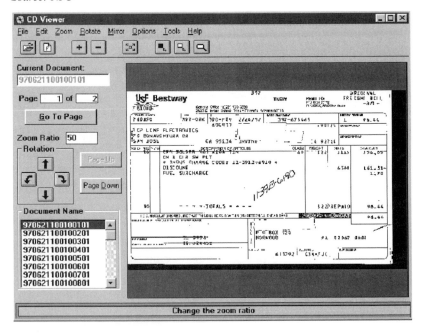

in CD-ROM format. The CD-ROM is distributed to each shipper with software that permits online freight and shipping volume trend tracking. A screen shot from NPC's freight bill assessment software is provided in Figure 7-47.

Auditing Freight Bills
Auditing freight bills is necessary to recover mistakes and overcharges made by carriers in their invoicing process. Third-party freight bill auditors typically receive a percentage of the overcharges they identify as their fee. Done internally, freight bill auditing can pay for itself through the savings in overcharge recovery fees. However, auditing freight bills internally requires the shipper to maintain freight rates internally.

7.10   TRANSPORTATION MANAGEMENT SYSTEMS (TMSs)
The marketplace for TMSs is perhaps the most fragmented of all the marketplaces for logistics software. Most transportation applications accomplish a single execution or planning task for a single mode of transportation. We have learned this the hard way trying to find a minimum set of transportation packages to integrate into an entire corporate transportation solution.

Based on the world-class transportation practices described earlier, our recommended set of TMS requirements is summarized here:

- Transportation data warehousing and data mining
- Transportation performance measurement
- Transportation network design and simulation
- Inbound/outbound consolidation planning
- Shipment and load planning
- Mode and carrier selection
- Optimal and dynamic routing and scheduling
- Online shipment bidding, rating, and tracing
- Carrier management and measurement
- Fleet/container tracking, management, and maintenance
- Dock/yard/port management
- Freight bill payment and audit

7.11   TRANSPORTATION ORGANIZATION DESIGN AND DEVELOPMENT

The transportation industry and the transportation activity within most major enterprises are stressed today beyond any other day in recent memory. Any transportation professional working today feels the stress of the need to move more, smaller loads more often with less margin for error in the face of a severe driver shortage and increasing fuel costs. I am convinced that a major source of the difficulty is the lack of strategic planning and organization development within transportation companies, within the transportation activities of most major corporations, and within the government authorities that have regulated transportation activities over the years.

Though the oldest of what we now call logistics activities, somehow transportation is the least developed organizationally. The planning disciplines and supporting systems that are characteristic of the customer service organization, inventory management organization, supply organization, and even the warehousing organization are not as developed in transportation and distribution organizations. We recommend the following set of initiatives and programs be implemented within the transportation activities of our major clients.

Core Carrier Programs and Carrier Relationship Management

Similar to supplier relationship management programs, carrier relationship management programs are designed to formalize the communication, partnering, negotiating, and performance monitoring aspects of carrier management. At the heart of most carrier relationship management programs is a set of guidelines for selecting core carriers, the minority of carriers who carry a majority of the enterprise's weight, cube, and shipments.

Corporate Traffic Councils

Corporate traffic councils bring together all personnel working in the area of transportation within an enterprise. The traffic council sets corporate transportation policy and explores opportunities for leveraging transportation spending across the corporation.

Training and Certification in Transportation Management

Because transportation is heavy-laden with changing regulations, complex terminology, multiple personnel issues, and layers of required documentation, on-going training and certification for transportation managers helps insure that transportation remains transparent to the public, customers, and internally. Corporations should make and maintain transportation as a value-added activity.

Driver Certification and Quality of Life Programs

Due to increasing demands for all modes of trucking, low unemployment, and pending regulatory constraints on driving hours and schedules, the economy is facing a severe driver shortage. Recent estimates suggest that there will be a shortfall of nearly 100,000 truck drivers during the upcoming Christmas season. As demands on drivers increase, as traffic congestion increases, and as the transportation infrastructure begins to falter, the need for certified, more experienced, and more highly qualified drivers has never been more severe. In fact, those organizations that have maintained a highly qualified driving staff are experiencing a significant competitive advantage in some industries.

For example, with driver tenures sometimes averaging less than one year, a recent client leveraged a driving team with an average tenure of more than 13 years to establish a dominant industry position in customer service and related market share. When I asked the fleet manager how he had been able to maintain such a low turnover amongst the drivers, he shared that he had designed the transportation network and related schedules around the quality of life of the drivers. (The network design allowed the drivers to return home most nights and always on the weekends.) Though perhaps slightly more expensive in fuel than some possible network designs, this organization's driver-friendly network design paid overwhelming dividends in market share, safety, customer service, and reduced driver turnover.

Joint Procurement of Transportation Services

Significant savings in freight payments can be achieved if the purchase and negotiation of transportation services is consolidated across inbound/outbound transportation activities within a business unit, across business units, and even with noncompetitors servicing similar markets. One example of joint transportation procurement is the global transportation services agreement that two large food companies utilize. One company manufactures cereal, the other, confections and pet food. Both serve the same marketplaces yet do not compete. Their joint procurement program yields seven-figure savings each year. Another example is a joint fleet procurement program utilized by a large beverage company and a large rental car company.

Logistics Compliance and Security Officer
Though "deregulated" in the early 1980s, transportation is still fraught with international, federal, and state regulations. Maintaining compliance is key to maintaining good public, government, and business relations. With increasing numbers of transportation transactions more and more likely to traverse multiple borders, regulatory compliance is more and more difficult to maintain. To help an organization stay in step with regulatory developments, we typically recommend that a logistics compliance officer be put in place to develop enterprise guidelines, programs, and systems to insure enterprise-wide compliance with global, federal, and state regulations that relate to transportation and logistics.

A recent client recruited an attorney with a special interest in logistics to serve in this role. The individual graduated from our Logistics Management Series as a prerequisite to his accepting the position and as a supplement to his legal training. Another client sent his corporate director of safety and security through the Logistics Management Series to prepare him for a role as vice-president of logistics security and compliance. One global consumer electronics firm established the position of Chief Logistics Intelligence Officer to help them comply with global logistics law and to anticipate security lapses within the logistics network.

Participation in Transportation Industry Forums
One means of anticipating and staying in step with developments in transportation regulation is to participate actively in industry forums and professional associations where transportation issues are debated. Those forums include the *Council of Logistics Management* (CLM), *National Trucking Council* (NTC), NAASTRAC, and the *Intermodal Association of North America* (IANA).

Recruiting from Carriers
Transportation is not the core activity for most businesses, and it is a highly complex activity to manage. As a result, when staffing an internal transportation organization, we encourage our clients to recruit professionals with carrier experience, where transportation is a way of life.

8

WAREHOUSE OPERATIONS

> "They should collect all the food of these good years that are coming and store up the grain . . . This food should be held in reserve for the country, to be used during the seven years of famine that will come . . ."
>
> *Genesis 41:35–36*

FTER I WROTE THE *World-Class Warehousing*[1] book, many people asked me why I wrote a book on warehousing when there were so many projects and industry initiatives aimed at eliminating the warehouse. My response was and is that the warehouse is playing a more vital role in the success (or failure) of businesses today than it ever has.

Under the influence of e-commerce, supply chain collaboration, globalization, quick response, and just-in-time, warehouses today are being asked to

- Execute *more*, smaller transactions
- Handle and store *more* items
- Provide *more* product and service customization
- Offer *more* value-added services
- Process *more* returns
- Receive and ship *more* international orders

---

[1] Frazelle, E.H., *World Class Warehousing*, McGraw-Hill, New York, New York, 2002.

At the same time warehouses today have

- *Less* time to process an order
- *Less* margin for error
- *Less* young, skilled, English-speaking personnel
- *Less warehouse management system* (WMS) capability (a byproduct of Y2K investments in *enterprise resource planning* [ERP] systems)

I call this a "rock and a hard place scenario" the plight of the warehouse manager. Never has the warehouse been asked to do so much and at the same time been strapped for resources. One barometer we have for the focus of business on the warehouse is the number of requests for expert witness work we receive. In the last year, we have had an unprecedented number of requests for expert witness work related to failed warehouse management or material handling systems. The fault is about evenly divided between the vendors and users; however, the number of calls is a testimony to the value that corporations are placing on warehouse operations. Never before has it been so critical for the warehouse to work efficiently, quickly, and error free.

This chapter describes the principles of warehousing that yield world-class warehousing operations. (The principles are described and illustrated in more detail in the *World-Class Warehousing* book.) The principles follow our warehouse master planning methodology (see Figure 8-1) and cover warehouse performance metrics, receiving, putaway, storage, order picking, and shipping.

We present warehousing as the last of the five logistics activities (see Figure 8-2) for a variety of reasons. First, good planning in the other four areas of logistics may eliminate the need for warehousing. Second, requirements in the other four areas of logistics may suggest that a third party warehousing firm should be retained to operate the warehouse. Third, the warehouse must be designed to meet all the requirements of the customer service policy spelled out in the customer response master plan, house all the inventory required by the inventory master plan, work to receive in quantities stipulated by the supply master plan, and serve a mission stipulated by the transportation master plan. The warehouse is a service to all the other areas of logistics.

8.1   WAREHOUSING FUNDAMENTALS

This chapter begins with a description of the missions of a warehouse and the activities within its four walls.

FIGURE 8-1   Warehouse master planning methodology.

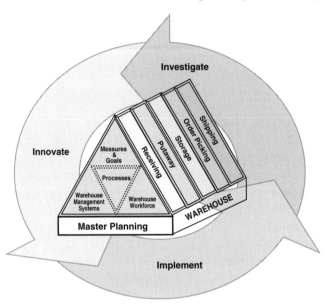

Missions of a Warehouse

In a distribution network, a warehouse may play one or more of the following roles:

- **Raw material and component warehouses**   Hold raw materials at or near the point of induction into a manufacturing or assembly process.
- **Work-in-process warehouses**   Hold partially completed assemblies and products at various points along an assembly or production line.
- **Finished goods warehouses**   Hold inventory used to balance and *buffer* the variation between production schedules and demand. For this purpose, the warehouse is usually located near the point of manufacture and is often characterized by the flow of full pallets in and full pallets out assuming that product size and volume warrant pallet-sized loads. A warehouse serving only this function may have demands ranging from monthly to quarterly replenishment of stock to the next level of distribution.
- **Distribution warehouses and distribution centers**   Accumulate and *consolidate* products from various points of manufacture within a single firm or from several firms for combined shipment to common customers. Such a warehouse may be located central to either production locations or the customer base. Product movement may be

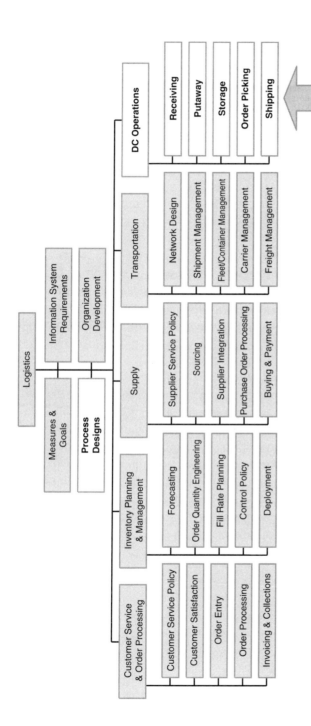

FIGURE 8-2   Warehousing in the logistics framework.

typified by full pallets or cases in and full cases or broken case quantities out. The facility is typically responding to regular weekly or monthly orders.

*   **Fulfillment warehouses and fulfillment centers**   Receive, pick, and ship small orders for individual consumers.
*   **Local warehouses**   Distributed in the field in order to shorten transportation distances to permit *rapid response* to customer demand. Frequently, single items are picked, and the same item may be shipped to the customer every day.

Figure 8-3 illustrates warehouses performing these functions in a logistics network. Unfortunately, in many of today's networks, a single item will pass in and out of a warehouse serving each of these functions between the point of manufacture and the customer. When feasible, two or more missions should be combined in the same warehousing operation. Current changes in the availability and cost of transportation options make the combination possible for many products. In particular, small high-value items with unpredictable demand are frequently shipped world-wide from a single source using overnight delivery services.

FIGURE 8-3   **Roles of a warehouse in the logistics chain.**

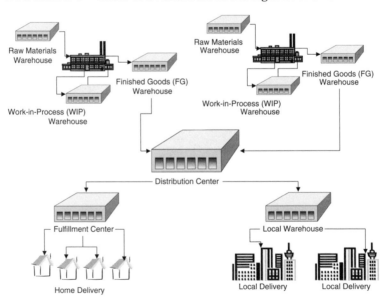

Functions in the Warehouse

No matter the name or role, warehouse operations have a fundamental set of activities in common. The following list includes the activities found in most warehouses. These tasks, or functions, are also indicated on a flow line in Figure 8-4 to make it easier to visualize them in actual operation.

1. Receiving
2. Prepackaging (optional)
3. Putaway
4. Storage
5. Order picking
6. Packaging and/or pricing (optional)
7. Sortation and/or accumulation
8. Packing and shipping

The functions may be defined briefly as follows:

1. *Receiving* is the collection of activities involved in (a) the orderly receipt of all materials coming into the warehouse, (b) providing the assurance that the quantity and quality of such materials are as ordered, and (c) disbursing materials to storage or to other organizational functions requiring them.

2. *Prepackaging* is performed in a warehouse when products are received in bulk from a supplier and subsequently packaged singly, in merchandisable quantities, or in combinations with other parts to form kits or assortments. An entire receipt of merchandise may be processed at once, or a portion may be held in bulk form

FIGURE 8-4 **Common warehouse activities.**

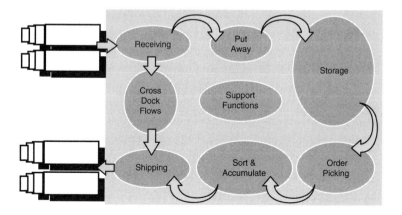

to be processed later. This may be done when packaging greatly increases the storage-cube requirements or when a part is common to several kits or assortments.

3. *Putaway* is the act of placing merchandise in storage. It includes the material handling, location verification, and product placement.

4. *Storage* is the physical containment of merchandise while it is awaiting a demand. The storage method depends on the size and quantity of the items in inventory and the handling characteristics of the product or its container.

5. *Order picking* is the process of removing items from storage to meet a specific demand. It is the basic service a warehouse provides for customers and is the function around which most warehouse designs are based.

6. *Packaging and/or pricing* may be done as an optional step after the picking process. As in the prepackaging function, individual items or assortments are boxed for more convenient use. Waiting until after picking to perform these functions has the advantage of providing more flexibility in the use of on-hand inventory. Individual items are available for use in any of the packaging configurations right up to the time of need. Pricing is current at the time of sale. Prepricing at manufacture or receipt into the warehouse inevitably leads to some repricing activity as price lists are changed while merchandise sits in inventory. Picking tickets and price stickers are sometimes combined into a single document.

7. *Sortation* of batch picks into individual orders and *accumulation* of distributed picks into orders must be done when an order has more than one item and the accumulation is not done as the picks are made.

8. *Packing and shipping* may include the following tasks:
   - Checking orders for completeness
   - Packaging merchandise in an appropriate shipping container
   - Preparing shipping documents, including the packing list, address label, and bill of lading
   - Weighing shipments to determine shipping charges
   - Accumulating orders by outbound carrier
   - Loading trucks (in many instances, this is a carrier's responsibility)

For discussion purposes, this chapter includes in *receiving* those activities described previously as receiving, prepackaging, and putaway; in *order picking*, those activities described previously as order picking, packaging, and sortation/accumulation; and in *shipping*, those activities described as packing and shipping.

8.2 WAREHOUSE ACTIVITY PROFILING

A warehouse activity profile is made up primarily of an order activity profile and an item activity profile. The order activity profile includes the

- Order mix distributions
- Lines per order distribution
- Cube per order distribution
- Lines and cube per order distribution

The best way to explain each of these distributions and their interpretations is to review a series of examples.

Order Mix Distributions

There are a variety of order mix distributions that are helpful for plotting warehouse operating strategy. Three of the most helpful are the family mix distribution, the handling unit distribution, and the order increment distribution.

Family Mix Distribution

In many cases, the overall operating strategy of the warehouse is dictated by the order mix—the extent to which orders require items from multiple families of items. If the orders are pure, that is, tend to have just one of the families of items on them, then it is an early indicator that zoning the warehouse on that basis will create a virtual warehouse within the warehouse and will lead to good productivity and customer service.

The family mix distribution in Figure 8-5 comes from a wholesale distributor of fine papers, copy/laser paper, and envelopes. Category A is a family of merchandise called flat stock. Printers make high quality brochures from these flat stocks of fine papers. A carton of flat stock is about 30 inches long, 24 inches wide, and 9 inches deep. A carton weighs about 80 pounds. Category B is cut stock, 8 1/2 × 11 copier and laser printer paper. A carton of cut stock is about 24 inches long, 10 inches wide, and 10 inches deep. A carton weighs about 20 pounds. Category C is envelopes and labels—extremely small and lightweight merchandise.

In this example, we are trying to figure out if it makes sense to zone the warehouse by those three item families—flat stock, cut stock, and envelopes. If the orders are mixed, that is, flat stock, cut stock, and envelopes tend to

FIGURE 8-5   Family mix distribution.

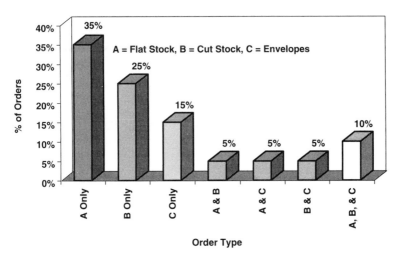

appear together on customer orders, then in pallet building, we would start with flat stock, put cut stock on top of that, and put envelopes on top of that. If that is the way we zone the warehouse, we may pay a big travel time penalty because we will have to travel across those zones or pass a pallet from one zone to the next.

If the orders are pure, that is, they tend to be completable out of just one item family, then zoning the warehouse along these lines will establish efficient warehouse processing cells, especially because products tend to be received by the warehouse as flat stock, cut stock, and envelope shipments. In Figure 8-5, 35 percent of the orders can be completed out of flat stock alone; 25 percent of the orders can be completed out of cut stock alone, and 15 percent out of envelopes alone. The good news is that 75 percent (35 percent + 25 percent + 15 percent) of the orders can be completed out of a single item family, suggesting that zoning the warehouse by item family will yield good productivity, customer service, and storage density performance.

Full/Partial Pallet Mix Distribution

With the full/partial pallet mix distribution, we try to determine if we need separate areas for pallet picking and case picking. In some warehouses, pallet and case picking are performed out of the same item location, aisle, and/or area of the warehouse. In general, it is a good idea to establish separate areas for pallet and case picking—replenishing a case picking line/area from a pallet reserve/picking area. This distribution simply helps reinforce the point and helps to identify warehouse within a warehouse opportunities.

FIGURE 8-6   **Full/partial pallet mix distribution.**

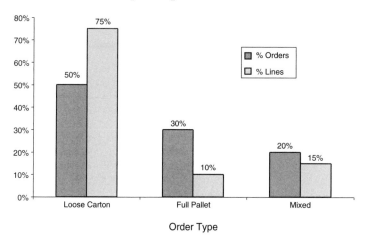

Order Type

In Figure 8-6, 50 percent of the orders are completable from partial pallet quantities, that is, just case picks; 30 percent of the orders are fillable from full pallet quantities, and the remaining 20 percent of the orders require both partial and full pallet quantities.

Should we have a separate case picking and pallet picking area? If we did, would we pay a big penalty for mixed orders that require merging of the partial and full pallet portions of the order? No, we really won't. That only happens 20 percent of the time. For 80 percent of the orders, zoning based on pallet/case picking creates a warehouse within the warehouse. When the orders come into the warehouse management system, it should classify them immediately as a pallet pick order, a carton pick order, or a mixed order. For mixed orders, the warehouse management system should create a pallet portion, a case pick portion, and either pass the full pallet portion to the case pick area or merge the case pick and pallet portions downstream from picking.

You now begin to see how we can quickly address the major planning and design decisions by having the right information available to us in the right format.

Full/Broken Case Mix Distribution

With this distribution (see Figure 8-7), we try to determine if we should create separate areas for full and broken case picking. In some warehouses, full and broken case picking are performed in the same item location, aisle, and/or area of the warehouse. In general, it is a good idea to establish separate areas for full and broken case picking—replenishing a broken case

FIGURE 8-7   Full/broken case mix distribution.

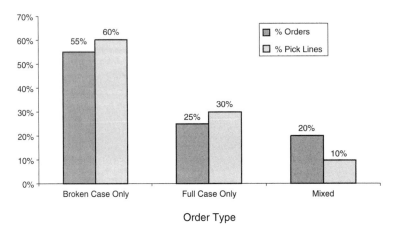

Order Type

picking line/area from a case reserve/picking area. This distribution simply helps reinforce the point and helps to identify warehouse within a warehouse opportunities. As was the case with the pallet/case mix distribution in Figure 8-6, the distribution in Figure 8-7 indicates that only a small portion of the orders require both a full and broken case quantity. Hence, to create separate areas for full and broken case picking will yield two order completion zones with very little mixing between them.

Order Increment Distributions

With the order increment distribution (see Figure 8-8), we determine the portion of a unit load (in this case a pallet) requested on a customer order. For example, suppose there are 100 cartons on a pallet and a customer orders 50 cartons. In that case, he ordered 50 percent of the pallet. If there are 80 cartons on a pallet and a customer orders 20, he ordered 20 percent of the pallet.

What do you notice that is unusual about this distribution? (In almost all of these distributions, the key insights are in the peaks and valleys.) Where are the peaks? The peaks are around 25 percent and 50 percent of a pallet.

Suppose there are 100 cartons on a pallet and a customer places an order for 100 cartons. Would you rather pick a full pallet or 100 individual cartons? You didn't have to buy this book to figure out that you would prefer to pick a whole pallet at a time. That is not only good practice for you, but it is good practice for your customer as well. The customer would rather receive a full pallet quantity that they can handle in one unit load as opposed to having to handle 100 loose cartons.

Now, what operating decision should we make to take advantage of the distribution in Figure 8-8? Right, we should build some quarter- and

FIGURE 8-8   Pallet order increment distribution.

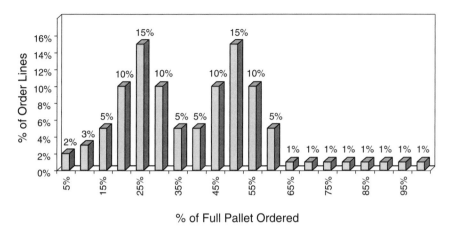

% of Full Pallet Ordered

half-pallet unit loads. Then, when a customer places an order for a quarter pallet, we have that unit load preconfigured. If a customer places an order for a half-pallet, we have that unit load preconfigured.

How can we build half- and quarter-pallet unit loads? In this particular case, the manufacturing facility is attached to the warehouse. There is a palletizer that sits on the border, and all we have to do is set the palletizer to put a pallet in place about four times as often to build quarter pallets and twice as often to build half pallets. If the warehouse is not attached to manufacturing, the next best scenario is to have the supplier build the quarter- and half-pallet loads; if not the supplier, then we can preconfigure the unit loads at receiving.

Can we encourage people to order in half, quarter, and/or layer quantity increments? Absolutely. In many cases, by simply making the pallet/layer quantities accurate and visible to the customer and the order entry personnel via the logistics information system, we can encourage the practice of ordering in preconfigured unit loads. We can further encourage the practice by offering price discounts designed around efficient handling increments. In this case, there was a representative from the sales organization on the cross-functional team who literally reset the price breaks on the quarter- and half-pallet quantities the next day.

With the case order increment distribution (see Figure 8-9), we determine the portion of a full carton that is requested on customer orders. For example, if there are 100 pieces in a carton and a customer orders 50, the customer ordered half the carton. What do you notice that is unusual about this distribution? In this case (see Figure 8-9), customers tend to order around

FIGURE 8-9   Case order increment distribution.

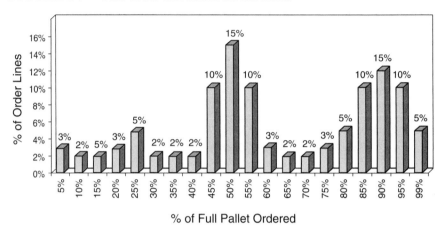

% of Full Pallet Ordered

half a carton and a quantity close to a full carton. As a result, we would like to set price breaks at a half carton (and create an inner pack for a half-carton) and at a full carton to encourage customers who are almost ordering that quantity now to order in full carton increments.

The general principle is to prepackage in increments that people are likely to order in and to encourage customers to order in intelligent handling increments. A higher level principle is that the supplier should do as much as possible to help prepare the product for picking and shipping. After we negotiate to have the supplier do as much for us as possible, then we should do as much as possible at the receiving dock to get product ready for shipping and packing, because it is at that moment that we have the largest time window available for picking/shipping preparation. As soon as the order drops for that product, the handling and preparation of the product should be at a minimum to meet the ever shrinking time window for product delivery.

Lines per Order Distribution

The lines per order distribution in Figure 8-10 indicates that 50 percent of the orders in the warehouse are for one line item, 15 percent for two, 15 percent for three to five, 10 percent for six to nine, and 10 percent for ten or more. Where is the peak? It is around single line orders. This is not uncommon, especially in the mail order industry or in cases where individual consumers or technicians are placing orders on the warehouse. We now need to consider the operating strategies that take advantage of this order profile.

First, *singles* may be backorders. Backorders are an excellent opportunity for cross-docking. Second, singles may be small, emergency orders.

FIGURE 8-10   Example lines per order distribution.

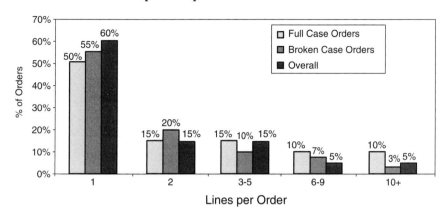

Those orders can be batched together for picking on single-line picking tours, and by printing single line orders in location sequence, we create very efficient picking tours. In addition, the order batches naturally zone the warehouse into zones defined by the length of the picking tour. Third, single line orders may also represent an opportunity to create a dynamic forward pick line. In this operating scenario, an automated look ahead into the day's or shift's orders may yield a number of *stock-keeping units* (SKUs) for which there is at least a full-carton's worth of single line orders. Those SKUs can be batch picked and set up along fast pick-pack lines.

Another common lines per order distribution is the mirror image of Figure 8-10. The peak is around ten plus lines per order. This is common in retail/grocery/dealer distribution where the customer is a retail store/grocery store/dealership. In that case, there is typically enough work to do within an order so that the order itself represents an efficient workset. Or, the order may be so large that it may be split across multiple order fillers for zone-wave picking.

Item Activity Profile

The item activity profile is used primarily to slot the warehouse, to decide for each item (1) what storage mode the item should be assigned to, (2) how much space the item should be allocated in the storage mode, and (3) where in the storage mode the item should be located. The item activity profile includes the following activity distributions:

* Item-popularity distribution
* Cube-movement/volume distribution
* Popularity-volume distribution
* Order completion distribution

Again, the best way to describe each distribution and its interpretation is by example.

Item-Popularity Distribution—Close to the Door, Close to the Floor

Just like a minority of the people in the world have a majority of the wealth, a minority of the items in a warehouse generate a majority of the picking activity. The popularity distribution (sometimes called an ABC curve or a Pareto Distribution) indicates the x percent of picks associated with y percent of the SKUs (ranked by descending popularity). Figure 8-11 is a classic popularity distribution indicating that the 10 percent most popular items represent 70 percent of the picking activity, the 50 percent most popular items represent 90 percent of the picking activity, and so on.

Dramatic breakpoints in the distribution may suggest item popularity families. For example, the top 5 percent of the items (Family A) may make up 50 percent of the picking activity, the next 15 percent of the items (Family B) may take us to 80 percent of the picking activity, and the remaining 80 percent of the items (Family C) cover the remaining picking activity. These families may in turn suggest three alternative storage modes: Family A in an automated highly productive storage mode, Family B in a semi-automated moderately productive picking mode, and Family C in a manual picking mode that offers high storage density. The family breakpoints may also suggest the location of the items within a storage mode—A items located in the *golden zone* (close to a travel aisle and/or at or near waist level), B items in the *silver zone*, and C items in the remaining spaces.

FIGURE 8-11   Item-popularity distribution.

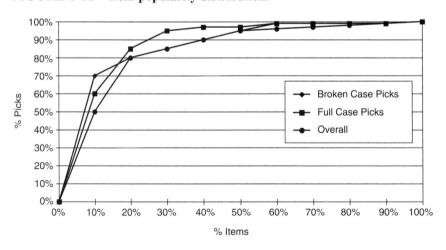

The overriding principle is to assign the most popular items to the most accessible warehouse locations. Unfortunately, many warehouse operators use the wrong measure of popularity. Some use dollar sales, some use usage, and some use the number of requests for the item. In the end, all of these are wrong. The number of requests for an item is the true measure of popularity; however, it is not enough information to assign items to storage modes or even to locate items within storage modes. The proper assignment of items to storage modes and allocation of space within the assigned storage mode is based on the popularity distribution and the cube-movement distribution. A joint popularity-cube-movement distribution follows in Figure 8-12. From the joint popularity-cube- movement distribution, we can make appropriate slotting assignments.

Popularity-Cube-Movement Distribution

Done properly, slotting takes into account both the item-popularity distribution and the cube-movement distribution. These distributions can be combined into a joint distribution. An example popularity-cube-movement distribution for broken case picking is presented in Figure 8-12.

In the example, those items exceeding a certain cube-movement threshold are assigned to carton flow rack. Items with high cube movement, turnover frequently, need to be restocked frequently, and need a larger storage location as compared to items with medium and low cube movement. Hence, they need to be assigned to a storage mode that facilitates restocking and con-

FIGURE 8-12   **Popularity-cube-movement distribution for broken case picking.**

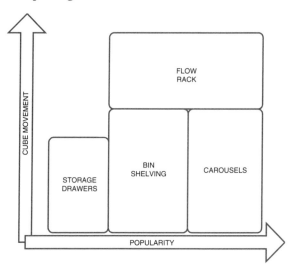

denses large storage locations along the pick line-carton flow rack. Items with low cube movement and high popularity are generating many picks per unit of space that they occupy and do not occupy much space along the pick line. They need to be in a highly productive picking mode. In this case, light directed carousels are recommended because the picking productivity is high and we can afford the carousels for items that do not need large storage housings on the pick line and do not need to be restocked frequently. (Carousels do not lend themselves to restocking and are expensive per cubic foot of space.) Items with low popularity and low cube movement cannot be justifiably housed in an expensive storage mode. Hence, they are candidates for bin shelving and modular storage drawers. Once the storage mode assignments have been made, the preference regions for each storage mode become their popularity-cube movement distributions. Those items in the bottom right-hand portion of the distribution generate the most picking activity per unit of space they occupy in the storage mode. Hence, they should be assigned to positions in the golden zone. Those items in the upper right hand and lower left hand generate a moderate number of picks per unit of space they occupy in the storage mode. Hence, they should be assigned to positions in the silver zone. Finally, those items in the upper left hand quadrant of the distribution generate the fewest picks per unit of space they occupy and they should be assigned positions in the bronze (least accessible) zone.

This example is not meant to make an end-all recommendation for slotting broken case picking systems. That depends on many other factors, including the wage rate, the cost of space, the cost of capital, the planning horizon, and so on. Instead, this example is presented to illustrate how the popularity-cube-movement distribution is used in the slotting process. Once in place, the distribution provides most of the insights required for slotting the entire warehouse.

Item-Order Completion Distribution
The item-order completion distribution (see Figure 8-13) identifies small groups of items that can fill large groups of orders. Those small groups of items can often be assigned to small *order completion zones* in which the productivity, processing rate, and processing quality are two to five times better than that found in the general warehouse.

The item-order completion distribution is constructed by ranking the items from most to least popular. Beginning with the most popular item, then the two most popular items, then the three most popular items, and so on, the items are put against the order set to determine what portion of the orders a given subset of the items can complete. In this example, 10 percent of the items can complete 50 percent of the orders. Suppose I walk into your

FIGURE 8-13   **Item-order completion distribution.**

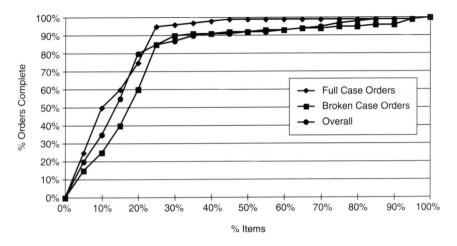

warehouse and identify 10 percent of the items that can completely fill 50 percent of the orders. What would you do with those 10 percent? I hope you would create a warehouse within the warehouse or order completion zone for those 10 percent.

The design principle is similar to that used in agile manufacturing, where we look for small groups of parts that have similar machine routings. Those machines and those parts make up a small group technology cell wherein the manufacturing efficiency, quality, and cycle time are dramatically improved over those found in the factory as a whole.

I recently worked with a large media (compact discs, cassettes, videos, and so on) distributor and helped to identify 5 percent of its 4,000 SKUs that could complete 35 percent of the orders. We assigned those 5 percent to carton flow rack pods (three flow rack bays per pod, one operator per pod) at the front of the distribution center. Operators could pick-pack orders from the flow rack at nearly six times the overall rate of the distribution center. The distribution center has won its industry's productivity award for the last two years.

8.3   WAREHOUSE PERFORMANCE MEASURES

We encourage our clients to consider and measure the performance of warehouse operations as if each warehouse was a standalone business. Essentially, each warehouse is competing with the warehouse operations among its business competitors, any third-party warehouse operator who would like to do the job, and with internal business operations for funding. Because businesses compete on the basis of financial, productivity, quality, and cycle time performance, we recommend that warehouse performance be captured in those four categories of indicators.

Warehouse Financial Performance

In financial performance, we recommend that each warehouse establish a warehouse activity based costing program. An example appears in Figure 8-14. In the example, a cost for each warehousing activity (receipt, putaway, store, pick, ship, and load) is established. The activity costs become the basis for comparing third-party warehousing proposals, budgeting, measuring improvement, and menu-based pricing for warehousing services.

In this particular analysis, the cost of storing and handling an item in the warehouse for a year was estimated to be $340.37. This warehouse managed over 70,000 items, 40,000 of which did not yield $340.37 in sales per year, not even enough to cover their storage and handling costs. Needless to say, the finding was taken up with the marketing area and a SKU reduction ensued.

Warehouse Productivity Performance

For productivity performance, we recommend that our clients monitor the productivity and utilization of the key assets in the warehouse – labor, space, material handling systems, and warehouse management systems.

FIGURE 8-14   Warehouse activity based costing example.

	Labor Cost	Space Cost	MHS Cost	WMS Cost	Total Cost	Cost per Transaction	
Receiving	$ 1,963,055	$ 238,125	$ 569,820	$ 218,333	$ 2,989,333	$ 1.38	$ per receipt
Putaway	$ 1,090,534	$ -	$ 416,000	$ 240,333	$ 1,746,867	$ 3.56	$ per line
Storage	$ 999,640	$ 1,933,250	$ 1,650,710	$ 123,833	$ 4,707,433	$ 86.93	$ per SKU
Picking	$ 1,946,966	$ -	$ 1,830,782	$ 161,833	$ 3,939,581	$ 1.10	$ per line
Consolidation	$ 287,188	$ 100,500	$ 135,000	$ 38,333	$ 561,021	$ 61.45	$ per load
Delivery	$ 68,225	$ 50,000	$ 69,000	$ 38,333	$ 225,558	$ 24.71	$ per load
Marketing	$ 3,534,218	$ 105,000	$ 222,200	$ 113,833	$ 3,975,251	$ 0.22	$ per piece
Returns	$ 68,225	$ 99,250	$ 6,000	$ 113,000	$ 286,475		
Total	**$ 9,958,052**	**$ 2,526,125**	**$ 4,899,512**	**$ 1,047,831**	**$18,431,520**	**$ 368.63**	**$ per line**
% of Total	54.03%	13.71%	26.58%	5.68%	100.00%		
Cost/Sales	4.05%	1.03%	1.99%	0.43%	7.49%		
Cost/Order	$ 199.16	$ 50.52	$ 97.99	$ 20.96	$ 368.63		
Cost/Case	$ 4.58	$ 1.16	$ 2.25	$ 0.48	$ 8.47		
Cost/Line	$ 2.79	$ 0.71	$ 1.37	$ 0.29	$ 5.16		
Cost/Piece	$ 0.11	$ 0.03	$ 0.06	$ 0.01	$ 0.21		
Cost/CF	$ 2.77	$ 0.70	$ 1.36	$ 0.29	$ 5.12		
Cost/Pound	$ 0.35	$ 0.09	$ 0.17	$ 0.04	$ 0.64		
Cost/SKU	$ 183.89	$ 46.65	$ 90.48	$ 19.35	$ 340.37		

We typically measure overall labor productivity as the ratio of units, orders, lines, or weight shipped out of the warehouse to the number of hours spent in operating, supervising, and managing the warehouse. Labor utilization is normally measured as the percent of operating capacity for the workforce.

Storage density, the ratio of the amount of inventory storage capacity to the square footage in the warehouse, is our recommended productivity indicator for floorspace. It is normally expressed as the value, cube, pieces, or positions of inventory that can be accommodated per square foot. In addition, we suggest that each warehouse continuously monitor the percent of available storage locations that are occupied (location utilization) and the percent of available storage cube that is occupied (cube utilization).

Warehouse Quality Performance

There are four key quality indicators for warehouse performance we recommend for implementation:

- **Putaway accuracy**   The percent of items put away correctly
- **Inventory accuracy**   The percent of warehouse locations without inventory discrepancies
- **Picking accuracy**   The percent of order lines picked without errors
- **Shipping accuracy**   The percent of order lines shipped without errors

Warehouse Cycle Time Performance

For cycle time, we recommend the warehouse track performance in two key areas:

- *Dock-to-Stock Time* **(DTS)**   The elapsed time from when a receipt arrives on the warehouse premises until it is ready for picking or shipping
- *Warehouse Order Cycle Time* **(WOCT)**   The elapsed time from when an order is released to the warehouse floor until it is picked, packed, and ready for shipping

We often assess our client's performance in the form of a warehouse performance gap analysis (see Figure 8-15) indicating to the client their standing versus world-class norms in the key performance indicators and the cost savings that are available if the gaps can be closed (see Figure 8-16).

8.4   RECEIVING PRINCIPLES

Receiving is the setup for all other warehousing activities. If we don't receive merchandise properly, it will be very difficult to handle it properly in putaway, storage, picking, or shipping. If we allow damaged or inaccurate deliveries in the door, we are likely to ship damaged or inaccurate shipments out the door.

FIGURE 8-15   Warehouse performance gap analysis.

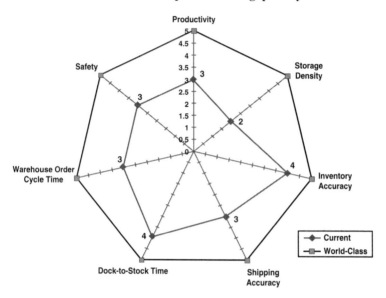

FIGURE 8-16   Warehouse opportunity assessment.

	Productivity	Storage Density	Inventory Accuracy	Shipping Accuracy	Dock-to-Stock Time	Warehouse Order Cycle Time	Safety
Annual Volume	360,000 lines/year	29,000 SKUs	26,000 locations	360,000 lines/year	$120,000,000 on-hand inventory	$120,000,001 on-hand inventory	
Current Performance	4 lines/PH	1.89 SF/SKU	85% % locations	99.7% % lines	48 hours	24 hours	5 accidents/year
Current Resource Requirement	90,000 person-hours	54,810 SF	3,900 locations	1,080 locations			
World-Class Performance	6 lines/PH	1 SF/SKU	95% % locations	99.97% % lines	24 hours	12 hours	1 accidents/year
World-Class Resource Requirement	60,000 person-hours	29,000 SF	1,300 locations	108 lines/year			
Resource Savings	30,000 person-hours	25,810 SF	2,600 locations	972 lines/year	24 hours	12 hours	4
Rate	$25 $/PH	$11 $/SF *Yr.	$100 $/location	$300 $/line	0.1% %/day	0.1% %/day	$10,000 $/accident
Annual Savings	$750,000	$283,910	$260,000	$291,600	$120,000	$60,000	$40,000

Total Savings ($s/year) $1,805,510
Payback Period (Years)   1.5
Justifiable Investment $2,708,256

LOGISTICS RESOURCES
INTERNATIONAL, INC.

The world-class receiving principles presented here are meant to serve as guidelines for streamlining receiving operations. They are intended to simplify the flow of material through the receiving process and to insure the minimum work content is required. Minimizing work content, mistakes, time, and accidents is accomplished in logistics by reducing handling steps. Figure 8-17 illustrates the reduction in handling steps that can be achieved by applying advanced receiving practices.

The world-class receiving practices are as follows:

- Direct shipping
- Cross-docking
- Receiving scheduling
- Prereceiving
- Receipt preparation

Direct Shipping

For some materials, the best receiving is no receiving. In direct (or drop) shipping, vendors bypass our warehouse completely and ship directly to the customer. Hence, all the labor, time, and equipment normally consumed and all the mistakes and accidents that often occur in the warehouse are eliminated.

Large, bulky items lend themselves to drop shipping. For example, a large camp and sportswear mail order distributor drop ships all the canoes and large tents that are advertised in their catalog instead of shipping from their central DC. The food industry is also adopting more direct shipping. More and more food and consumer products manufacturers are making and assembling store orders at their factories for direct delivery to their retail customers' store locations.

FIGURE 8-17   **Touch analysis for alternative receiving practices.**

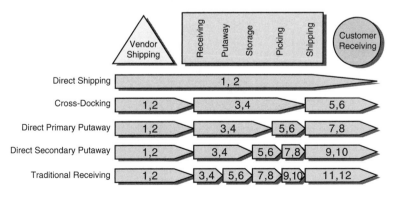

By bypassing the warehouse completely, all the warehouse handling steps are eliminated, as well as the opportunities to mishandle product accordingly.

Cross-Docking
When material cannot be shipped directly, the next best option may be cross-docking. In cross-docking,

- Loads are scheduled for delivery into the warehouse from vendors
- Inbound materials are sorted immediately into their outbound orders
- Outbound orders are transported immediately to their outbound dock
- There is no receiving staging or inspection
- There is no product storage

In so doing, the traditional warehousing activities involving receiving inspection, receiving staging, putaway, storage, pick location replenishment, order picking, and order assembly are eliminated.

An example of cross-docking is illustrated in Figure 8-18. The example is from a large consumer products manufacturer.

Certain load and communication requirements must be met before high-volume cross-docking can be implemented. First, each container and product must be automatically identifiable through a bar code label or RF tag. Second, loads must be scheduled into the DC and assigned to dock doors

Figure 8-18   Cross-docking example.
Source: James M. Apple, Jr.

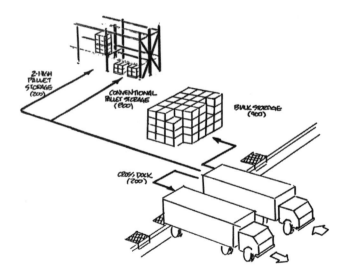

automatically. Third, inbound pallets or cases that will be cross-docked should contain only a single SKU or be preconfigured for their destination to minimize sortation requirements.

In addition to normal order flows, backorders, special orders, and transfer orders are good candidates for cross-docking because the sense of urgency to process those orders is high. The inbound merchandise is prepackaged and labeled for delivery to the ultimate customer, and the merchandise on those orders does not have to be merged with other merchandise to complete a customers requirements.

Receiving Scheduling

It is true that premeditated cross-docking requires the ability to schedule inbound loads to match outbound requirements on a daily or even hourly basis. In addition, balancing the use of receiving resources—dock doors, personnel, staging space, and material handling equipment—requires the ability to schedule carriers and to shift time-consuming receipts to offpeak hours. Through Internet, EDI, and/or fax links, companies have improved access to schedule information on inbound and outbound loads. This information can and should be used to proactively schedule receipts and to provide *advance shipping notice* (ASN) information.

Prereceiving

The rationale for staging at the receiving dock, the most time and space intensive activity in the receiving function, is often the need to hold material for location assignment, product identification, and so on. This information can often be captured ahead of time by having the information communicated by the vendor at the time of shipment via the Internet, EDI link, or via fax notification. In some cases, the information describing an inbound load can be captured on a smart card, enabling immediate input of the information at the receiving dock. Load contents can also be communicated in RF tags readable by antennae located along major highways, at each receiving dock, on lift trucks, and/or conveyors.

Figure 8-19 depicts an optical memory card used to download the contents of an entire trailer load into a PC at a receiving dock.

Receipt Preparation

The most time we ever have available to prepare a product for shipment is at the moment it is received. Once the demand for a product has been received, there is precious little time available for additional preparation of the product prior to shipment. Hence, any material processing that can be accomplished ahead of time should be accomplished. Those preparatory activities include

FIGURE 8-19   **Optical memory card.**
Source: U.S. Army Logistics Command

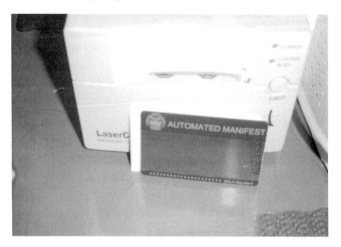

- *Prepackaging in issue increments.* At a large office supplies distributor, quarter, and half-pallet loads are built at receiving in anticipation of orders being received in those quantities. Customers are encouraged to order in those quantities by quantity discounts. A large distributor of automotive aftermarket parts conducted an extensive analysis of likely order quantities. Based on that analysis, the company is now prepackaging in those popular issue increments.
- *Applying necessary labels and tags.*
- *Cubing and weighing for storage and transport planning.* Product cube and weight information is used to make a myriad of key warehouse design and operating decisions, yet few organizations have reliable cube information on their products. If suppliers cannot produce cube and weight, the information can and should be captured at the receiving dock. A device called a Cubiscan is often used at receiving to capture and automatically communicate inbound carton dimensions and weights (see Figure 8-20).

8.5 PUTAWAY

Putaway is order picking in reverse. Many of the principles that streamline the picking process work well for putaway. In order, the world-class principles for putaway are

- Direct putaway
- Directed putaway

FIGURE 8-20   Automatic cubing and weighing.

- Batched and sequenced putaway
- Interleaving

Direct Putaway
   Putaway directly to primary or reserve locations.

One of our large healthcare clients does not allow staging space in their warehouse layouts. They force warehouse operators to put goods away immediately upon receipt as opposed to the delays and multiple handlings that are characteristic of traditional receiving and putaway activities.

When material cannot be cross-docked, material handling steps can be minimized by bypassing receiving staging and putting material away directly to primary picking locations, essentially replenshing primary locations from the receiving dock. When there are no severe constraints on product rotation, this may be feasible. Otherwise, material should be directly putaway to reserve locations.

In direct putaway systems, staging and inspection activities are eliminated. Hence, the time, space, and labor associated with those operations is eliminated.

Vehicles that serve the dual purpose of truck unloading and product putaway facilitate direct putaway. For example, counterbalanced lift trucks can be equipped with scales, cubing devices, and online RF terminals to streamline the unloading and putaway function.

FIGURE 8-21   Automated, direct putaway.

The world's most advanced logistics operations are characterized by automated, direct putaway to storage locations. The material handling technologies that facilitate direct putaway include roller-bed trailers and extendable conveyors (see Figure 8-21). (The prequalification of vendors to support direct putaway and prereceiving was described in Chapter 6, "Supply Management.")

Directed Putaway

Left to their own devices, most putaway operators naturally choose putaway locations that are easiest to locate—nearest the floor, nearest their friend, nearest the break room—using any criteria except where the putaway should be located to maximize storage density and operating productivity. The *warehouse management system* (WMS) should direct the putaway operators to place each pallet or case in the location that maximizes location and cube utilization, insures good product rotation, and maximizes retrieval productivity (see Figure 8-22).

Batched and Sequenced Putaway

Sort inbound materials for efficient putaway.

Just as zone picking and location sequencing are effective strategies for improving order picking productivity, inbound materials can and should be sorted for putaway by warehouse zone and by location sequence.

FIGURE 8-22   RF directed putaway operation.

Figure 8-23 illustrates an example of putaway batching at a large Dutch shoe distributor. All shoes that will be put away in the same aisle are sorted down a particular conveyor lane and stacked in putaway location sequence automatically.

Interleaving and Continuous Moves
Combine putaways and retrievals when possible.

To further streamline the putaway and retrieval process, putaway and retrieval transactions can be combined in a dual command to reduce the amount of empty travel (deadheading) by lift trucks (see Figure 8-24). This technique is especially geared for pallet storage and retrieval operations. Counterbalance lift trucks that can unload, putaway, retrieve, and load are an efficient means for executing dual commands. (Interleaving is similar to backhauling in transportation.) The practice of interleaving should be extended to continuous moves within the warehouse, where warehouse operators are directed from most-efficient-task to most-efficient-task by the WMS.

FIGURE 8-23   Batched and sequenced putaways.

FIGURE 8-24   Interleaving concept.

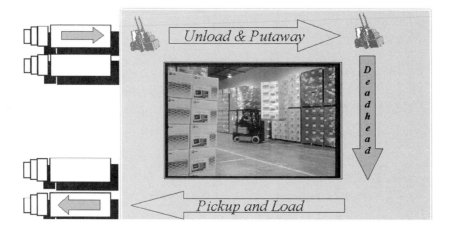

8.6   STORAGE OPERATIONS

Because there are still good reasons to hold inventory, we still need efficient means for storing inventory. The four basic techniques for optimizing storage operations by maximizing storage density and retrieval productivity are

- Storage mode optimization
- Storage space optimization

- Storage location optimization
- Storage layout optimization

Storage Mode Optimization
Assign each item to its least cost storage mode.

Based on each item's demand and dimensional characteristics, each storage mode's capabilities and costs, and general planning parameters, each item should be housed in the storage mode that minimizes the cost of storage and handling for the item. For pallet storage, a decision must be made for each item as to whether to assign it to positions in floor storage, single-deep rack, double-deep rack, drive in/thru rack, push-back rack, or mobile rack (see Figure 8-25). For small item storage, a decision must be made for each item as to whether to assign it to positions in bin shelving, storage drawers, flow rack, horizontal carousels, vertical carousels, miniload automated storage/retrieval systems, or automated dispensing machines (see Figure 8-26).

An example storage mode optimization is in Figure 8-27. In the example, the least cost storage mode for the item including the cost of picking, restocking labor, equipment, space, and errors is a vertical carousel.

In Figure 8-28, an example of pallet storage mode optimzation is illustrated. In the example, the drive-thru rack using a single-deep counterbalance truck is the least cost alternative.

Storage Space Optimization
Assign each item its optimal allocation of space.

One of the key decisions in storage system design is whether or not to establish a forward picking area separate from the reserve picking area. Because a minority of the items in a warehouse generate a majority of pick requests, a condensed picking area containing some of the inventory of popular items should normally be established. (Otherwise, the pick-from-storage scheme described in Section 8.7, "Order Picking Operations," may be justified.)

The smaller the allocation of inventory to the forward area (in terms of the number of SKUs and their inventory allocation), the smaller the forward picking area, the smaller the travel times, and the greater the picking productivity. However, the smaller the allocation, the more frequent the internal replenishment trips between forward and reserve areas, and the greater the staffing requirement for internal replenishments. Figure 8-29 illustrates the cost tradeoffs in forward-reserve planning.

FIGURE 8-25   Pallet storage systems.

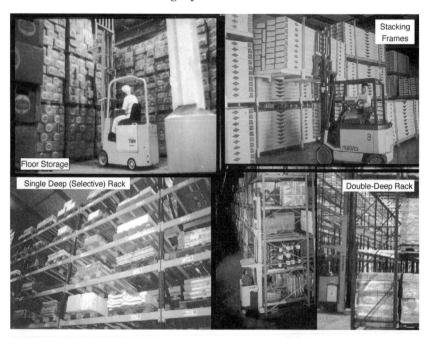

FIGURE 8-26 Small item storage systems.

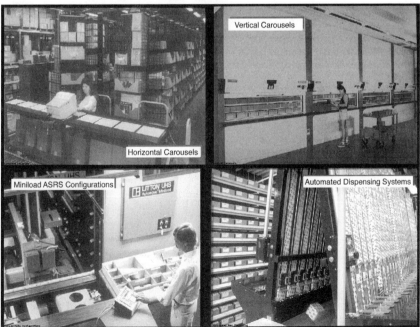

FIGURE 8-27   **Storage mode optimization for small items.**
Source: LRI's item slotting optimization tool

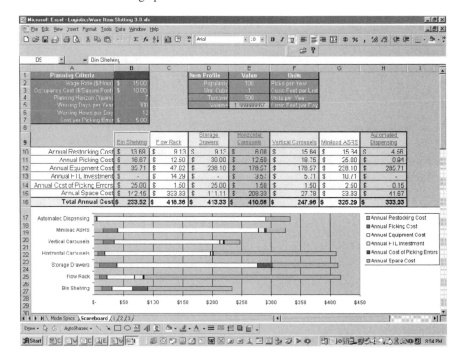

Storage Location Optimization

> *Assign the most popular items to the most easily accessed locations in the warehouse.*

A minority of the items (the A's or fast movers) in a warehouse generate a majority of the picking activity. We prefer that most of the picking activity take place in the picking locations that are easiest to pick from and yield the highest picking productivity (the golden zones). Hence, to maximize picking productivity and to minimize picking costs, the A items should be assigned to locations in the golden zone.

The location of the golden zone for a particular warehouse depends on many factors, including the location of shipping docks, order profiles, and the design of picking tours. For a pallet storage/retrieval system, the golden zone is often comprised of the 20 percent of the storage locations nearest the floor and near the shipping dock. For an item picking system with long picking tours, the golden zone is often comprised of the 20 percent of the storage locations nearest the waist level of the operator (see Figure 8-30).

FIGURE 8-28   Pallet storage optimization.

Source: LRI's pallet storage optimization tool

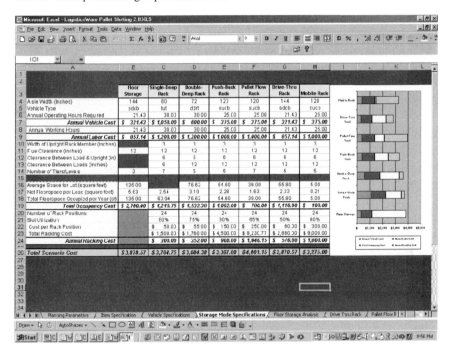

FIGURE 8-29   Forward-reserve space planning tradeoffs.

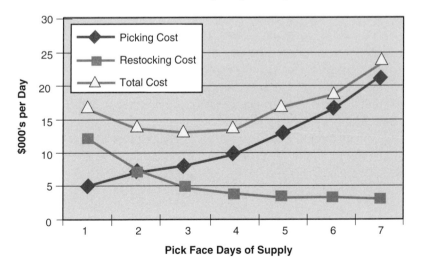

FIGURE 8-30   Golden zone picking from a horizontal carousel.
Source: White Systems

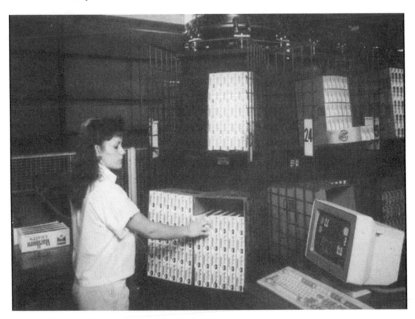

Just like a minority of items in a warehouse generate a majority of the picking frequency, there are items in the warehouse that are likely to be requested together. Examples include items in repair kits, items from the same supplier, items in the same subassembly, items of the same size, and so on. Correlations can be identified from order profiles and can be capitalized on by storing correlated items in the same or in nearby locations. Travel time is in turn reduced because the distance between pick locations on an order is reduced.

At a major mail-order apparel distributor, nearly 70 percent of all orders can be completed from a single size (such as, small, medium, large, and extra large) regardless of the type of item ordered (such as, shirts, pants, and belts, and so on). At a major distributor of healthcare products, a majority of the orders can be filled from a single vendor. Because material is also received that way, correlated storage by vendor improves productivity in picking and putaway.

A simple way to begin the process of identifying demand families is to rank pairs of items based on the number of times the pair appears together on an order. The pairs at the top of the list often reveal the rationale for demand family development.

8.7   ORDER PICKING OPERATIONS

A recent survey of warehousing professionals identified order picking as the highest priority activity in the warehouse for productivity improvements.[2] There are several reasons for their concern. First, order picking is the most costly activity in a typical warehouse (see Figure 8-31). A recent study in the United Kingdom[3] revealed that 63 percent of all operating costs in a typical warehouse can be attributed to order picking.

Second, the order picking activity has become increasingly difficult to manage. The difficulty arises from the introduction of new operating programs such as *just-in-time* (JIT), cycle time reduction, quick response, and new marketing strategies such as micromarketing and megabrand strategies. These programs require that (1) smaller orders be delivered to warehouse customers more frequently and more accurately, and that (2) more SKUs must be incorporated in the order picking system. As a result, both throughput, storage, and accuracy requirements have increased dramatically. Third, renewed emphasis on quality improvements and customer service have forced warehouse managers to reexamine the order picking activity from the standpoint of minimizing product damage, reducing transaction times, and further improving picking accuracy. Finally, the conventional responses to these increased requirements, to hire more people or to invest in more automated equipment, have been stymied by labor shortages and high hurdle rates due to uncertain business environments. Fortunately, there are a variety of

FIGURE 8-31   **Operating cost distribution in a typical warehouse.**

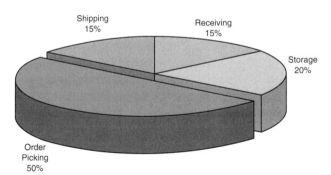

[2] Annual member survey of the Warehousing Education and Research Council.
[3] Frazelle, E.H., "Small Parts Order Picking: Equipment and Strategy," Material Handling Research Center Technical Report Number 01-88-01, Georgia Institute of Technology, Atlanta, Georgia, 30332-0205.

ways to improve order picking productivity without increasing staffing or making significant investments in highly automated equipment. A variety of ways to improve order picking productivity in light of the increased demands now placed on order picking systems are described in the following:

- Issue pack optimization
- Pick-from-storage
- Pick task simplification
- Order batching
- Pick sequencing

Issue Pack Optimization

Encourage and design for full-pallet as opposed to loose case picking and full-case as opposed to broken case picking.

By encouraging customers to order in full-pallet quantities, or by creating quarter- and/or half-pallet loads, much of the counting and manual physical handling of cases can be avoided both in your warehouse and also in your customers' warehouses. In similar fashion, by encouraging customers to order in full-case quantities, much of counting and extra packaging associated with loose case picking can be avoided. A pick line profile illustrating the distribution of the portion of a full-pallet or full-case requested by customers frequently reveals an opportunity to reduce the amount of partial pallet and/or partial case picking in the warehouse. An example profile was illustrated in Figure 8-7.

Pick-from-Storage

Because a majority of a typical order picker's time is spent travelling and/or searching for pick locations, one of the most effective means for improving picking productivity and accuracy is to bring storage locations to the picker, preferrably reserve storage locations. A large cosmetics distributor recently installed systems that bring reserve storage locations to stationary order picking stations for batch picking of partial case quantities and direct induction into a cross-belt sortation system (see Figure 8-32). In so doing, order picking travel time has been virtually eliminated. In addition, the same system can transfer storage locations to/from receiving, prepackaging, and inspection operations, virtually eliminating travel throughout the warehouse. Though expensive, the systems may be justified by increased productivity and accuracy.

Pick Task Simplification

Eliminate and combine order picking tasks when possible.

FIGURE 8-32   Pick-from-storage concept.

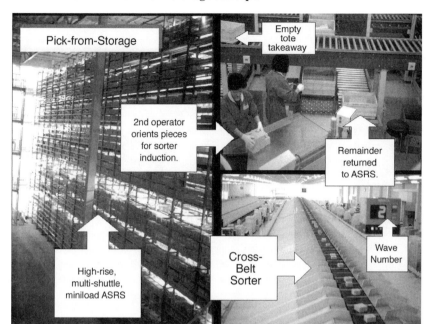

The human work elements involved in order picking may include

- *Traveling* to, from, and between pick locations
- *Extracting* items from storage locations
- *Reaching* and *bending* to access pick locations
- *Documenting* picking transactions
- *Sorting* items into orders
- *Packing* items
- *Searching* for pick locations

A typical distribution of the order picker's time among these activities is provided in Figure 8-33. Means for eliminating the work elements are outlined in Table 8-1.

When work elements cannot be eliminated, they can often be combined to improve order picking productivity. Some effective combinations of work elements are outlined in the following sections.

Travelling and Extracting Items   *Stock-to-picker* (STP) systems such as carousels and the miniload automated storage/retrieval system are designed to keep order pickers extracting while a mechanical device travels to, from,

FIGURE 8-33   **Typical distribution of an order picker's working time.**

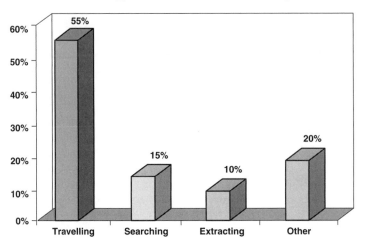

TABLE 8-1   **Order Picking Work Elements and Means for Elimination**

Work Element	Method of Elimination	Equipment Required
Travelling	Bring pick locations to picker	Stock-to-picker system -Miniload AS/RS -Horizontal carousel -Vertical carousel
Documenting	Automate information flow	Computer-aided order picking Automatic identification systems Light-aided order picking Radio frequency terminals Headsets
Reaching	Present items at waist level	Vertical carousels Person-aboard AS/RS Miniload AS/RS
Searching	Bring pick locations to picker Take picker to pick location Illuminate pick locations	Stock-to-picker systems Person-aboard AS/RS Pick-to-light systems
Extracting	Automated dispensing	Automatic item pickers Robotic order pickers
Counting	Weigh count Prepackage in issue increments	Scales on picking vehicles

and between storage locations bringing pick locations to the order picker. As a result, a man-machine balancing problem is introduced. If the initial design of STP systems is not accurate, a significant portion of the order picker's time may be spent waiting on the storage/retrieval machine to bring pick locations forward.

Travelling and Documenting   Because a person-aboard storage/retrieval machine is programmed to automatically transport the order picker between successive picking locations, the order picker is free to document picking transactions, sort material, or pack material while the storage/retrieval machine is moving.

Picking and Sorting   If an order picker completes more than one order during a picking tour, picking carts equipped with dividers or totes may be designed to allow the picker to sort material into several orders at a time.

Picking, Sorting, and Packing   When the cube occupied by a completed order is small, say less than a shoe box, the order picker can sort directly into a packing or shipping container. Packing or shipping containers must be setup ahead of time and placed on picking carts equipped with dividers and/or totes.

Order Batching

Batch orders to reduce total travel time.

By increasing the number of orders (and therefore items) picked by an order picker during a picking tour, the travel time per pick can be reduced. For example, if an order picker picks one order with two items while travelling 100 feet, the distance travelled per pick is 50 feet. If the picker picked two orders with four items, the distance travelled per pick is reduced to 25 feet.

Single line orders are a natural group of orders to pick together. Single line orders can be batched by small zones in the warehouse to further reduce travel time. A profile of the number of lines requested per order helps identify the opportunity for batching single line orders. An example profile is illustrated in Figure 8-34.

Other order batching strategies are depicted in the order batching decision tree in Figure 8-35 and described in the following text. Note that when an order is assigned to more than one picker, the effort to reestablish order integrity is significantly increased. The additional cost of sortation must be evaluated with respect to the travel time savings generated with batch picking.

Single Order Picking   In single order picking, each order picker completes one order at a time. For picker-to-stock systems, single order picking is like

FIGURE 8-34   Lines and cube per order profile used in batch-wave planning.

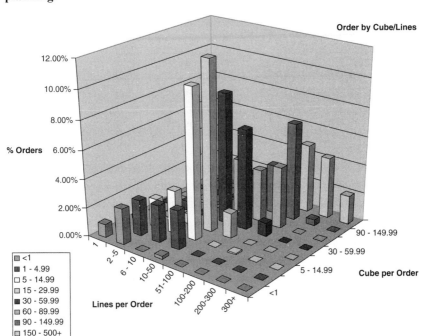

going through the grocery store and accumulating the items on your grocery list into your cart. Each shopper is concerned with only his or her list.

The major advantage to the single order picking strategy is that order integrity is never jeopardized. The major disadvantage is that the order picker is likely to have to travel over a large portion of the warehouse to pick the order. Consequently, the walking time per line item picked is high. However, for large orders (that is, those greater than 10 line items), a single order may yield an efficient picking tour. In addition, in some systems, response time requirements do not enable orders to build up in queue to create efficient batches for order picking.

Batch Picking   A second operating strategy for order picking is batch picking. Instead of an order picker working on only one order at a time, orders are batched together. Order pickers take responsibility for retrieving a batch of orders during a picking tour. In the grocery store example, batch picking can be thought of as going to the grocery store with your shopping list and those of some of your neighbors. In one traversal of the grocery store, you

FIGURE 8-35   Order batching decision tree.

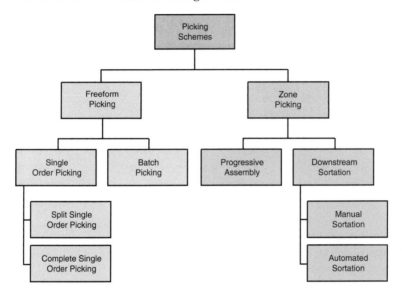

will have completed several orders. As a result, the travel time per line item picked will be reduced by approximately the number of orders per batch. The major advantage of batch picking is a reduction in travel time per line item.

The major disadvantages of batch picking are the time required to sort line items into customer orders and the potential for picking errors.

Orders may be sorted in one or two ways. First, the order picker may use separate containers to sort the line items of different orders as he or she traverses the warehouse. Special pick carts and containers are available to facilitate this approach. Second, the line items and quantities of different orders may be grouped together to be sorted later. It is the cost of this sortation process, not required in strict order picking, that determines whether batch picking is a cost effective strategy.

Batch picking can also be used in stock-to-operator systems. In those cases, all the line items requested in the batch of orders are picked from a location as it is presented to the picker. Again, the benefits of reduced travel time must be weighed against the cost of sortation and the potential for order filling orders. Batch picking is especially effective for small orders (one to five line items).

Zone Picking   In zone picking, an order picker is dedicated to pick the line items in his or her assigned zone, one order at a time or in batches. In the grocery store context, zone picking can be thought of as assigning one individual to each aisle in the grocery store. The individual would be responsible for picking all the line items requested in that aisle regardless of the customer order that generated the request.

One advantage of zone picking is travel time savings. Because each picker's coverage has been reduced from the entire warehouse to a smaller area, the travel time per line item should be reduced from that of strict order picking. Again, however, these travel time reductions must be weighed against the costs of sorting and the potential for order filling errors. Additional benefits of zone picking include the order picker's familiarity with the product in his or her zone, reduced interference with other order pickers, and increased accountability for productivity and housekeeping within the zone.

Two methods for establishing order integrity in zone picking systems are progressive assembly and wave picking. In *progressive assembly* (or pick-and-pass) systems, complete orders are established as their components are passed from zone-to-zone in tote pans or cartons along a conveyor or on a cart. In *downstream sortation,* order pickers truely work in an item picking mode. In a typical downstream sortation system, an order picker applies a bar code label to each unit picked. Unit-by-unit or in batch, labelled units are placed on a takeaway conveyor for induction into a sortation/accumulation system. As before, the productivity gains in order picking must be weighed against the investment in sortation/accumulation systems.

Pick Sequencing
Sequence pick location visits to reduce travel time.

In both operator-to-stock and stock-to-operator systems, sequencing pick location visits can dramatically reduce travel time and increase picking productivity. For example, the travel time for a man-aboard AS/RS picking tour can be reduced by 50 percent by simply dividing the rack into upper and lower halves and visiting pick locations in the lower half in increasing distance from the front of the rack on the outbound leg, and in decreasing distance in the upper half on the rack during the inbound leg (see Figures 8-36 and 8-37).

Location visits should also be sequenced in walk-and-pick systems. In case picking operations, when an order may occupy one or more pallets, the picking tour should be sequenced to enable the picker to build a stable load and to reduce travel distance. A major distributor of photographic supplies uses an expert system to solve this complex problem.

Paperless Picking
Eliminate paperwork from the order picking activity.

Paperwork is one of the major sources of inaccuracies and productivity losses in order picking. Pick-to-light systems, radio frequency data communication,

FIGURE 8-36   Picking tour prior to pick sequencing.

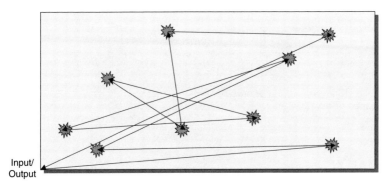

FIGURE 8-37   Picking tour after pick sequencing.

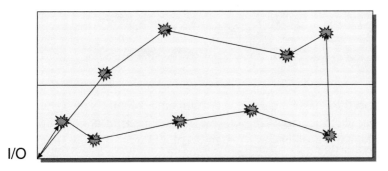

and voice input/output are existing technologies that have been successfully used to eliminate paperwork from the order picking function (see Figure 8-38).

8.8   SHIPPING PRINCIPLES

Many of the world-class receiving principles apply in reverse in shipping, including direct loading (the reverse of direct unloading), advanced shipping notice preparation (prereceiving), and staging in racks. To those we add the following practices in defining a world-class shipping activity:

- Container optimization
- Automated loading
- Dock management

Container Optimization

Select cost and space effective handling units.

FIGURE 8-38   Paperless picking.
Source: Vocollect, Symbol Technologies, Kingway

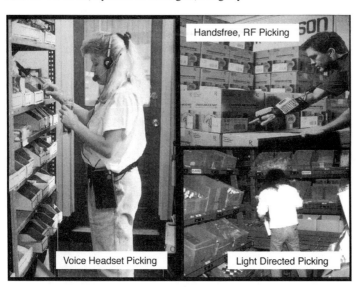

The impact of the design and selection of shipping containers throughout the entire supply chain is one of the most neglected areas of opportunities for increasing logistics efficiencies. Containers of all kinds—cartons, totes, pallets, trailers, 20- and 40-foot ocean containers, rail cars, and air containers—are the building blocks of the supply chain. Containers should protect, secure, and identify the merchandise they contain (see Figure 8-39). Containers should stack and nest easily, collapse when they are empty, handle comfortably, fit together naturally with other containers, and provide easy means for tracking and tracing. Containers should be reuseable and/or returnable to minimize the impact of logistics on the environment (see Figure 8-40).

Automated Loading

Eliminate shipping staging and direct load outbound trailers.

As was the case in receiving, the most space and labor intensive activity in shipping is staging activity. To facilitate the automated loading of pallets onto outbound trailers, pallet jacks and counterbalance lift trucks can serve as picking and loading vehicles enabling a bypassing of staging. To go one step further, automating pallet loading can be accomplished with pallet conveyor interfacing with specially designed trailer beds to enable pallets to be automatically conveyed onto outbound trailers with automated fork trucks and/or

FIGURE 8-39   **Container dunnage and void fill.**

FIGURE 8-40   **Returnable and reusable containers.**

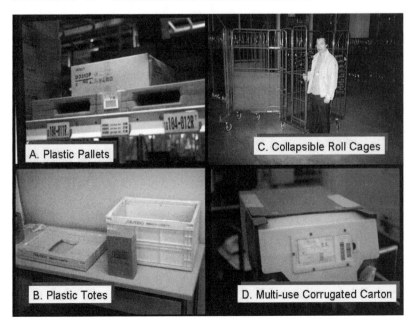

FIGURE 8-41 Automated, direct vehicle loading.

automated guided vehicles (see Figure 8-41). Direct, automated loading of loose cases is facilitated with an extendable conveyor.

Dock Management

Automate and optimize dock assignments and route on-site drivers through the site with minimum paperwork and time.

A variety of systems are now in place to improve the management of shipping and receiving docks and trailer drivers. Inbound trailers should be assigned to the dock closest to the centroid of the putaway locations on-board (see Figure 8-42). Outbound trailers should be assigned to the dock door closest to the contents of the load it will pick up.

8.9 WAREHOUSE MANAGEMENT SYSTEMS

The increased attention placed on warehouse and fulfillment operations in the last few years yielded a harvest of improvements in technology and functionality in warehouse management systems. What we used to put in the "wish-list" column we now place in the "must-have" column in developing WMS requirements. A brief summary of "must-haves" for WMS requirements follows. Descriptions of the various requirements were the focus of Sections 8.2–8.8.

• Warehouse activity profiling
  • Order activity profiling

FIGURE 8-42   Dock door assignment.

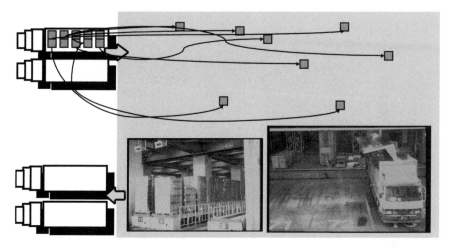

- Item activity profiling
- Warehouse performance measures
  - Warehouse activity based costing
  - Warehouse resource utilization
- Receiving
  - Cross-docking
  - Receiving scheduling
  - Automatic cubing and weighing
  - Vendor compliance
- Putaway
  - Directed putaway
  - Batch putaway
  - Putaway sequencing
  - Interleaving and continuous moves
- Storage
  - Storage mode optimization
  - Storage space optimization
  - Storage location optimization
  - Rewarehousing
  - Cycle-counting
- Order picking
  - Batch picking

- • Zone picking
- • Dynamic replenishment
- • Shipping
  - • Container optimization
  - • Load planning
  - • Dock management
- • Workforce management
  - • Time standards
  - • Workload planning and scheduling

8.10   WAREHOUSE WORKFORCE DESIGN AND DEVELOPMENT

The plight of the warehouse manager is not much better and perhaps worse than the plight of the transportation manager. Required to execute more transactions in less time, with more items, with less margin for error, and with less skilled labor, the warehouse manager's role has risen to mission critical. The capabilities of the warehouse workforce have also risen to mission critical status. Unfortunately, the development and capabilities of most warehouse workforces and supporting information systems are lacking in the face of e-commerce, same-hour delivery, and no-fault performance. We recommend the following practices as supporting initiatives in what should be a strategic and on-going program of warehouse workforce development.

Safety and Ergonomic Training

One reason the turnover of warehouse personnel is so high is a basic tenant of human psychology. When people feel threatened or unsafe in any environment, their natural reaction is to flee. If the dock is unsafe, if order pickers sustain back injuries, or if the workforce is infiltrated by drug users and/or pilferers, the instinct of the most qualified workers will be to flee. My experience with our clients is that the ones with the most stable and productive warehouse working teams are the ones with the most developed programs for safety training, ergonomics, drug and substance-abuse screening, and housekeeping.

Time Standards, Incentives, and Personnel Scheduling

With warehouse worker availability at a premium and time of the essence, the ability to monitor, motivate, and schedule each task within the warehouse is a critical capability in warehouse workforce management. Time standards enable warehouse managers to develop staffing requirements in each area within the warehouse. Incentives for productivity and quality help to motivate excellent performance and reward outstanding performance. Personnel scheduling minimizes the likelihood of bottlenecking in the warehouse and facilitates the movement of personnel between activities within the warehouse.

Optimal Management—Operator Ratios

There was a move a few years ago toward self-directed work teams in warehouse operations. As warehouse activities have become more complex, as the availability of qualified warehousing professionals has declined, and as the fallacies of self-direction without adequate training and tools have been exposed, there has been a renewed interest in the fundamentals of warehouse workforce management. One of the most important fundamentals of warehouse management is the span of control within the operations. Our experience shows that operator-supervisor ratios in excess of 17–18 do not permit adequate supervision and that ratios less than 13–14 are too costly.

Cross-Training

Cross-training is the practice of preparing warehouse operators to work in multiple areas within the warehouse. The practice is especially effective when the timing of activity peaks do not coincide in the operating areas in the warehouse. In those scenarios, the cross-trained workers can move between the peak activity areas as workload mandates. Cross-training can reduce the overall staffing requirements in proportion to the ratio of the peak to average activity levels.

Soko Circles

Quality circles are nothing new. The concept originated in Japanese automobile factories where groups of workers would meet in small teams to coordinate problem solving for quality issues on the production floor. More than ten years ago, I borrowed the Japanese word for warehouse, soko, to coin the phrase Soko Circles. Soko circles are quality circles working in warehouse operations. I have only seen the concept applied in a few warehouse operations in the United States. One of those is the JC Penney catalog distribution centers, where problem solving teams meet regularly to resolve quality issues on the warehouse floor. Another example is the Walt Disney World attractions merchandise DC, where workers meeting in continuous improvement teams to develop floor-level implementation plans for new warehousing initiatives. In both instances, the concept is the foundation for the management philosophy and works to foster excellent relationships between the warehouse management and the warehouse workforce.

At a time when warehouse quality and accuracy have become competitive differentiators, it is time for the warehouse workforce to become more prepared for and more involved in warehouse solution design and implementation. We worked recently with a large retailer in the design of a range of new warehousing initiatives. Part of the implementation plan was a series of training sessions for the entire warehouse workforce that shared the warehousing principles underpinning the new initiatives. The workforce could then understand the motivation for the new systems and procedures, and embrace the new operating concepts based on their understanding as opposed to their directives.

1/2 × 2 × 3

There is an organizational philosophy that theorizes if you take the top 1/2 of the workforce and pay each of them twice as much, then you accomplish three times as much work as was previously being accomplished. I'm not sure where the theory came from, but I do believe the underlying principle has some merit. Our clients who focus rewards and attention on the top performers, who pay higher than the industry norms for qualified warehouse personnel, and who work to weed out the operators who are impeding the overall effectiveness of the entire workforce, have much lower overall operating costs and much higher shipping accuracy.

III

IMPLEMENTING LOGISTICS SYSTEMS

C H A P T E R

LOGISTICS AND SUPPLY CHAIN INFORMATION SYSTEMS

"... come back to me with definite information."

1 Samuel 23:23

TRUE BREAKTHROUGHS in logistics performance are achieved when new ways are identified to substitute information for inventory and work content. This phenomenon was demonstrated in the United States in the early 1980's, when the greatest improvements in logistics productivity were achieved (see Figure 9-1). It was during that timespan that personal computers were mainstreamed, enabling logisticians real-time and broad access to demand, supply, inventory, and shipment information. Access to that information enabled logisticians to take advantage of powerful optimization tools for forecast optimization in inventory management, network and routing optimization in transportation, slotting optimization in warehouses, and so on. Optimized forecasts, transportation networks, routes, and warehouse layouts in turn yield lower inventory levels and less material handling throughout the supply chain.

The merge-in-transit logistics model (see Figure 9-2) is another concrete example of how information can be substituted for inventory and work content. Online information concerning production schedules and capacities at

276

FIGURE 9-1   Total U.S. logistics costs versus GNP – 1960-1996.
Source: Bob Delaney, Cass Logisitics

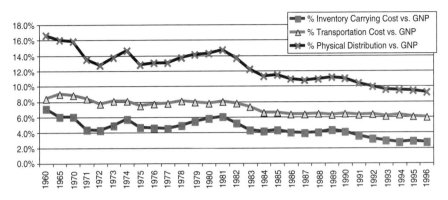

FIGURE 9-2   Merge-in-transit logistics model.

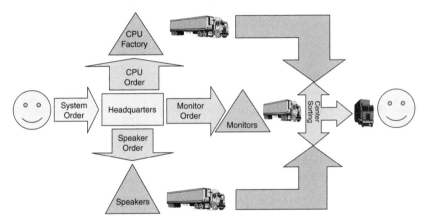

multiple assembly locations, transportation schedules and capacities at multiple assembly and pickup locations, inventory availability from multiple online suppliers, and customer leadtime requirements enable companies like Dell and Micron Computers to make and keep an online promise to deliver a complete computer system configuration and to assemble computer systems in-route.

In the merge-in-transit model, customer requirements for individual components (that is, monitor, keyboard, CPU, and printer) are submitted to each component factory. Carrier pickup times are designed to ensure that each component comes through the carrier's main sorting hub on the same

day so that each component may be sorted into the same destination sortation lane. The system's components may be put together at the main hub,
the destination hub, or at delivery. In so doing, Dell or Micron avoid the need
to anticipate and house finished goods inventory in large warehouses and
avoid the in-house sortation work that would be required but is already being
done in the carrier's sorting center anyway. This new logistics model has
enabled Dell and Micron to operate with less than seven days of on-hand
inventory and to achieve significantly higher financial returns than their
competitors. The key to success is the substitution of information for inventory and work content.

The last examples I want to share come from the world of warehousing.
There, information about daily shipping requirements from a DC, online
links to suppliers, the ability to automatically identify unit loads, the ability to assign dock doors to inbound loads in real time, and the ability to
schedule inbound receipts can all be used to implement a cross-docking program, enabling a warehouse to ship each day what it receives each day and
to bypass the traditional warehouse activities of receiving staging, putaway,
pick-face replenishment, order picking, and packing. In traditional warehouse operations, popularity, cube, and turnover information for each item
can be used to assign items to warehouse locations in such a way as to minimize the travel time in the warehouse. Again, the breakthroughs come when
we find ways to substitute information for inventory and work content.

It is difficult to substitute information for inventory and work content
if we don't have access to the information. *Logistics information systems*
(LISs) are the means by which we capture, analyze, and communicate information related to logistics and supply chain management. This chapter is not
meant to be a comprehensive treatment of the subject, but it is intended to
cover five key aspects of logistics and supply chain information systems:

- Logistics and supply chain management system functionality and
  architecture
- Logistics data mining and decision support systems
- Web-Based logistics
- Paperless logistics systems
- Logistics and supply chain management system justification, selection
  and implementation

9.1 LOGISTICS INFORMATION SYSTEM (LIS) FUNCTIONALITY AND ARCHITECTURES

Our presentation of the functionality and architecture of a LIS (see Figure 9-3) follows directly from our definition of logistics—logistics is the

FIGURE 9-3   **Logistics information system architecture.**

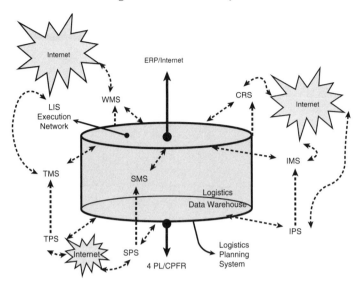

planning and execution of customer response, inventory management, supply, transportation, and warehousing.

To execute logistics, we need a *customer response system* (CRS), an *inventory management system* (IMS), a *supply management system* (SMS), a *transportation management system* (TMS), and a *warehouse management system* (WMS). We call these modules working in unison the execution layer of a LIS or the *logistics execution system* (LES). In some circles, the TMS and WMS modules are referred to as logistics or *supply chain execution systems* (SCES). The specific functionality and a sample list of vendors for each execution system is provided in Table 9-1. A complete listing of vendors of LISs is published each year by the Council of Logistics Management[1].

To plan customer response, we need a *customer response planning system* (CRPS), an *inventory planning system* (IPS), a *supply planning system* (SPS), a *transportation planning system* (TPS); and a *warehouse planning system* (WPS). These planning systems we call jointly a *logistics planning system* (LPS). An even higher level planning system that may or may not make use of information from the LPS is a supply chain or *advanced planning system* (APS). The specific functionality and a sample list of vendors for each planning system is provided in Table 9-1.

---

[1] Logistics Software CD-ROM, Council of Logistics Management, Schaumberg, Illinois.

TABLE 9-1 Logistics Information Systems Functions and Vendors

		Planning	Execution	Collaboration	ERP
Supply Chain	Functions	DC location, strategic location, sourcing, supply chain simulation, inventory deployment	OnLine supply chain communications	Supply chain scheduling and optimization, supply chain conflict resolution	
	Vendors	Aspentech, CAPS Logistics, i2, Logility, Manugistics	i2, Logility, Manugistics	Aspentech, i2, Logility, Manugistics, SyncraSystems, SupplyPoint.com	JD Edwards, QAD, SAP
Customer Response	Functions	Customer relationship management, market segmentation, RFM analysis, customer service policy	Order entry, order processing, contact management, customer yield management and pricing, customer tracking, service call scheduling, returns processing, order status	Online customer service	
	Vendors	Act, Goldmine, SalesLogix, Siebel	Cambar, Goldmine, i2, Siebel	Goldmine, SalesLogix, Siebel	JD Edwards, QAD, SAP
Inventory Management	Functions	Demand planning, forecasting, safety stock optimization, assortment planning, inventory plan simulation	Cycle counting, production scheduling, Available-to-promise, lot tracking, MRP	Inventory auctions, forecast sharing	
	Vendors	Aspentech, Cambar, Great Plains, i2, Logility, Manugistics	Aspentech, Cambar, Great Plains, i2, Logility	Aspentech, Cambar, Great Plains, i2, Logility, Manugistics, SyncraSystems	JD Edwards, QAD, SAP
Supply Management	Functions	Replenishment planning, DRP, sourcing, order quantities, negotiations	Purchase order creation, purchase order entry, purchase order processing, purchase order tracking, supplier management	Procurement marketplaces, global sourcing, online catalog management	

		Planning	Execution	Collaboration	ERP
Supply Management	Vendors	i2, Logility, Manugistics	i2, Logility, Manugistics,	i2, PurchaseCenter.com purchasepro.com, commerceone.net, GEIS.com	JD Edwards, QAD, SAP
Transportation Management	Functions	Load planning, routing and scheduling, mode/carrier selection, consolidation planning	Shipment tracking, freight payment/audit, shipment rating, carrier management, container tracking, fleet tracking	Transportation exchanges, transportation auctions	
	Vendors	Cambar, Great Plains, i2, Logility, Manugistics, Roadnet	Cambar, Great Plains, i2, Logility, Manugistics, nte.net, Qualcomm	nistevo.com, nte.net, celarix.com, qualcomm	JD Edwards, QAD, SAP
Warehouse Management	Functions	Slotting, work measurement, warehouse simulation	Cross-docking, dock management, receiving, storage, order picking, shipping, returns, MHE interface	Storage capacity availability, third-party warehousing availability	
	Vendors	LRI, Manhattan Associates, ROM	Cambar, EXE, Great Plains, Manhattan Associates, McHugh, HK Systems, RGTI, TRW, Logility	GoWarehouse.com, 3Plex.com	JD Edwards, QAD, SAP

281

A popular phrase in logistics circles these days is collaborative planning, a reference to two or more corporations communicating and developing logistics plans together. Our LIS architecture shows links to the Internet in general and collaborative planning/fourth-party logistics sites in particular as means for collaborative planning. The specific functionality and a sample list of vendors of collaborative planning systems is provided in Table 9-1.

We recommend that a real or virtual *logistics data warehouse* (LDW) serve as the foundation for the architecture of the LIS. The execution systems should feed data to the LDW and the LPS should take data from the logistics data warehouse. Eventually, the execution and planning modules will be linked, permitting automatic and real-time changes in execution rules based on learnings and analysis carried out in planning systems.

9.2 LOGISTICS DATA WAREHOUSING, DATA MINING, AND DECISION SUPPORT SYSTEMS

Logistics data warehousing, data mining, and decision support systems are often an afterthought in the design and development of *logistics information systems* (LISs). Most organizations and software providers focus the majority of their logistics I/T attention on execution systems. The focus is on automating or institutionalizing logistics transactions. Unfortunately, very little thought or analysis is applied to the effectiveness or efficiency of the transactions that are being automated. The irony is that system paybacks accrue primarily from new efficiencies gained in improving, not automating tasks. The opportunities for improvement are learned and gleaned via data mining and the application of decision support systems.

Logistics Data Warehousing

We typically recommend that a virtual or physical LDW serve as the foundation for specifying the entire LIS. The reason is that if the underlying data structures are anticipated and developed ahead of the requirements for the other execution and planning systems, the design, selection, and implementation of those systems becomes much easier, less time consuming, and less likely to fail. In addition, it is the access to data that is typically the bottleneck, the cause of most system failures, and the underlying reason for most system delays and response time problems. Finally, the design of the data structures and/or corporate I/T strategy will suggest a database provider(s). The execution and planning systems must be compatible with the selected provider's database. For all these reasons, we begin designing LISs by designing logistics data structures.

Another reason we begin the LIS design with the underlying data structures is that the process of logistics activity profiling and data mining can't really begin until the *logistics data warehouse* (LDW) has been designed and populated. It is also in the process of logistics data mining that we normally reveal the greatest opportunities for improvement in logistics performance.

Logistics Data Mining

Suppose you were sick and went to the doctor for a diagnosis and prescription. When you arrived at the doctor's office, he already had a prescription waiting for you, without even talking to you, let alone looking at you, examining you, doing blood work, and so on. In effect, he diagnosed you with his eyes closed and a random prescription generator. Needless to say, you would not be going back to that doctor for treatment.

Unfortunately, the prescriptions for many sick logistics systems are written and implemented without much examination or testing. For lack of knowledge, lack of tools, and/or lack of time, the majority of logistics re-engineering projects commence without any understanding of the root cause of the problems and without exploration of the real opportunities for improvement.

Logistics activity profiling (or logistics data mining) is the systematic analysis of supply and demand activities. The *logistics data mining* (LDM) process is designed to quickly identify the root cause of material and information flow problems, to pinpoint major opportunities for process improvements, and to provide an objective basis for project-team decision making. Done properly, profiling quickly reveals logistics design and planning opportunities that might not naturally be in front of you. It quickly eliminates options that really aren't worth considering to begin with. Many reengineering projects go awry because we work on a concept that never really had a chance in the first place. Profiling provides the right baseline to begin justifying new investments. It gets key people involved. During the profiling process, it is natural to ask people from many affected groups to provide data, to verify and rationalize data, and to help interpret results. My partner, Hugh Kinney, says that, "People will only successfully implement what they design themselves." To the extent people have been involved, they feel that they have helped with the design process. Finally, profiling permits and motivates objective decision making as opposed to biased decisions made with little or no analysis or justification. I worked with one client whose team leader we affectionately called Captain Carousels. No matter what the data said, no matter what the order and profiles looked like, no matter what the company could afford, we were going to have carousels in the new design. You can imagine how successful that project was.

LDM is key to the success of any logistics improvement initiative, but it is normally the activity in a logistics project that our clients are the least enthusiastic about, and the internal I/T group is least likely to want to support. To help overcome both barriers, we have developed a streamlined methodology and Web-based tools to facilitate logistics data mining. We begin with a standard representation of LDW and data mining requirements. Those requirements are presented in Table 9-2. Those data and profile elements also spell out the underlying requirements for the logistics data structure and decision support capabilities. If the I/T group is unable to develop these profiles due to limited resources or technology constraints, we oftentimes create the logistics activity profiles for our clients via a Web-based data mining service (see Figure 9-4). Organizations transfer specified files and the Web-based tools produce an online logistics activity profile. The profile is updated as often as the client resends the required files. In that role, we are an example of a *logistics application service provider* (LASP). We will talk more about ASPs in the section on Web-based logistics.

Logistics Decision Support Systems

I took a class in my Ph.D. program on complexity theory. I had no exposure to the subject prior to taking the course and given my pragmatic nature, I expect I won't have any additional exposure. The reason is that we spent an entire quarter in a quantitative course never solving a quantitative problem. We only studied problems to find out how difficult or complex they were.

FIGURE 9-4   **Web-based logistics activity profiling.**
Source: LRI Logistics

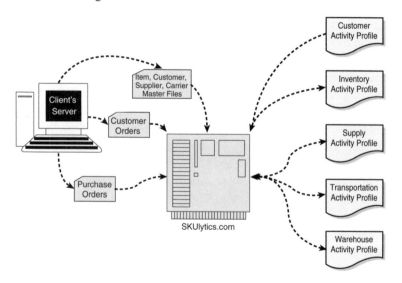

TABLE 9-2 Specifications for Logistics Activity Profiling and Data Mining

Profile	Files/Sources	Queries	Profiles	Decisions
Customer Activity Profile	• Customer order history • POS data • Customer master file	• **Sales by customer and customer location** in dollars, pallets, cases, pieces, weight, volume, frequency, orders, lines, and deliveries • **Sales by SKU** in dollars, pallets, cases, pieces, weight, volume, and lines • **Sales by customer and SKU** in dollars, pallets, cases, pieces, weight, and volume	• **Customer activity**—ABC Customers by dollar sales and volume • **SKU activity**—ABC SKUs by dollar sales and volume • **Customer-SKU activity**—ABCxABC customers and SKUs by dollar sales and volume • **Customer order profile**—dollar sales, volume, cube, weight, and lines per order	• Customer response measures • Customer classifications • SKU classifications • Customer-SKU classifications • Customer service policy design
Inventory Activity Profile	• Item master file—snapshots of on-hand inventory • POS data • Customer order file	• **On-hand inventory** in—turns, days-on-hand, dollar value, cube, space, pieces by—location and commodity by—vendor, SKU popularity, SKU usage, and SKU age • **Forecasting**—leadtime, demand variability and forecast accuracy by SKU by location	• **Demand variability** by SKU popularity and SKU age • **On-hand inventory** by location and commodity by—SKU popularity ranking, SKU age ranking, SKU popularity and age rankings, and vendor rankings	• Inventory management performance measures • SKU categories for inventory management • Inventory turnover and fill rate targets by logistics segments • Forecasting models by SKU category • Inventory reduction opportunities by logistics segment
Supply Activity Profile	• Purchase order history file • Supplier master file	• **Purchasing by supplier** and supplier location in dollars, cases, pieces, weight, volume, frequency, orders, lines, and deliveries • **Purchasing by SKU** in dollars, cases, pieces, weight, volume, and lines • **Purchasing by supplier and SKU** in dollars, pallets, cases, pieces, weight, and volume	• **Supplier activity**—ABC by $Purchases, Volume, SKUs • **SKU Activity**—ABC by dollar purchasing, volume, and frequency • **Supplier-SKU activity**—ABCxABC by dollar purchasing, volume, and SKUs • **Purchase order profile**—purchasing, volume, cube, weight, and lines per purchase order	• Supplier performance measures • Supplier categories • SKU categories for supply planning • Supplier-SKU rationalization • Sole versus primary-secondary versus competitive sourcing • Make-buy analysis • Supplier service policy design

(continued)

285

TABLE 9-2 Specifications for Logistics Activity Profiling and Data Mining *(continued)*

Profile	Files/Sources	Queries	Profiles	Decisions
Transportation Activity Profile	• Shipping manifest history file • Carrier master file • Customer master file • Supplier master file	• **From-to matrix** between all pickup-deliver to points including, frequency, volume, weight, dollar value, carriers, carrier capacity, carrier availability, distance, time, freight paid, on-time delivery, damages, and claims	• **Lane activity profile**—ABC lanes by dollar freight, volume, and claims • **Carrier activity**—ABC carriers by dollar freight, volume, and shipments • **Inbound transportation activity**—ABC by dollar freight, volume, value, and frequency • **Outbound transportation activity**—ABC by dollar freight, volume, value, and frequency • **Carrier-shipment activity**—ABCxABC by dollar purchasing, volume, and SKUs • **Manifest profile**—shipping, volume, cube, weight, and lines per manifest	• Transportation performance measures • Logistics hierarchy design • Logistics network design • Inbound freight management • Consolidation design • Routing and scheduling • Fleet configuration • Mode and carrier selections • Potential roles for third parties
Warehouse Activity Profile	• Item master file • Customer order history file	• **SKU Activity by:** popularity, usage, cases, pallets, cube, and weight • **Orders by** dollar value, lines, cube, and units	• **Order profile**—lines, cube, pieces, dollar value, and weight per order distribution • **Lines and cube per order distribution** • **Item activity profile**—ABC SKUs by picks, usage, and volume by SKU • **Item-order completion profile**	• Warehouse performance measures • SKU categories for warehouse master planning • Slotting • Storage mode selection • Order picking policies • Warehouse layout

We learned that there is a category of problems known as NP-Hard problems for which no algorithm can be invented that will solve the problem in less than infinite time with the fastest computer that can be imagined by mankind. Guess what? Most logistics problems, including vehicle routing, production scheduling, and slotting a warehouse are NP-Hard problems. All of this to say that due to the inherent interdependencies, multiple constraints, hundreds to thousands of item numbers, and sometimes complex and non-linear objective functions, logistics problems do not lend themselves to back-of-the-envelope kinds of solutions. In fact, due to the inherent complexity, oftentimes solutions to logistics problems are counterintuitive. As a result, the best (though usually not optimal) solutions to logistics problems are developed with computer-based decision support tools. In Table 9-1, the capabilities and vendors of a variety of logistics decision support tools were enumerated. Sample output from a variety of decision support tools has been provided throughout this book. A more detailed review of logistics decision support tools was recently published by the Warehousing Education and Research Council.

9.3   WEB-BASED LOGISTICS

We have already discussed that real breakthroughs in logistics are achieved when new ways are found to substitute information for inventory and work content. It follows then that a tool that enables exponentially greater access to logistics information than we have previously enjoyed would receive wide and rapid adoption. That tool we know today as the Internet.

For some benchmarks illustrating the rate of adoption of Internet services, consider the following:[2]

- It took 38 years for radio to reach 50 million users, 13 years for TV, 10 years for cable, and five years for the Internet.
- In 1970, 5 percent of the U.S. economy was agrarian, 10 percent electronic, and 85 percent industrial. In 2000, two percent of the U.S. economy was agrarian, 38 percent was electronic, and 60 percent industrial.
- In 1998, 8 percent of all purchase orders were placed via the Internet; in 2000, 40 percent of all purchase orders were placed via the Internet.
- 150,000 organizations trading more than $1.8 trillion per year are expected to participate in Web-based supply chain exchanges in 2001.
- Transportation bookings over the Internet are expected to increase by 80 percent per year for next few years.

[2]*Business Week,* Morgan Stanley, Marvin Zosis and Associates.

The world-wide Web connects stationary and mobile computers and wireless devices in a $7 \times 24 \times 365$ network permitting global visibility of real-time logistics transactions. It is a great resource for logisticians. However, at the same time, the nature of e-commerce increases the demands on all logistics systems in all areas of capability. In this section, we will study both the extra requirements for logistics to support e-commerce and the extra resources provided to logisticians by e-logistics solutions.

Web-Based Customer Response

E-commerce has dramatically raised the expectations for customer service in the areas of

- *Response time* (kozmo.com and aerodelivery.com provide one hour delivery.)
- *Product customization* (levistrauss.com custom engineers a pair of jeans online, landsend.com custom engineers a swimsuit online, callawaygolf.com custom engineers a pair of golf clubs online.)
- *Convenience* (Grocers deliver groceries and other items and auto makers delivery custom specified automobiles directly to your doorstep.)
- *Returns processing* (It is $3 \times$ more likely that an item purchased over the Internet will be returned than an item purchased via traditional mail order or in retail stores.)
- *Order status visibility* (Amazon and Dell, among many others, provide e-mail status reporting as your order moves through the major milestones of the supply chain.)

E-commerce dramatically increases the demands on customer response. However, e-commerce also provides a variety of Web-based solutions for customer response that enable e-tailers and traditional retailers alike to respond to more demanding customers. Customer service Web sites post solutions and links for the 20 percent of issues that generate 80 percent of the inquiries (see Figure 9-5). Online customer service representatives and online chat forums are dedicated to particular types of customer concerns. Online auctions are natural vehicles for selling returned merchandise. Many vendors and carriers offer Web-based returns processing. Highly detailed product information that can be presented online (and may not be available in a retail store or catalog) can actually reduce product returns. Proactive order status reporting via e-mail and/or paging relieves much of the burden of customer service where a majority of incoming calls are related to order status inquiries.

FIGURE 9-5   Wishbook.com customer service screen.
Source: Sears Corporation

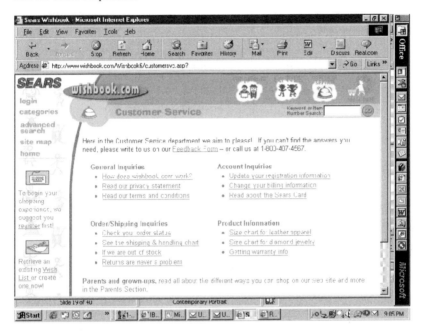

Federal Express has been one of the most aggressive and successful in applying Internet technologies to the customer service function. Of the 1.2 billion customer transactions processed each year by Federal Express, 800 million are handled by their Web site. They estimate that without the online customer service capability, they would require more than 22,000 additional customer service representatives.

Web-Based Inventory Management

The nature of e-commerce makes many aspects of inventory management more difficult than in past times. First, e-commerce creates a new distribution channel for most businesses. Hence, overall demand is fragmented into an even less predictable channel. Second, because it is difficult to control Web-site exposure (as opposed to targeted mailings for traditional mail order catalogs), Internet demand is by nature highly volatile. One of our e-commerce clients predicted sales of 3,000 units per month via a new feature they were adding to their Web site. At the end of the first three months, sales were in excess of 300,000 units. They eventually had to turn the Web site off to curtail the demand. Finally, higher return rates for Web sales add another degree of uncertainty in inventory planning.

As was the case with customer response, there are a variety of Web-based solutions for inventory management that improve the ability to cope with the increase uncertainty. The Web permits online forecast sharing between supply chain partners (www.cpfr.org). Online auctions provide a means for purging excess inventory (www.ebay.com). Links with wireless devices provide perpetual inventory visibility. Digital media (text, maps, music, and video) delivered over the Internet even eliminates many physical inventories.

Web-Based Supply

As a vendor, one of the most challenging aspects of e-commerce is the wide availability of price information and procurement auctions that make it easier for a supplier to pull the rug out from under a marketplace. Vendors are forced to become increasingly price competitive. Some vendors (with shallow understandings of their own cost structures) have offered unprofitable pricing to the detriment of buyers and sellers alike.

In this marketplace, it is not necessarily the strong that survive, but the nimble and the most efficient. The wide availability of price information stems from Web-based marketplaces that also make it increasingly convenient to click to an alternate source. As a result, the margin for error in supply chain management, particularly in the area of inventory availability, has decreased by an order of magnitude.

The supply side of logistics management is one of the great beneficiaries of e-commerce breakthroughs. Vendor Web sites make the vendor selection process more convenient and reliable. Online marketplaces make shopping for materials from alternate sources easier than it has ever been. Online catalogs for nearly all products make product selection less time consuming. Online RFPs and electronic bidding make the bid process many times faster and much less costly. The sum total of these benefits has permitted a 300 percent to 500 percent reduction in purchase order costs for the organizations most aggressive in applying Web-based solutions for supply management.

Another Web-based capability for supply management is *collaborative planning, forecasting, and replenishment* (CPFR). In the CPFR logistics model manufacturers, wholesalers, retailers, carriers, financial institutions, and customers exchange information related to the demand and supply of their resources and work together to optimize the performance of each participant's assets and to maximize the levels of customer service throughout the supply chain. Coming on the heals of the ECR initiative, the food industry has been one of the most aggressive in implementing CPFR practices and technologies. The CPFR pilot between Wegmans and Planters yielded dramatic reductions in inventory levels for both organizations and significant reductions in lost sales at the retail level. The computing industry's rosettanet.com initiative is another example of CPFR at work. There, organizations such as Intel, Microsoft, Compaq, Dell, Ingram-Micro, CompUSA, Siemens, and a variety of major organizations in the computer industry use a common platform, logistics transaction standards, and a Web-based bulletin board to streamline the logistics of the computer industry.

We have participated in a variety of client engagements recently requiring us to design industry exchange concepts. In each case, we noticed that there are a mix of exchanges offering limited logistics services, but no single exchange offering one-stop shopping for all logistics services. This opportunity led us recently to design and promote the concept of the *total logistics exchange* (TLE) depicted in Figure 9-6. Manufacturers, wholesalers, retailers, consumers, and third-party logistics companies are connected

FIGURE 9-6   **Total logistics exchange concept.**

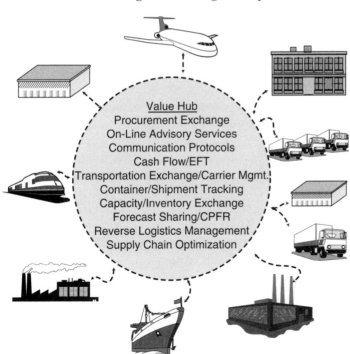

in the exchange. The exchange provides the following services on a per-transaction basis:

- E-procurement
- Electronic RFPs and product bidding
- Electronic funds transfer
- Transportation services bidding
- Reverse logistics management
- Freight payment and audit
- On-line carrier management
- Container and shipment tracking
- Capacity and inventory exchange
- Forecast sharing and CPFR
- Supply chain optimization
- On-line logistics decision support tools
- Online advisory services

Web-Based Transportation Management
E-commerce has placed the transportation industry under tremendous pressure. Because e-procurement yields low (sometimes inconsequential) purchase order costs, order sizes at every level of the supply chain are declining rapidly. Hence, shipment sizes are declining rapidly and shipment frequencies are increasing rapidly. Direct-to-consumer Web sites of all kinds require carriers to deliver products more frequently to customers' homes and to locations that were not necessarily configured for high truck traffic. Same-hour and same-day shipping promises bring increased expectations for short and sure delivery times. In addition, online auctions for transportation services and widely available pricing information increase the pressure on carriers to offer lower prices. It is a difficult environment to manage in, but it bodes well for the carriers with the best capabilities in transportation optimization and information technology.

Web technologies have also permitted a multiplicity of breakthroughs in transportation management. Carriers, transportation service providers, and transportation portals make shipping rates and shipment tracking information widely available (see Figure 9-7). Online transportation auctions, bidding, and booking yield lower transportation rates, increased asset utilization for carriers, and lower booking/tracking costs for shippers (see Figure 9-8). Online transportation service providers provide online bill payment, audit-

FIGURE 9-7 Online container and shipment tracking.
Source: Bridge-Point.com

Container	Associated Document Information						
ID	ID	Type	Transit	Origin	Depart	Destination	Arrive
RSK0190213	KCP1102	dkrcpt	Int	Tokyo	03, Oct 2000 09:00 GMT	Savannah	17, Oct 2000 17:00 GMT
	MRU9845	ocnbk	Pre	Tokyo	05, Oct 2000 11:00 GMT	Seattle	14, Oct 2000 10:00 GMT
	XKG5522	ocnbk	Pre	Taiwan	11, Oct 2000 04:00 GMT	Los Angeles	22, Oct 2000 12:00 GMT
	WSJ1963	ocnbk	Pre	Taiwan	01, Nov 2000 07:00 GMT	Portland	12, Nov 2000 17:00 GMT
	APP3588	ocnbk	Pre	Hong Kong	14, Nov 2000 03:00 GMT	Miami	01, Dec 2000 11:00 GMT

FIGURE 9-8 Online rating.
Source: TransRater Network

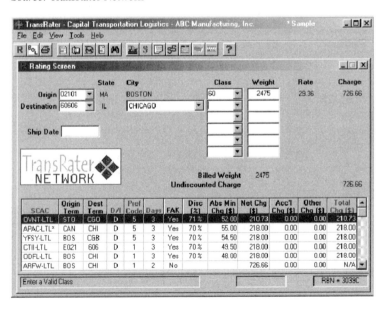

ing, analysis, and claims collection (see Figure 9-9). New GPS systems permit transportation assets to be tracked physically within a few feet across the U.S. and functionally across a variety of activities including loading, unloading, traveling empty, traveling full, idling, and so on (see Figure 9-10).

FIGURE 9-9   Online freight bill payment and audit.
Source: NPC

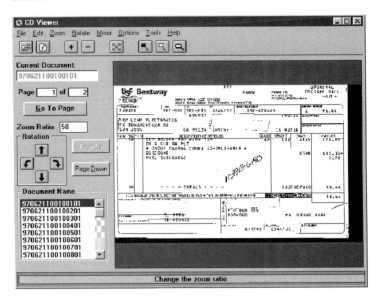

FIGURE 9-10   Web-based truck tracking.
Source: Qualcomm

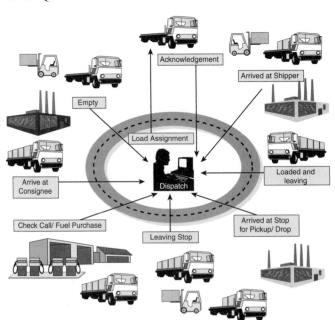

Web-Based Warehouse Management

Due to significant increases in the number of inbound purchase and outbound customer orders, increases in product and packaging customization, and significant decreases in order sizes and available processing times, e-commerce has wreaked havoc in most warehouse operations. In addition, Web exposure makes it increasingly likely that an outbound order is destined for an international customer, therefore requiring additional paperwork, packaging, and internal handling. In the face of low unemployment and high turnover among warehouse personnel, times are tough for warehouse managers.

Unfortunately, the warehouse has experienced the least benefit of Web-based technologies. Some WMS vendors are offering subscriptions to warehouse management systems as application services via the Internet. LRI offers some Web-based warehouse activity profiling and slotting services.

A summary of the impact of the e-commerce on logistics and Web-based logistics solutions is provided in Table 9-3.

9.4 PAPERLESS AND WIRELESS LOGISTICS SYSTEMS

Digital and real-time logistics require an enabling set of devices and technologies. These devices are the data collection and communication devices forming the backbone of integrated logistics information systems. Because

TABLE 9-3   **The Impact of E-commerce on Logistics and Web-based Logistics Solutions**

	New and Increased Requirements	Web-based Solutions
Customer Response	• Returns management • Short-cycle deliveries	• Online response to customer inquiries
Inventory Management	• Fragmented demand streams • SKU proliferation	• Forecast sharing • Inventory auctions
Supply Management	• Profit erosion	• E-procurement • CPFR
Transportation Management	• Home delivery • Short lead times • Smaller shipments • Profit erosion	• Shipment bidding, booking, and tracking • Online freight payment
Warehouse Management	• Returns handling • Short cycle times • Smaller order sizes	• Warehouse application service providers

the list of devices grows daily, it is impossible to present a current picture of the state of paperless logistics technologies in textbook form. The logistics industry trade shows and related Web sites are the best and perhaps only continually updated presentation of the current state of paperless logistics technologies.

Though the set of devices is changing and being upgraded rapidly, the general categories of technologies have remained fairly stable over the last few years. To support paperless logistics, we need a way to automatically *identify* a logistics object (that is, a container, document, or location), a way to *communicate* information to a logistics operator, and a way to *present* information to a logistics operator. Those major categories of technologies are described and illustrated in this section:

- Automatic identification technologies
  - Bar codes and bar code scanners
  - Radio frequency tags and antennae
  - Smart cards and magnetic stripes
  - Vision systems
- Automatic communication and presentation technologies
  - Radio frequency data communications
  - Synthesized voice
  - Virtual displays
  - Pick-to-light systems

Automatic Identification Technologies

Bar Codes and Bar Code Scanners   A bar code system includes a bar code *symbology* to represent a series of alphanumeric characters, bar code *readers* to interpret the bar code symbology, and bar code *printers* to reliably and accurately print bar codes on labels, cartons, and/or picking/shipping documents. The review is included here because bar code systems are the foundation of many paperless warehousing systems, but the review is meant only as a brief introduction to bar code systems.

Bar Code Symbologies   A bar code (see Figure 9-11) is a series of printed bars and intervening spaces. The structure of unique bar/space patterns represents various alphanumeric characters. The same pattern may represent different alphanumeric characters in different codes.

The primary codes or symbologies for which standards have been developed include

FIGURE 9-11   **Bar code.**

- **Code 39**   An alpha-numeric code adopted by a wide number of industry and government organizations for both individual product identification and shipping package/container identification.
- **Interleaved 2 of 5 Code**   A compact, numeric-only code still used in a number of applications where alpha-numeric encoding is not required.
- *Universal Product Code* **(UPC)**   Used to record the unique product identifier on retail products.
- **Codabar**   One of the earlier symbols developed, this symbol permits encoding of the numeric-character set, six unique control characters, and four unique stop/start characters that can be used to distinguish different item classifications. It is primarily used in non-grocery retail point of sale applications, blood banks and libraries.
- **Code 93**   Accommodating all 128 ASCII characters plus 43 alpha-numeric characters and four control characters, Code 93 offers the highest alpha-numeric data density of the six standard symbologies. In addition to enabling for positive switching between ASCII and alpha-numeric, the code uses two check characters to ensure data integrity.
- **Code 128**   Provides the architecture for high density encoding of the full 128 character ASCII set, variable length fields and elaborate character-by-character and full symbol integrity checking. Provides the highest numeric-only data density. Adopted in 1989 by the Uniform Code Council (U.S.) and the International Article Number Association (EAN) for shipping container identification.
- **UPC/EAN**   The numeric-only symbols developed for grocery supermarket point-of-sale applications and now widely used in a variety of other retailing environments. Fixed length code suitable for unique manufacturer and item identification only.
- **Stacked Symbologies**   Although a consensus standard has not yet emerged, the health and electronics industries have initiated programs to evaluate the feasibility of using Code 16K or Code 49, two micro-symbologies that offer significant potential for small item encoding.

Packing data in from two to sixteen stacked rows, Code 16K accommodates the full 128-character ASCII set and permits the encoding of up to 77 characters in an area of less than .5 square inches. Comparable in terms of data density, Code 49 also handles the full ASCII character set. It encodes data in from two to eight rows and has a capacity of up to 49 alpha-numeric characters per symbol.

- **Two-Dimensional Codes**   Two-dimensional bar codes, sometimes referred to as high-density bar codes, are the latest development in a rapidly advancing field. Two-dimensional codes are overlapping linear bar codes, one horizontal and the other vertical in the same field. These codes permit the automatic encoding of nearly a printed page's worth of text in a square inch of page space. Examples include Code 49, Code 16k, PDF 417, Code One, Datamatrix, and UPS's Maxicode.

Bar codes can be and are used for

- Product identification
- Container identification
- Location identification
- Operator identification
- Equipment identification
- Document identification

The tendency is to get caught up in bar coding for the sake of bar coding, trying to bar code anything and everything. The key to success is to minimize the amount of bar coding required to achieve the automatic communications objectives of logistics. If there is too much bar coding and too much bar code scanning, the costs and time to print and scan all the codes can quickly negate potential productivity and accuracy benefits.

Bar Code Readers   Bar codes are read by both contact and noncontact scanners. Contact scanners must contact the bar code. They can be portable or stationary and typically come in the form of a wand or a light pen. The wand/pen is manually passed across the bar code. The scanner emits either white or infrared light from the wand/pen tip and reads the light pattern that is reflected from the bar code. This information is stored in solid-state memory for subsequent transmission to a computer.

Contact readers (see Figure 9-12) are excellent substitutes for keyboard or manual data entry. Alphanumeric information is processed at a rate of up to 50 inches per minute, and the error rate for a basic scanner connected to

FIGURE 9-12   Light-pen bar code scanner.

its decode is 1 in 1,000,000 reads. Light pen or wand scanners with decoder and interface cost around $700.

Noncontact readers may be handheld (see Figure 9-13) or stationary (see Figure 9-14) and include fixed-beam scanners, moving-beam scanners, and *charged couple device* (CCD) scanners. Noncontact scanners employ fixed-beam, moving beam, video camera or faster scanning technology to take

FIGURE 9-13   Handheld laser scanner.
Source: Symbol Technologies

FIGURE 9-14   In-line bar code scanner.
Source: Computer Identics

from one to several hundred looks at the code as it passes. Most bar code scanners read codes bidirectionally by virtue of sophisticated decoding electronics that distinguish the unique start/stop codes peculiar to each symbology and decipher them accordingly. Further, the majority of scanner suppliers now provide equipment with an autodiscrimination feature that permits recognition, reading, and verification of multiple symbol formats with no internal or external adjustments. Finally, suppliers have introduced omnidirectional scanners (see Figure 9-15) for industrial applications that are

FIGURE 9-15   Omnidirectional bar code scanning.

capable of reading bar codes passing through a large viewfield at high speeds, regardless of the orientation of the bar code. These scanners are commonly used in high-speed sortation systems.

Fixed-beam readers use a stationary light source to scan a bar code. They depend on the motion of the object to be scanned to move past the beam. Fixed-beam readers rely on consistent, accurate code placement on the moving object.

Radio Frequency Tags *Radio frequency* (RF) tags encode data on a chip encased in a tag. When a tag is within range of a special antenna, the chip is decoded and read by a tag reader (see Figure 9-16). RF tags can be programmable or permanently coded and can be read from up to 70 feet away. *Surface acoustical wave* (SAW) tags are permanently coded and can be read only within a 10-foot range.

RF tags are often used for permanent identification of a container, where advantage can be taken of the tag's durability. RF tags are also attractive in harsh environments where printed codes may deteriorate and become illegible. A tag reader costs around $5,000. Nonprogrammable tags range in price from $1 to $50, programmable tags, from $5 to $75.

At a large textiles manufacturer, the contents of a truckload are encoded into a RF tag located in the windshield of the truck. The tag can be read by antennae placed at 10 mile increments along the highway to enable a customer to watch the progress of its load and to prelocate the contents of the truckload. This technology facilitates cross-docking and direct (no-staging) putaway of truckload contents to primary and reserve picking locations.

FIGURE 9-16   **RF tag application in yard management.**

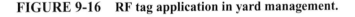

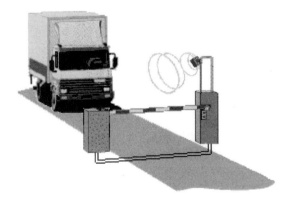

Magnetic Stripes and Optical Cards   Magnetic stripes commonly appear on the back of credit or bank cards. They are used to store a large quantity of information in a small space. The magnetic stripe is readable through dirt or grease. Data contained in the stripe can be changed. The stripe must be read by contact, thus eliminating high-speed sortation applications. Magnetic stripe systems are generally more expensive than bar code systems. In warehousing, magnetic stripes are used on smart cards in a variety of paperless applications. Smart cards are now used in logistics to capture information ranging from employee identification, to the contents of a trailer load of material (see Figure 9-17), to the composition of an order picking tour. For example, at a large cosmetics distribution center, order picking tours are downloaded onto smart cards (see Figure 9-18). The smart cards are in turn inserted into a smart card reader built into each order picking cart. In so doing, the picking tour is illuminated on an electronic map of the warehouse appearing on the front of the cart.

Vision Systems   Vision system cameras take pictures of objects and codes and send the pictures to a computer for interpretation. Vision systems "read" at moderate speeds with excellent accuracy, at least for limited environments. Obviously, these systems do not require contact with the object or code. However, the accuracy of a read is highly dependent on the quality of light. Vision systems are becoming less costly but are still relatively expensive.

FIGURE 9-17   Optical memory card used for automated truck manifesting and RF tag used in container identification.

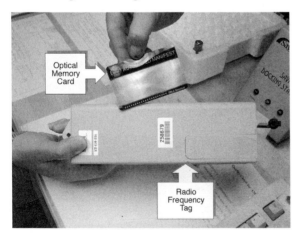

FIGURE 9-18   Smart cards in an order picking application.

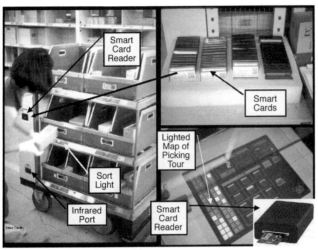

FIGURE 9-19   Vision system used in automated receiving inspection.
Source: Siemens

A large mail order operator recently installed a vision system at receiving (see Figure 9-19). The system is located above a telescoping conveyor used to convey inbound cartons from a trailer into the warehouse. The system recognizes those inbound cartons that do not have bar codes, reads the product and vendor number on the carton, and directs a bar code printer to print and apply the appropriate bar code label.

Automatic Communication and Presentation Technologies

Radio Frequency Data Communications   Handheld, lift-truck mounted (see Figure 9-20), and hands-free *radio data terminals* (RDTs) (see Figure 9-21) are rapidly emerging as reliable tools for both inventory and vehicle/driver management. RDTs incorporate a multicharacter display, full keyboard, and special function keys. They communicate and receive mes-

FIGURE 9-20   **Vehicle-mounted radio frequency terminals.**

FIGURE 9-21   **Handsfree radio frequency terminals.**
Source: Symbol Technologies

sages on a prescribed frequency via strategically located antennae and a host computer interface unit. Beyond the basic thrust toward tighter control of inventory, improved resource utilization is most often cited in justification of these devices. Further, the increasing availability of software packages that permit RDT linkage to existing plant or warehouse control systems greatly simplify their implementation. The majority of RDTs installed in plants and warehouses use handheld wands or scanners for data entry, product identification, and location verification. This marriage of technologies provides higher levels of speed, accuracy, and productivity than could be achieved by either technology alone.

Synthesized Voice   The use of synthesized voice (see Figure 9-22) is increasingly popular in warehouse operations. In stationary systems, a synthesized voice is used to direct a stationary warehouse operator. For example, at a wholesale grocery distribution center, carousel operators are directed by lights and a broadcast synthesized voice speaks the correct picking location and quantity.

In mobile voice-based systems, warehouse operators wear a headset with an attached microphone. Via synthesized voice, the WMS talks the operator through a series of transactions. For example, for a pallet putaway, the lift truck operator hears a command to put away a particular pallet into a particular warehouse location. When the transaction is complete, the operator speaks, "putaway complete," into the microphone. Then the system speaks

FIGURE 9-22   **Voice headset.**
Source: Vocollect

the next transaction to the operator. If the operator forgets the transaction, he simply speaks, "repeat transaction," and the system repeats the instruction.

The advantages of voice-based systems include hands-free operations, the operator's eyes are free from terminals or displays, and the system functions whether or not the operator is literate. Another advantage is the ease with which the system is programmed. A simple Windows-based software package is used to construct all necessary transaction conversations. To operate every area of the warehouse with a voice-based system would require conversations for receiving, putaway, restocking, order picking, and shipping. Once those conversations have been developed, the system is a WMS unto itself. This approach can be an inexpensive way to achieve a majority of the functionality of a typical WMS. A typical mobile voice-based system costs approximately the same as a RDT-based system, in the range of $1,000 to $3,000 per terminal.

Virtual "Heads Up" Displays   Virtual (or "heads up") displays (see Figure 9-23) present an operator with virtual overlays on the warehouse floor, products, or layouts to direct an operator through travel paths and/or to perform specific transactions on specific products. The displays can also be used to present the operator with a virtual computer display and or to take an operator on a virtual tour of a 3D warehouse layout (see Figure 9-24). That application can be used in training warehouse operators in working the full range of warehouse transactions in each area within the warehouse.

FIGURE 9-23   **Heads-up warehouse display.**
Source: VRwarehouse.com

FIGURE 9-24   Virtual warehouse picking tour.
Source: VRwarehouse.com

FIGURE 9-25   Pick-to-light systems.

Pick-to-Light Systems   Light directed operations (see Figure 9-25) use indicator lights and lighted alphanumeric displays to direct warehouse operators in order picking, putaway, and/or sortation. The most popular use is in broken case picking from flow racks, shelving, and/or carousels. In the case of flow rack or bin shelving, a light display is placed at the front of each pick location (in the place of a location label). The light is illuminated if a pick is required from that location. The number of units to pick appears on the same display or on a display at the top of the flow rack or shelving bay. A typical light display system costs in the range of $100 to $200 per SKU position. Typical picking rates are in the range of 300 to 600 lines per person —hour and accuracy is in the range of 99.97 percent. In incremental justification, these rates and accuracies must pay for the incremental computer hardware and software costs.

In carousels, a light tree is placed in front of each carousel. A light display appears on the tree to correspond to every picking level on the carousel. As a carrier is positioned in front of the order picker, the light display corresponding to the level to be picked from is illuminated. A typical light tree for carousel picking costs in the range of $100,000. However, if we normalize the cost by the number of items on a typical carousel, say 5,000, then the cost per SKU position is only $20.

Lights can also be used to direct case picking and pallet storage and retrieval operations.

9.5 LIS JUSTIFICATION, SELECTION, AND IMPLEMENTATION

You may be familiar with the proverb that says when we are faithful with the little things, then we can handle the big things. That proverb also holds with logistics projects. Under the pressures of short term financial performance and increasing competition, we may yield to the instinct to bite off more than we can individually or corporately chew with respect to financial and/or human resources. To assist our clients with an incremental justification approach, we typically perform an incremental economic analysis of a proposed project. Figure 9-26 illustrates an example analysis.

In the figure, the initial project under consideration required a capital investment of $1,000,000 with a potential annual savings of $1,000,000. The payback on the project would be 1.0 years, strong enough to be funded in most U.S. organizations. However, a more detailed analysis of the initial proposal typically reveals a less expensive option that may yield a majority of the savings associated with the initial proposal. The reason is that the initial project proposal is typically derived from an automation plan proposed by a vendor, consultant, or an internal resource excited by a recent conference, magazine article, or vendor presentation. It is easy to justify automation for a poorly conceived process. It is almost impossible to be successful with automation in a poorly conceived process!

In incremental justification, we consider every possible alternative that could improve the current process. That discipline usually reveals a small capital investment combined with a variety of simplification techniques that

FIGURE 9-26   **Incremental project justification approach.**

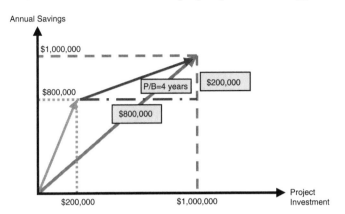

can yield a dramatic improvement for a fraction of the investment and risk. In the example, a $200,000 investment was found to yield $800,000 in annual savings. The payback period on the low-risk proposal is 0.25 years or three months. This proposal should almost certainly be pursued because the risk is low, the payback is high, and the underlying process should be simplified before any automation is deployed. In addition, by exposing the second option, the true economics of the initial proposal are revealed. That is, for an incremental investment of $800,000, an annual savings of $200,000 is available. The payback on this incremental proposal is 4.0 years, exposing the reality that a majority of the initial proposal was related to infrastructure that may or may not be required.

There is also a tendency in most organizations to run as fast as they possibly can with a project implementation. The Big Bang approach is popular in many organizations. My experience with the Big Bang is that the banging is either the project staffing banging their heads against the wall or the door banging as the project staff departs the project or organization for greener pastures. We have worked with some of the largest ERP implementations in the United States. In each case, the organizations who yielded to the temptation to run too fast with the implementation nearly ran out of money and personnel in the process. Instead, we work diligently with our clients to map out an implementation plan that will not strap the organization financially or morale wise. In addition, the incremental implementation plan may reveal that a majority of the benefits of the project can be achieved

FIGURE 9-27   **Incremental implementation plan.**

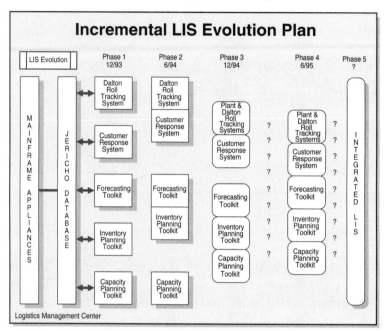

Copyright: Edward H. Frazelle, Ph.D.

at very early phases of the project and may call into question the work required in the latter phases of the project. An example incremental project plan is illustrated in Figure 9-27.

10

LOGISTICS ORGANIZATION DESIGN AND DEVELOPMENT

SEVEN DISCIPLINES OF HIGHLY SUCCESSFUL LOGISTICS ORGANIZATIONS

> "Any kingdom divided against itself will be ruined, and a house divided against itself will fall."
>
> *Luke 11:17*

LESS THAN ONE-THIRD of all logistics projects are ever "successful," meaning that the goals developed for the project in the beginning of the project were met in retrospect. Those projects include logistics reengineering efforts, facility reconfigurations, outsourcing to third-party logistics providers, and restructuring of the transportation network. If the project involves software, the success rate is less than 15 percent. I can speak first-hand to the high failure rate because our job oftentimes as consultants is to help "fix" a broken project and/or to assist with a project from the outset to maximize the likelihood of success.

In considering the 100-plus projects I have been involved in personally, and the many more I have second hand knowledge of through our professional education program, I can say without hesitation that the fundamental reason a project, program, or enterprise fails is organizational dysfunction. I was first made starkly aware of this when the managing partner of the one of the nation's largest logistics consulting firms quit his position abruptly and went back to school to study industrial psychology and Christian counseling. I was introducing him to an industry audience sometime after he completed his course of study and I asked him why he quit so suddenly and why he chose his program of study. He shared that most of the logistics assignments his firm had completed had resulted in thick binders and very limited results. His observation was that the barrier to implementation was nearly always organizational in nature.

As I thought back over the project successes and failures I was aware of, I had to agree. That motivated my interest and personal study of organizational disciplines that lead to logistics successes. Pulling from a variety of previous consulting assignments, experiences from the students in our professional education program, and an intense literature search, I put names and descriptions into seven disciplines that have distinguished logistics organizations in the areas of project success rates, contributions to total corporate performance, and the ability to adapt logistics processes to new business strategies and tactics. The seven disciplines tie together enterprises across the supply chain, logistics activities within the enterprise, and personal/community development objectives within the logistics organization.

1. Supply chain organization management–enterprise to enterprise
2. Corporate logistics organization alignment–logistics to enterprise
3. Logistics strategic planning and project management–logistics to enterprise
4. Logistics process and activity management–logistics to enterprise
5. Logistics professional development–professional to logistics
6. Human-friendly logistics–professional to logistics
7. Community-friendly logistics–community to logistics

10.1 SUPPLY CHAIN ORGANIZATION MANAGEMENT

We define the supply chain as the network of enterprises, individuals, facilities, and information/material handling systems that connect our supplier's supplier to our customer's customer. From that perspective, there is no stand-alone logistics organization. Logistics organizations across any supply chain must collaborate and act in concert with one another to yield the mutually desired result of maximizing shareholder and customer value across the chain.

Our experience shows that seven supply chain management practices distinguish truly world-class logistics organizations and lead to superior logistics and corporate performance:

- Supply chain scoreboards to measure supply chain value creation virtual vertical integration
- Benchmarking and collaborative logistics service purchasing with noncompetitors
- *Collaborative Planning, Forecasting, and Replenishment* (CPFR)
- Supply chain optimization
- Collaborative purchasing
- Strategic outsourcing to third-party logistics service providers

Supply Chain Scoreboards

People behave based on the way they are measured. (Even if a system is designed to force a process to be carried out one way, if that way leads to a lower performance score for the affected individual, the individual will work around the system.) The principle holds within an organization as well as across a supply chain. If the supply chain participants cannot come to agreement on a mutually satisfactory set of performance metrics, the supply chain managers will not make decisions that benefit overall supply chain performance.

A recommended framework for a supply chain scoreboard addressing financial, productivity, quality, and cycle time performance is provided in Figure 10-1.

We recently completed a supply chain assignment in the healthcare industry. Just the process of documenting the total supply chain performance led to major improvements. Figure 10-2 shows the results of the scoreboard analysis.

Once we were able to bring together all the major players in the supply chain and they could jointly see the significant cost reductions and service improvements that were available to them, they were all motivated to begin working together to realize the benefits. For example, the number of weeks of inventory coverage at the healthcare providers (four to eight weeks for most SKUs) was more than the manufacturing lead time for a large majority of the SKUs. Simply communicating the consumption of the merchandise and surgery schedules was identified as a means of taking more than half the inventory out of the supply chain. Those savings were estimated to be worth $10,000,000 per year per healthcare manufacturer, $30,000,000 per year per distributor/wholesaler, and $400,000 per year per hospital.

Supply Chain Benchmarking

Once the metrics and performance relative to those metrics has been documented, benchmarking with logistically similar supply chains will help to identify appropriate targets for each metric. Without benchmarking acting as a check and balance for the goal setting process, the members of the supply

FIGURE 10-1   Supply chain scoreboard framework.

	Inbound to Supplier	Supplier	Supplier to Manufacturer	Manufacturer	Manufacturer to Wholesaler	Wholesaler	Wholesaler to Retailer	Retailer	Retailer to Consumer	Consumer	Reverse Logistics	Total Supply Chain
	⇨	▽	⇨	△	⇨	☐	⇨	◔	⇨	◉	⇦	∑
Finance												
Productivity												
Quality												
Cycle Time												
	Total Supply Performance		Total Manufacturing Performance		Total Wholesaling Performance		Total Retailing Performance		Total Consumer Satisfaction			Total Supply Chain Performance

FIGURE 10-2   Healthcare supply chain scoreboard.

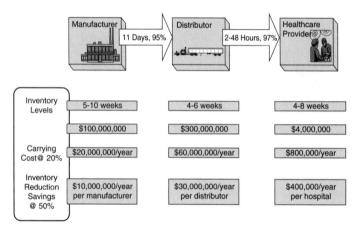

	Manufacturer	Distributor	Healthcare Provider
	11 Days, 95%	2-48 Hours, 97%	
Inventory Levels	5-10 weeks	4-6 weeks	4-8 weeks
	$100,000,000	$300,000,000	$4,000,000
Carrying Cost@ 20%	$20,000,000/year	$60,000,000/year	$800,000/year
Inventory Reduction Savings @ 50%	$10,000,000/year per manufacturer	$30,000,000/year per distributor	$400,000/year per hospital

chain may settle for inappropriately low expectations. If the logistics performance of the supply chain is low relative to its potential, improvement targets may fall short of what can and should be realized. Rich Rankin, logistics manager with SBC, calls it being named Queen of the Hogs—if you are the best performer in a group of underachievers.

Collaborative Planning, Forecasting, and Replenishment (CPFR)

The information that must flow between supply chain partners include item descriptions, order quantities, forecasts, origins, destinations, freight rates, ETAs, performance metrics, dimensions, and so on. That much information cannot flow efficiently through the restricted communication openings in typical supply chains where two individuals, few systems, and a multiplicity of phone calls and faxes make up the entire flow path between players in most supply chains (see Figure 10-3).

FIGURE 10-3   **Typical point-to-point supply chain communications.**

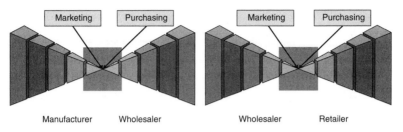

Both organizationally and via new supply chain information system architectures, it is possible and necessary to open up supply chain communications. One organizational structure that lends itself to open supply chain communications is the horizontal process management structure illustrated in Figure 10-4.

The principle in the CPFR organization structure is that, just like the three logistics flows (material flow, information flow, and cash flow) need to be coordinated within an organization, material flow, information flow, and cash flow can and should be coordinated across the supply chain with the chief logistics officers in a supply chain meeting regularly to work out kinks in the material flows; chief information officers meeting regularly to work out kinks in the information flows, and chief financial officers meeting regularly to work out kinks in the cash flows.

The RosettaNet (**www.RosettaNet.org**) initiative connecting the major players in the computing industry supply chain is one example of a CPFR

FIGURE 10-4   **Horizontal supply chain management organization structure.**

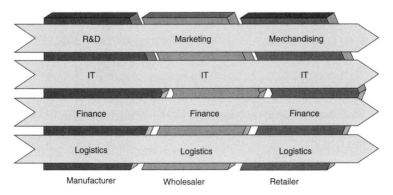

organization structure (see Figure 10-5). There, the major suppliers (Intel and Microsoft), manufacturers (Compaq and Dell), wholesalers (Arrow, Avnet, IngramMicro, and TechData), retailers (CompUSA, MicroAge, and Office Depot), and carriers (UPS and Fedex) meet face-to-face and electronically to determine common metrics and communication protocols for their supply chain.

The information architecture that facilitates the CPFR supply chain organization model is aptly named the *value hub* by i2. The principle of a value hub (see Figure 10-6) is that a neutral third/fourth party adds value to the value chain by creating a hub for electronic communications between major supply chain players. The hub eliminates the need for each party to create individual connections with each of the supply chain players. In addition to the communication links, the hub operator can offer a variety of related services, including transportation/procurement exchanges, application hosting, *electronic funds transfer* (EFT), and *supply chain optimization* (SCO).

Supply Chain Optimization
The best analogy I have found for the principle of SCO is production planning and scheduling. The objective in production planning and scheduling is to maximize the yield of factory (or minimize total production and inventory costs) subject to the constraints of labor availability, raw material availability, machine tool production capacity, material handling system capacity,

FIGURE 10-5 **RosettaNet.org organization structure.**

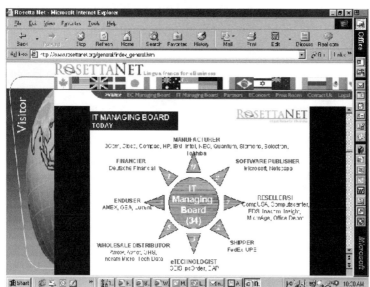

FIGURE 10-6   Value hub concept.
Source: Modified from i2

staging area storage capacities, and due date requirements for production jobs. There are many mathematical formulations for production optimization, and even though there may be thousands of constraints and variables, the algorithms are typically implemented on personal computers. In supply chain planning and scheduling, the objective is to maximize the yield of the supply chain (or minimize total delivered cost) subject to the constraints of labor availability, raw material availability, factory production capacities, transportation system capacities, warehouse storage/handling capacities, and total order cycle time restrictions. It is as if the supply chain was a factory where the machine tools are factories, material handling systems are physical distribution systems (tractor-trailers, ocean vessels, airplanes, and trains), staging areas are standalone warehouses, and production job due dates are order deliver by requirements.

SCO requires each factory in the chain to report production capacities, each carrier in the chain to report transport capacities along each lane, each warehouse in the chain to report storage and handling capacities, and each retailer in the chain to report POS data and time windows for receiving. This dataset is used to form the constraints in a SCO model. A fourth party (typically a consulting firm, software company, or professional association working on behalf of the supply chain) takes the dataset (usually over an intranet) and the agreed upon supply chain objective function and produces an optimized recommendation for retail operating hours, warehouse storage requirements, warehouse operating hours and material handling plans, transportation schedules, production schedules, and order flows. Discrepancies and disagreements can be worked out electronically or in face-to-face meetings. The SCO concept is illustrated in Figure 10-7.

Collaborative Purchasing

Another means for supply chain partners to participate together in logistics initiatives is via collaborative purchasing. In collaborative purchasing, non-competitors going into similar marketplaces may purchase anything from packaging materials to logistics services in collaborative purchasing agreements. As an example, one of the nation's largest cereal companies purchases global transportation services collaboratively with one of the nation's largest pet food companies. The products are going into the same grocery market-places all over the world, yield higher container utilizations, and require the same transportation modes. Coming together in this joint negotiation enables each party to enjoy a 15 percent savings in transportation costs as compared to what could have been negotiated separately.

Strategic Outsourcing

World-class logistics organizations also partner with strategic providers of various logistics services, including transportation management, transportation services, freight forwarding, customs brokerage, warehousing, logistics information systems, logistics exchanges, logistics application service providers, benchmarking, logistics consulting, and logistics professional education. The outsourcing decision for any one of these logistics services

FIGURE 10-7   **Supply chain optimization concept.**

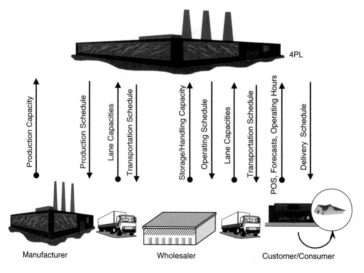

must be made continuously (as the business and logistics environment is changing perpetually) and carefully (because it is much more difficult to re-insource an activity). That said, we are typically cautious in outsourcing rec-ommendations and suggest the following decision criteria to justify outsourcing a logistics activity. We recommend logistics outsourcing if *all* of the following apply:

- There is a *proven* 3PL provider in your industry
- There are *economies* of scope and scale available for the 3PL
- The 3PL has a significant *cost* (-20 percent) and *service advantage*
- Outsourcing is acceptable to the *customer base*
- The 3PL has a better warehouse management system
- There is a culture match between the 3PL and the user

10.2   CORPORATE LOGISTICS ORGANIZATION ALIGNMENT

We often have a "question of the day" contest in our professional education programs. The winner one day and perhaps the winner of all time was a question asked by Roger Montgomery, a logistics manager with QWEST. He sim-ply asked me, "Ed, in your experience with your consulting clients, what is the first, best, and least expensive opportunity for improvement?" Roger made me focus on the fact that the most common and most severe barrier to suc-cess in logistics for nearly all logistics organizations is that they are aligned organizationally and/or via metrics against themselves. Jesus Christ said in Mark 3:25, "If a house is divided against itself, that house cannot stand."

A classic and common example of logistics misalignment occurs when procurement reports through the finance organization and inventory man-agement reports through the logistics organization. In that scenario, the head of procurement is often given the charge to find lower unit cost merchan-dise, and the head of inventory management is given the charge to reduce turns, increase service levels, and reduce lead times. The head of procure-ment charges out to find the lowest cost, sometimes fly-by-night, far-flung vendors in the world offering low unit costs but unreliable service, large bulk buys, and unreachable by most forms of transportation and/or communica-tion. The low unit cost objective is achieved but the poor inventory manager is left holding the bag.

Another common misalignment occurs in retail operations where the store's objective is based on revenue per store and the merchandisers are often working to increase inventory turns. In that scenario, the retail man-ager's worst nightmare is to run out of inventory in the store. In turn, they call in as much inventory for the store floor and back room as possible, thus increasing overall inventory levels in the network and perhaps denying the stores that need the inventory the most.

For political, technical, and cultural reasons, bringing the logistics organization into alignment is easier said than done. To assist our clients with the transition, we normally recommend the gradual approach depicted in Figure 10-8.

Logistics Council

The five-step restructuring typically begins with the creation of a corporate logistics council comprised of the individuals whose decisions impact the flows of material, information, and money across the organization. A typical corporate logistics council would include representation from inbound and outbound transportation, warehousing, procurement, inventory planning, customer service, manufacturing, information technology, and finance. The council should meet at least quarterly (preferably monthly) to begin coordinating the planning and execution of all activities that affect logistics.

Performance Measure Alignment

The second step along the evolutionary path is taken by the logistics council. That step is to develop a set of measures that will align the goals of the individuals and their internal organizations toward a common purpose of satisfying customers at the lowest total logistics cost and maximizing shareholder value through logistics value added concepts. We typically recommend our logistics scoreboard framework of indicators as a starting point in developing the initial set of indicators. The metrics in that framework can

FIGURE 10-8   **Evolutionary steps to an aligned logistics organization.**

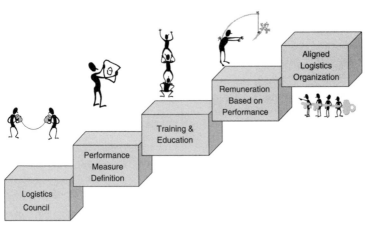

and should be tailored to the particular industry, culture, and existing indicators. The logistics scoreboard framework is illustrated in Figure 10-9. An adaptation of the logistics scoreboard for a recent retail client is illustrated in Figure 10-10.

The logistics scoreboard framework presents a holistic set of indicators for aligning logistics performance toward the unifying goals of reducing total logistics cost, decreasing the logistics labor content per order (measured as the total logistics hours per order shipped), increasing total logistics quality (measured as the perfect order percentage), and decreasing total logistics cycle time. The summary indicators are computed by adding or multiplying the subindicators in the five logistics activities of customer response, inventory planning and management, supply, transportation, and warehousing. Detailed descriptions of each indicator were provided in Chapter 3.

Figure 10-10 illustrates an adaptation of the logistics scoreboard for a recent retail client. The adaptation is based on the flow of product from the creation of the inventory plan for the product to its eventual sell in a store. Metrics are summarized across those activities into total logistics performance measures.

FIGURE 10-9 **Logistics scoreboard framework of indicators.**

	Customer Response	Inventory Planning & Management	Supply	Transportation	Warehousing	Total Logistics
Finance	Total Response Cost (TRC) +	Total Inventory Cost (TIC) +	Total Supply Cost (TSC) +	Total Transportation Cost (TTC) +	Total Warehousing Cost (TWC) =	Total Logistics Cost (TLC)
Productivity	Total Response Hours +	Total Inventory Hours +	Total Supply Hours +	Total Transportation Hours +	Total Warehousing Hours =	Total Logistics Hours/Order
Quality	Perfect Order Entry % x Perfect Order Status % x Perfect Documents % x On-Time Collections % Perfect Response Percentage (PRP)	Order Fill Rate % (OFR)		On-Time Arrival Percentage (OTAP)\ x % Orders without Damage/Claims x % Orders Delivered to Correct Location Perfect Delivery Percentage (PDP)	% Orders without Wrong SKUs x % Orders without Wrong Packaging x % Orders without Wrong Quantities Perfect Shipping Percentage (PSP)	Perfect Order Percentage (POP) = PRP x OFR x PDP x PSP
Response Time	Total Response Time (TRT) = Order Entry Time (OET) + Order Processing time (OPT) + Order Collections Time (OCT)	Purchase Order Cycle Time (POCT)		In-Transit Time (ITT)	Warehouse Order Cycle Time (WOCT)	Total Logistics Cycle Time (TLCT) = TRT + POCT x (1- OFR) + ITT + WOCT

FIGURE 10-10   Adaptation of the logistics scoreboard for retail operations.

	Planning ➧	Buying ➧	Inbound Transportation ➧	Warehousing ➧	Delivery ➧	Store Operations ➧	LOGISTICS
Finance	◆ Property Turns ◆ % time Above Inventory Maximums ◆ AGM=GM–TLC ◆ GMROI		◆ Freight Cost per Unit	◆ Warehousing cost per Unit ($/unit)	◆ Delivered Cost per Unit ($/unit)	◆ Store Turns ◆ AGM=GM - ICC	◆ Total Logistics Cost ◆ TLC/ Sales, Order, SKU, Unit ◆ LGM=GM-TLC
Productivity	◆ SKUs per Full-Time Equivalent ◆ $s per Full-Time Equivalent		◆ Inbound Container Utilization	◆ Warehousing Units per Person-Hour	◆ Delivered Units per Person-Hour ◆ Delivered Units per Operating Hour ◆ Delivery Vehicle Utilization	◆ Units per Person Hour	◆ Units per Logistics Person-Hour ◆ Sales per Logistics FTE ◆ Perfect Orders per Logistics Person-Hour
Quality	◆ Vendor Fill Rate ◆ % Time Below Inventory Minimum		◆ In-Transit Damage % ◆ On-Time Arrival %	◆ Shipping Accuracy ◆ Inventory Accuracy	◆ % In-Transit Damage	◆ Time In-Store Above Presantation Inventory	◆ Perfect Order Percentage
Cycle Time	◆ Receiving to Shipping Weeks Ratio ◆ Purchase Order Prepartion Time		◆ Domestic In - Transit Time ◆ Import In-Transit Time	◆ Dock-to-Stock Time ◆ Warehouse Order Cycle time	◆ % On-Time Arrival	◆ Stocking Cycle Time	◆ Total Logistics Cycle Time

The measurement process should also include on-going external and internal benchmarking to assure appropriate goals are established for each key performance indicator. Gillette's Latin American logistics organization is one of the very best examples of internal logistics alignment and benchmarking. Each year, the logistics managers for each country in Latin America are measured on ten key logistics performance indicators. The managers meet at the end of each year to compare performance results. The winner for each indicator receives an award, but more importantly, must share with the rest of the group the means by which he achieved the high performance score. As a result, the Gillette logistics systems continue to improve based on the measure-based learnings of the logistics professionals.

Logistics Organization Models

The third step in the evolution in corporate logistics organization alignment is the training and education of the logistics council and other key elements of the organization in the principles of integrated logistics and supply chain management. That training is typically the catalyst for the members of the council to ask for a restructuring of the logistics organization. The members of the council see for themselves the benefit to themselves and to the organization for their activities and organization to be integrated. As a part of that training, we typically share with the team a variety of logistics organizational models. Based on the organization's culture, existing organization structure, and business environment, the team begins to naturally gravitate toward a preferred model. The model alternatives include

- Functional organization
- Process organization

- Matrix organization
- Integrated logistics organization
- Global logistics organization
- Business unit logistics organization
- Distributed logistics organization
- Hybrid model

Functional Organization Model

The functional or *silo* organization model is a carryover from the post World War II manufacturing organizations and is an extension of the academic disciplines that are still maintained in most U.S. universities. The functional management philosophy is an advance over the task management focus that the early work of Fred Gilbreath and Frank Taylor promoted.

A typical functional organization concept from a recent retail client is illustrated in Figure 10-11. In their case, logistics only incorporated the traditional transportation and warehousing functions. Because the key performance indicator for logistics was storage and handling cost per unit, the logistics organization would hold outbound store deliveries for as long as possible to create large picking waves and larger outbound shipments. In the meantime, the stores were starved for key products resulting in tremendous lost sales costs in the stores. In this particular case, the lost sales recovery opportunity available from revising the shipping schedule was more than $300,000,000 per year.

The premise of the silo/functional organizational model is that if each silo is optimized, then the entire enterprise performance must be optimized. Of course, this premise turned out to be false. Customers and shareholders are not interested in silo performance, and customer/shareholder value is only really enhanced when the functional, political, and technical silos are shattered and restructured/refocused to target customer, shareholder, and employee satisfaction. We recently named a logistics project Project Jericho because the focus was on bringing down the old walls in the organization.

Process Organization Model

The process organizational model structures people, metrics, and systems around critical business processes. Figure 10-12 illustrates Kraft Food's process organizational model with silo overlays. The model features five key business processes—brand development, consumer development, customer development, supplier development, and supply chain management—that focus the corporate resources—marketing, manufacturing, and logistics—on customer service.

FIGURE 10-11   Functional organization model for retail operations.

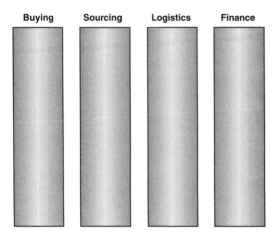

FIGURE 10-12   Kraft Food's process organizational model.

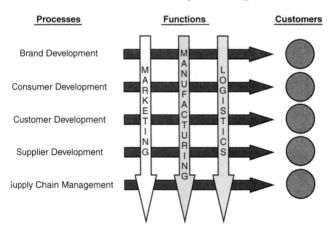

The model requires individuals from a variety of academic and business disciplines to work together toward common goals that relate directly to customer and shareholder value creation.

Matrix Organization Model

The matrix organizational model (see Figure 10-13) is an attempt to combine the functional and process models. It is oftentimes a transitional organization structure. My personal experience and the experience of most of our clients is that the matrix model serves neither the interests of the cus-

FIGURE 10-13   **Matrix organization structure.**

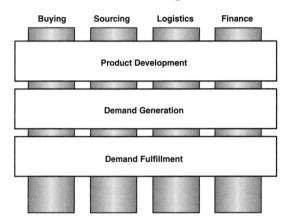

tomers, shareholders, or internal management. The proverb that says "You cannot serve two masters" holds true.

Integrated Logistics Organizational Model
The integrated logistics organizational model (see Figure 10-14) is really focused on the processes of customer satisfaction, supply development, and logistics cost/capital management. The model requires a *chief logistics officer* (CLO) or vice president of logistics who is responsible for the four key total logistics performance indicators: total logistics cost, perfect order percentage, total logistics cycle time, and logistics productivity. The CLO has four direct reports, one each in charge of customer response (customer service and order processing), supply (inventory planning and procurement), distribution (transportation and warehousing), and logistics planning/optimization. The model requires that each direct report deliver superior results in his/her elements of the cross-functional measures of total logistics cost, perfect order percentage, total logistics cycle time, and total logistics productivity. Sears Logistics, Caterpillar Logistics, Walt Disney World, and Keebler are structured in much this same way. Their results with this model have been impressive, and this a popular recommendation for us to make to our clients.

There are two reasons I believe this model works particularly well. First, the organization structure is cleanly aligned with well defined, reliable, and benchmarkable logistics performance indicators. Any time the metrics are vaguely presented and/or the organizational structure is at odds with the metrics that are in use, the total organizational performance will suffer. Second, individual personalities in logistics tend to fall into the three suborganizations: customer response, supply, and distribution. The customer

FIGURE 10-14   **Integrated logistics organization model with Chief Logistics Officer.**

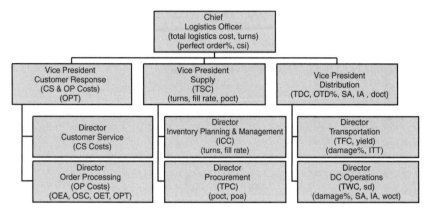

response team is typically and necessarily comprised of the happiest, most joyful, and most optimistic professionals in logistics. These are the individuals who are most adept at customer recovery and can patiently leave a complaining customer smiling at the end of a difficult conversation or series of e-mails. The supply team is typically and necessarily made up of the nerdy analysts with impressive academic credentials, expert spreadsheet skills, and thick glasses. These are the individuals that are the checks and balances between the high-minded objectives of the sales and marketing organization and the conservative concerns of the finance organization. The distribution team is typically and necessarily made up of the rolled-up shirtsleeves crowd that is not afraid to get their hands dirty driving a lift truck or fixing a tractor. These are the individuals who will get the job done, period. Any organizational model that works counter to human nature will fail. The integrated logistics organizational model tends to work in consideration of our God-given gifts and inclinations.

Global Logistics Organization Model

The global logistics organizational model is an extension of the integrated logistics model. In essence, the global logistics model includes an integrated logistics organization for global logistics planning and policy making, regional (that is, North America/NAFTA, Europe/E.U., Asia-Pacific, and Latin America) logistics planning and policy making, and in-country/local (that is, Canada, Spain, Korea, Peru) logistics planning and policy making. Each level has an individual responsible for total logistics, customer response, supply, and distribution. In a typical global logistics organization model, the global logistics management team makes global policy/plans (that is, communication standards, metrics definition, system selections, best-practice templates, vision setting, and so on), and the regional/local management teams adopt those global standards to the unique regional/local conditions. The global logistics organization model has been adopted successfully by Coca-Cola, Nestle, and a variety of pharmaceutical firms.

A recommended global logistics organization structure from a recent client in the health and beauty aids industry is provided in Figure 10-15.

Business Unit Logistics Organization Model

One of the most difficult questions to answer in logistics organization design and development is if and when a business unit should have its own logistics organization. The classic tradeoff is between the leveraging of assets that is available when multiple business units utilize the same logistics assets (distribution centers, transportation fleets, inventory, logistics information systems, and logistics personnel) and the control that may be lost to a particular business unit when a designated logistics infrastructure is not dedicated to those particular needs. The evaluation usually comes down to an analysis of the logistics synergies that are available across business units. Those synergies are created when different business units are logistically similar in key areas, including order profiles, response time requirements, customer base, supplier base, carrier base, and inventory profiles. If those similarities are not evident, it most often is advisable to dedicate a logistics organization to a business unit. Otherwise, the logistics similarities can be leveraged to create high efficiencies in the leveraging of logistics assets across business units. Most business unit managers will go along if the benefits of the leveraging are passed along to the business unit, if the logistics manager is competent and politically astute, and if there is no major barrier

FIGURE 10-15   **Global logistics organization model.**

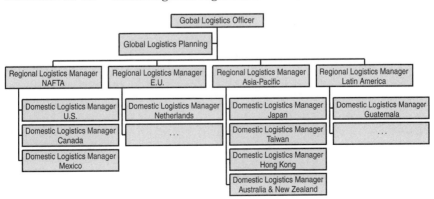

to customer satisfaction in the cross business unit model. In some situations, customer satisfaction may be improved due to the multiple business unit economies of scale that may permit the justification of advanced logistics information systems and material handling automation.

A recent client in the book distribution business was able to achieve both objectives simultaneously (see Figure 10-16). The logistics organization at Lifeway Christian Resources supplies retail stores, mail order customers, and thousands of churches with a variety of Christian media, including books, tapes, CDs, videos, magazines, and Bible lessons. All three business units are supplied from a common inventory and distribution center. The organization buys jointly for all business units and houses all reserve inventory in a common storage area. However, each business unit is supported with a standalone order picking area designed to accommodate the unique order profiles and customer service requirements of the unique business units. The processed orders then flow through a common sorting system for outbound deliveries.

Distributed Logistics Organizational Model

The distributed logistics organizational model (see Figure 10-17) eliminates any formal logistics organization other than a CLO. Instead, logisticians are recruited and developed by the CLO and placed in the other areas of the corporation with the responsibility to incorporate sound logistics practices into the traditional corporate activities of marketing, research and development,

FIGURE 10-16   Business unit logistics organization model.
Source: Lifeway Christian Resources

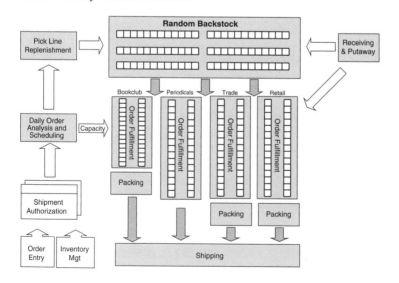

FIGURE 10-17   **Distributed logistics organization model.**

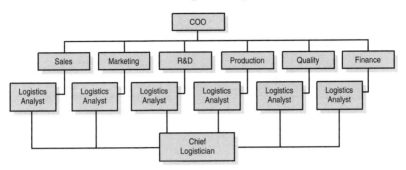

sales, manufacturing, information systems, finance, and so on. The model works similar to the concept of total quality management adopted by Motorola and Applied Signal where TQM experts (blackbelts) are placed in each area of the corporation to introduce quality management disciplines. Dell Computer is one of the most successful distributed logistics organizational models.

10.3   LOGISTICS STRATEGIC PLANNING AND PROJECT MANAGEMENT

Logistics is by nature a fire fighting business. Unfortunately, many organizations reward fire fighting at the exclusion of long-range planning. We worked on a project recently with a service parts logistics organization in Silicon Valley. Our client's customers were the chip factory managers at the likes of Intel, Motorola, Fujitsu, and IBM. If a fab line was shut down because our client was late in delivering, our client was charged $200,000 per hour of downtime. We were retained by our client to assist them in creating a long-range logistics strategy. As it turned out, each trip we made to the west coast was filled up with "hair on fire" issues to resolve. We were helpful with the "hair on fire" issues, but they really needed a strategy that would help them minimize the number of "hair on fire" issues. That's the purpose of a long-range strategy. I always think about the game at the arcades where the more gophers you beat back into their hole, the higher your score. In business, the real winners have the fewest gophers jumping up out of holes.

The need for a more formal approach to logistics strategy in U.S. industry was highlighted in recent surveys by the Ohio State University (see Figure 10-18) and KPMG (see Figure 10-19). Both surveys indicated that just around half of all U.S. enterprises have a formal logistics strategy. (The survey did not indicate whether the existing strategy was working or not, just that there was one.)

FIGURE 10-18 Strategic planning in corporate functions.
Source: Ohio State University

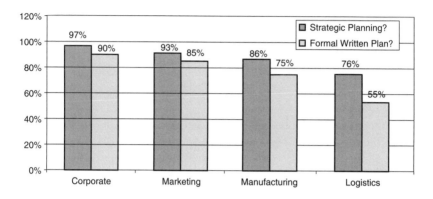

FIGURE 10-19 Portion of U.S. companies (by annual sales) with a logistics strategy.
Source: KPMG

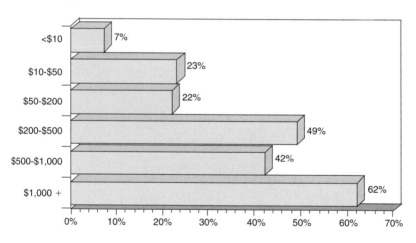

With logistics playing an increasingly important role in corporate growth, in determining competitive advantage, and in creating shareholder value, we have a lot of ground to make up in overcoming the historical neglect of logistics as a strategic focus for the corporation.

Our experience has revealed that effective logistics strategic planning and project management is characterized by

- Dedicated planning resources and programs
- Formal methodology for logistics strategic planning process

Dedicated Planning Resources and Programs

If the proper resources (money, time, staff, and systems) are not set aside for long-range planning, it will not be carried out to the level of detail necessary to truly assess the ways in which changes in the economic, technological, competitive, demographic, and regulatory environments are affecting long-range logistics requirements. In our recent project in Silicon Valley, I finally had to meet with the COO to suggest that we disengage unless they were willing to support the planning program with the necessary internal resources. Our corporate consulting philosophy says that, "People will only successfully implement what they design themselves." Therefore, we don't believe in handing off a long-range strategy to a client if the client has not been the primary source of resources in the planning program.

To formalize the logistics planning process, we typically recommend that a dedicated logistics planning team be organized to report to a CLO or to serve as a dedicated resource for a corporate logistics council. Figure 10-20 illustrates a logistics organization structure incorporating a logistics planning team. The logistics planning team should include the analytical and operational backgrounds required to resolve complex issues in supply chain engineering, customer service policy design, inventory planning, transportation operations design, warehouse engineering, and logistics performance metrics. In addition, the team members should have established credibility with the operational elements of the logistics organization.

A number of organizations have recently established project management offices and project management as a corporate discipline. The project management office provides, updates, and teaches best practices in project management that become standards throughout the organization. The standards

FIGURE 10-20   **Logistics organization with logistics planning team.**

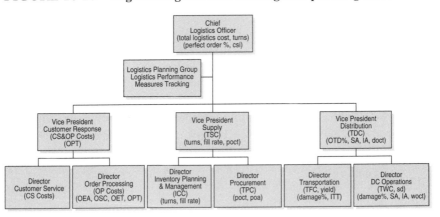

include selected project management tools, recommended project management review points, templates for timelines and presentations, spreadsheet formats for return-on-investment calculations, and guidelines for staffing and project funding.

Formalized Logistics Planning Methodology

Because logistics is fraught with interdependencies between its activities (customer response, inventory planning, supply, transportation, and warehousing) and the activities it impacts in other areas of the corporation (sales and marketing, regulatory compliance, human resources, research and development, and finance), if there is no formal methodology for planning, the planning process typically implodes, frustrates the planning team, and/or winds up with the most forceful member of the team driving the plan toward his/her objectives. Unfortunately, unlike information systems that have been around for some time and for which a variety of formal planning methodologies are available, logistics has really only been recognized in private industry since 1982, the year the *National Council of Physical Distribution Management* (NCPDM) was renamed the *Council of Logistics Management* (CLM). As a result, there are very few methodologies available for logistics strategic planning.

To assist our clients in navigating through the maze of long and short-term issues in logistics, LRI developed the *logistics master planning* (LMP) methodology (see Figure 10-21). The methodology uses a database of world-class practices to walk organizations through the process of developing (1) measures, (2) process designs, (3) system requirements, and (4) organization requirements for logistics as a whole, (a) customer response, (b) inventory management, (c) supply, (d) transportation, and (e) warehousing. Whether for an entire supply chain strategy or a single planning element for one logistics activity, we always work through the three phases of investigate, imagine, and implement. In the *investigation* phase, we compare the client's current performance, practices, and systems with world-class standards. We often conduct a logistics audit as a part of this phase to determine the overall return-on-investment opportunity associated with a world-class logistics initiative. In the *imagination* phase, we apply world-class practices to the current and anticipated business/logistics environment to recommend short and long-term designs and initiatives. In the *implementation* phase, we develop and monitor detailed project plans for completing the recommended initiatives. An example LMP stemming from LMP program is provided in Figure 10-22. The LMP defines specific initiatives in the five major areas of logistics, the cost of each initiative, the system requirements for each initiative, and the suggested timing.

FIGURE 10-21   Logistics master planning methodology.

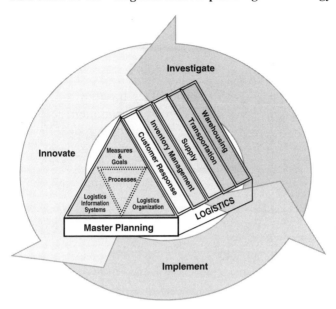

10.4   LOGISTICS PROCESS AND ACTIVITY MANAGEMENT

So far, we have been considering logistics between enterprises, between activities within the enterprise, and as a standalone activity. Now, we consider the organization of the activities within logistics—customer response, inventory management, supply, transportation and warehousing. There are unique aspects to each logistics activity that call for tailored management approaches.

Customer Response

Customer response is unique to the other logistics activities because it is the activity where most direct customer communications take place. That communications interface goes a long way toward determining overall customer satisfaction levels. As a result, there are a variety of practices that we recommend to clients to help them maintain the most effective customer communications possible.

Customer Focus Groups   Customer focus groups are small groups of customers that represent the overall business. The groups come together in face-to-face or online meetings to act as a sounding board for new products or service offerings the enterprise is considering. It is essentially a customer board of directors. The feedback is invaluable for developing reliable input for customer response planning.

Logistics Master Plan

Initiative	Recommendation	Estimated Expense	Estimated Duration	System Reqts.
Store Service				
Store Service Metrics	Create and implement store service performance measures.		3	LS
Store Service Segmentation	Segment store service policy by channel, store, commodity group, and SKU.		2	CAP
Store Service Optimization	Optimize store fill rate.	$24	4	FRP
	Optimize store delivery frequency.	$24	3	DFP
Store Replenishment	Implement vendor managed inventory or automated continuous replenishment to close the order entry gap.	$500	12	EDI
Inventory Management				
Inventory Performance Metrics	Implement inventory performance metrics.		3	LS
Intelligent Forecasting	Implement intelligent forecasting methodologies.		6	
	Establish dedicated forecasting personnel.		2	
	If required, select and implement forecasting package.	$200	6	
Supply				
Supply Performance Metrics	Implement financial, productivity, quality, and response time metrics for supply partners.		3	LS
	Implement productivity metrics for the supply process.		3	LS
Supply Flow Optimization	Determine DSD, XD, and DC flow paths based on total logistics cost and service implications.	$80	9	CAPS
	Determine potential benefits of inbound transportation consolidation, cross-trucking, backhauling, and mini-DCs.		3	CAPS
Collaborative Planning & Supply Chain Scheduling	Meet with key supply partners on an on-going basis to jointly plan logistics schedules and backhaul opportunities.		3	POS
	Share point-of-sale data with key suppliers.		4	EDI
	Integrate continuous replenishment with supplier production scheduling.		6	WMS EDI
	Implement receiving appointment scheduling.		3	EDI
	Establish annual supplier logistics conference.		1	
Transportation				
Transportation Performance Metrics	Implement and institute an formal transportation performance measures program.		3	TS
Optimal, Dynamic Routing	Implement a on-line, real-time, routing optimization software (e.g. Road show, CAPS Logistics, MANUGISTICS, Blast).	$80	6	RS
Roll Cages	Utilize collapsible roll cages for order picking and store shelf restocking.		3	
DC Operations				
Pre-Receiving	Eliminate receiving inspection for "green-light" vendors and sample receiving inspection for "yellow-light" vendors.		6	EDI
Slotting Optimization	Implement a PC-based tool for assigning SKUs to storage modes, allocating space within each mode, and locating an SKU within the mode.	$40	4	SP
WMS	Analyze WMS requirements beyond SAP capabilities.	$300	3	WMS
Pick and Price	Investigate the costs and benefits and pricing product during the picking process.	$20	3	WMS

Involvement columns: Customer Service, Inventory Management, Transportation, Warehousing. Timing columns: 1–12.

FIGURE 10-22 Logistics master plan example.

Dedicated, Personalized Account Teams   In the age of tele- versus personal communications, customers increasingly appreciate dedicated and personal response to their issues. The personalization may be carried out by an individual or a group of individuals who are familiar with their concerns, and it should be supported with advanced customer relationship management capability. Some transaction center management systems are sophisticated enough to route a call or incoming e-mail automatically to the most appropriate individual to respond to the transaction.

Multilingual, Multicultural   Economic globalization, political globalization, and the World Wide Web make it increasingly likely that an order and a customer will be from somewhere other than the United States. In fact, it is projected that by the year 2005, English will be a minority language on the Internet. That said, the culturally tailored customer is an increasingly important aspect of global customer response. Culturally tailored customers require speaking in the customers language and dialect, operating during their normal business hours ($7 \times 24 \times 365$), understanding the current and business events impacting them, and respectful protocols.

Transaction Center Monitoring   Each customer interface should be monitored to record the length of the transaction, the wait time experienced by the customer, the number of balks due to wait time or down time, and the overall satisfaction with the transaction experienced by the customer.

Inventory Management

Because inventory investment and availability is so critical to the overall success of a logistics-oriented enterprise, the organization of the inventory management activity is crucial to the success of the organization as a whole. Within the inventory management activity, we recommend the following organizational techniques. The techniques are designed to assist the enterprise with increasing inventory turns and service levels at the same time.

Dedicated Forecasting Organization   If forecasting is carried out in anything other than a dedicated forecasting organization, the forecast will carry some inherent biases. For example, if the forecast is developed in the sales organization, the forecast will be biased upward if the sales culture rewards optimism or biased downward if the culture rewards exceeding expectations. Knowing these inherent biases, the other parts of the organization—manufacturing, warehousing, transportation, and so on—begin to create their own forecasts, adjusted in their favor. All of sudden, there is no real forecast, just a variety of interpretations of projected sales adjusted in each party's favor. This is a result of human nature and individuals following the organization's spoken or unspoken system of metrics. We can borrow an analogy from music, where to get many instruments playing together in concert, all the musicians need to be working from the same sheet of music and under the direction of a single director.

We typically recommend that an individual or group of individuals be dedicated to the forecasting process. Their evaluation is based solely on the accuracy of the forecast at all levels. That forecast is produced and shared at all levels in the organization and in all relevant units of measure.

Certification in Inventory Management Principles   The tradeoffs in inventory management are many, varied, and oftentimes counterintuitive. The interdependencies and analytics involved in forecasting, lost sales computations, order quantity engineering, safety stock calculations, reorder points, combined replenishments, and so on have left many of the best logistics organizations in a supply chain quandary. The level of understanding of the tradeoffs and analysis imbedded in these critical inventory management decisions cannot be underestimated. Yet, many of the largest inventory management organizations in the United States are staffed with individuals who have not been formally trained in the science of inventory management.

We recommend that individuals in key inventory management roles be certified in inventory decision science through organizations like APICS or The Logistics Institute at Georgia Tech.

Integration with all Other Logistics Activities   The decisions made by individuals working in customer service, procurement, manufacturing, transportation, and warehousing all impact inventory investments and availability. Operating in isolation, those individuals and teams cannot possibly maximize the effectiveness of the inventory that is available to the enterprise. Those individuals and teams should operate with a common purpose and plan toward utilizing the inventory investment. That common purpose and plan should be established in shared meetings, metrics, and systems that give visibility and urgency to the inventory performance of the enterprise.

Evaluations Based on Performance to Target Fill Rates and Turn Objectives   Because there is a dual objective in inventory management—maximize service levels and minimize inventory investment—the individuals responsible for managing inventory should have individual evaluations based on the service level and inventory investment performance of the items under their management.

Supply

The customer response organization is responsible for developing and implementing a customer service policy addressing the inventory levels that will be made available to various classes of customers for various classes of items.

The inventory management organization is responsible for establishing the inventory targets throughout the supply chain that will satisfy the customer service policy, yet will minimize the overall inventory investment. The supply organization is responsible for acquiring the inventory that will meet the target levels established in the inventory plan, within the response time requirements of the customer service policy, at the quality levels established by the quality organization, and at the lowest possible total acquisition cost. That acquisition cost should include the unit cost paid to the supplier (or manufacturing cost transferred internally), transportation costs, importing costs, and related inventory carrying costs.

Integration with Other Logistics Activities   Due to misalignment in the logistics organization or a lack of education, supply specialists are often not aware of the impact of their decisions on the other logistics activities. One example is the common complaint from the warehouse when a shipment arrives that the warehouse management was not expecting and in a quantity that the warehouse cannot accommodate. The choice of suppliers, their location(s), and their systems/logistics capabilities have major impacts on total logistics costs, inventory investments, and overall customer satisfaction. Yet, many supply organizations do not coordinate their choice of suppliers or purchase quantities with the other logistics activities. Just the cost implications of the supply plan listed previously stresses the need for the supply organization to coordinate their decision making with the other logistics activities.

Supplier Logistics Certification   Unfortunately, it is common to promote individuals into supply specialist positions when they do not have adequate training or awareness of the impact of their decisions on the rest of the organizations. We recently completed an assignment with a large retailer where less than 15 percent of the buying staff had any formal training in logistics or inventory management. Because the decisions made by supply specialists have such a major impact on all the logistics activities, the supply specialists should have formal training in logistics and inventory management in addition to their formal training in procurement issues related to the commodities they are working with. The National Association of Purchasing Management, APICS, CLM, and The Logistics Institute at Georgia Tech are all excellent sources for professional education in logistics and inventory management.

Global Sourcing   Expensive and scarce domestic labor in developed countries and growing global centers of manufacturing excellence require organizations to search for global sources. Through trading companies, internal sourcing organizations, and/or sourcing consulting services, every enterprise should have an active program in place to search out new international sources of product. Once those sources have been identified, the sourcing evaluation should consider carefully the impact of the international source on transportation, inventory carrying, importing, administration, and warehousing costs. The advantage in initial unit cost can be lost quickly in the incremental costs of landing the product domestically.

Commodity Specialization in Buying Cells   Due to wide variation in packaging, material composition, dimensions, weight, order profiles, and supplier capabilities, every product and every supplier is logistically unique. As a result, a degree of special knowledge is required when dealing with logistically distinct products and suppliers. That special knowledge is best acquired on the job through an apprentice/mentoring program and professional education aimed at transferring special knowledge related to the product/supplier logistics issues. The buying cell concept, teams of buyers working together on inbound logistics for related items/suppliers, fosters the transfer of knowledge.

Supplier Relationship Management (SRM)   The supplier base is really an extension of the enterprise. As such, the supplier relationships (face-to-face, telecommunications, and the Internet) need to be developed as aggressively as the customer relationships. The reliability, predictability, and value added in the links with suppliers is the foundation for the ability to serve customers reliably, predictably, and with increasing value. Wal-Mart's supplier relationships (though criticized as heavy handed in many circles) are the foundation of their business success. Dell Computer and Harley-Davidson's on-site supplier community serve as the foundation for their successes in logistics. These relationships have been developed through a formal SRM program. Those SRM programs include annual conferences where logistics trends in all organizations are shared, upcoming business initiatives that will impact the supplier community are presented, and agreements are reached for future logistics standards and capabilities.

Transportation

The transportation industry and the transportation activity within most major enterprises are stressed today beyond any other day in recent memory. Any transportation professional working today feels the stress of the need to move more smaller loads more often with less margin for error in the face of a severe driver shortage and increasing fuel costs. I am convinced that a major source of the difficulty is the lack of strategic planning and organization development within transportation companies, within the transportation activities of most major corporations, and within the government authorities that have regulated transportation activities over the years. Though the oldest of what we now call logistics activities, somehow, transportation is the least developed organizationally. The planning disciplines and supporting systems that are characteristic of the customer service organization, inventory management organization, supply organization, and even the warehousing organization are not as developed in transportation and distribution organizations.

We recommend the following set of initiatives and programs be implemented within the transportation activities of our major clients.

Core Carrier Programs and Carrier Relationship Management   Similar to SRM programs, carrier relationship management programs are designed to formalize the communication, partnering, negotiating, and performance monitoring aspects of carrier management. At the heart of most carrier relationship management programs are a set of guidelines for selecting core carriers, the minority of carriers who carry a majority of the enterprise's weight, cube, and shipments.

Corporate Traffic Councils   Corporate traffic councils bring together all personnel working in the area of transportation within an enterprise. The traffic council sets corporate transportation policy and explores opportunities for leveraging transportation spending across the corporation.

Training and Certification in Transportation Management   Because transportation is heavy-laden with changing regulations, complex terminology, multiple personnel issues, and layers of required documentation, ongoing training and certification for transportation managers helps insure that transportation remains transparent to the public, customers, and internally, corporations make and maintain transportation as a value-added activity.

Driver Certification and Quality of Life Programs   Due to increasing demands for all modes of trucking, low unemployment, and pending regulatory constraints on driving hours and schedules, the economy is facing a severe driver shortage. Recent estimates suggest that there will be a shortfall of nearly 100,000 truck drivers during the upcoming Christmas season. As demands on drivers increase, as traffic congestion increases, as transportation infrastructure begins to falter, the need for certified, more experienced, and more highly qualified drivers has never been more severe. In fact, those organizations who have maintained a highly qualified driving staff are experiencing a significant competitive advantage in some industries.

For example, with driver tenures sometimes averaging less than one year, a recent client leveraged a driving team with average tenure of more than 13 years to establish a dominant industry position in customer service and related market share. When I asked the fleet manager how he had been able to maintain such a low turnover amongst the drivers, he shared that he had designed the transportation network and related schedules around the quality of life of the drivers. (The network design enabled the drivers to return home most nights and always on the weekends.) Though perhaps slightly more expensive in fuel than some possible network designs, this organization's driver-friendly network design paid overwhelming dividends in market share, customer service, and driver turnover.

Joint Procurement of Transportation Services   Significant savings in freight payments can be achieved if the purchase and negotiation of transportation services is consolidated across inbound/outbound transportation activities within a business unit, across business units, and even with noncompetitors servicing similar markets. One example of joint transportation procurement is the global transportation services agreement that two large food companies utilize. One company manufactures cereal, the other confections and pet food. Both serve the same marketplaces yet do not compete. Their joint procurement program yields seven-figure savings each year. Another example is a joint fleet procurement program utilized by a large beverage company and a large rental car company.

Logistics Compliance and Security Officer   Though "de-regulated" in the early 1980's, transportation is still fraught with international, federal, and state regulations. Maintaining compliance is key to maintaining good public, government, and business relations. With increasing numbers of transportation transactions more and more likely to traverse multiple borders, regulatory compliance is more and more difficult to maintain. To help an organization stay in step with regulatory developments, we typically recommend that a logistics compliance officer be put in place to develop enterprise guidelines, programs, and systems to insure enterprise-wide compliance with global, federal, and state regulations that relate to transportation and logistics.

A recent client recruited an attorney with a special interest in logistics to serve in this role. The individual graduated from our logistics management series as a prerequisite to his accepting the position and as a supplement to his legal training. Another client sent their corporate director of safety and security through the logistics management series to prepare him for a role as vice president of logistics security and compliance. One global consumer electronics firm established the position of chief logistics intelligence officer to help them comply with global logistics law and to anticipate security lapses within their logistics network.

Participation in Transportation Industry Forums   One means of anticipating and staying in step with developments in transportation regulation is to participate actively in industry forums and professional associations where transportation issues are debated. Those forums include the *Council of Logistics Management* (CLM), *National Trucking Council* (NTC), NAAS-TRAC, and the *Intermodal Association of North America* (IANA).

Recruiting from Carriers Transportation is not the core activity for most businesses, and it is a highly complex activity to manage. As a result, when staffing an internal transportation organization, we encourage our clients to recruit from carriers, where transportation is a way of life.

Warehousing

The plight of the warehouse manager is not much better and perhaps worse than the plight of the transportation manager. Required to execute more transactions, in less time, with more items, with less margin for error, with less skilled labor, the warehouse manager's role has risen to mission critical. The capabilities of the warehouse workforce have also risen to mission critical status. Unfortunately, the development and capabilities of most warehouse workforces and supporting information systems are lacking in the face of e-commerce, same-hour delivery, and no-fault performance.

Safety and Ergonomic Training One reason the turnover of warehouse personnel is so high is a basic premise of human psychology. When people feel threatened or unsafe in any environment, their natural reaction is to flee. If the dock is unsafe, if order pickers sustain back injuries, or if the workforce is infiltrated by drug users and/or pilferers, the instinct of the most qualified workers will be to flee. My experience with our clients is that the ones with the most stable and productive warehouse working teams are the ones with the most developed programs for safety training, ergonomics, drug and substance-abuse screening, and housekeeping.

Time Standards, Incentives, and Personnel Scheduling With warehouse worker availability at a premium and time of the essence, the ability to monitor, motivate, and schedule each task within the warehouse is a critical capability in warehouse workforce management. Time standards enable warehouse managers to develop staffing requirements in each area within the warehouse. Incentives for productivity and quality help to motivate excellent performance and reward outstanding performance. Personnel scheduling minimizes the likelihood of bottlenecking in the warehouse and facilitates the movement of personnel between activities within the warehouse.

Optimal Management-Operator Ratios There was a move a few years ago toward self-directed work teams in warehouse operations. As warehouse activities have become more complex, as the availability of qualified warehousing professionals has declined, and as the fallacies of self-direction without adequate training and tools have been exposed, there has been a renewed interest in the fundamentals of warehouse workforce management. One of the most important fundamentals of warehouse management is the span of control within the operations. Our experience shows that operator-supervisor ratios in excess of 1:17 do not permit adequate supervision and that ratios less than 1:14 are too costly.

Cross-Training   Cross-training is the practice of preparing warehouse operators to work in multiple areas within the warehouse. The practice is especially effective when the timing of activity peaks do not coincide in the operating areas in the warehouse. In those scenarios, the cross-trained workers can move between the peak activity areas as workload mandates. Cross-training can reduce the overall staffing requirements in proportion to the ratio of the peak to average activity levels.

Soko Circles   Quality circles are nothing new. The concept originated in Japanese automobile factories where groups of workers would meet in small teams to coordinate problem solving for quality issues on the production floor. More than ten years ago, I borrowed the Japanese word for warehouse, soko, to coin the phrase soko circles. Soko circles are quality circles working in warehouse operations. I have only seen the concept applied in a few warehouse operations in the United States. One of those is the JC Penney catalog distribution centers, where problem solving teams meet regularly to resolve quality issues on the warehouse floor. Another example is the Walt Disney World attractions merchandise DC where workers meet in continuous improvement teams to develop floor-level implementation plans for new warehousing initiatives. In both instances, the concept is the foundation for the management philosophy and works to foster excellent relationships between the warehouse management and the warehouse workforce.

At a time when warehouse quality and accuracy have become competitive differentiators, it is time for the warehouse workforce to become more prepared for and more involved in warehouse solution design and implementation. We worked recently with a large retailer in the design of a range of new warehousing initiatives. Part of the implementation plan was a series of training sessions for the entire warehouse workforce that shared the warehousing principles underpinning the new initiatives. The workforce could then understand the motivation for the new systems and procedures and embrace the new operating concepts based on their understanding as opposed to their directives.

1/2 × 2 × 3   There is an organizational philosophy that theorizes if you take the top 1/2 of the workforce and pay each of them twice as much, then you accomplish three times as much work as was previously being accomplished. I'm not sure where the theory came from, but I do believe the underlying principle has some merit. Our clients who focus rewards and attention on the top performers, who pay higher than the industry norms for qualified warehouse personnel, and who work to weed out the operators who are impeding the overall effectiveness of the entire workforce have much lower overall operating costs and much higher shipping accuracy.

The last three principles address the relationship of logistics professionals to their working environment and the community to the logistics of the enterprise.

10.5   LOGISTICS PROFESSIONAL DEVELOPMENT

One of my driving motivations for establishing The Logistics Institute at Georgia Tech was my observation that the level of understanding of logistics concepts was underdeveloped in most organizations. Yet, it is that understanding or lack thereof that ultimately determines the success or failure of logistics projects. Because less than one-third of logistics projects ever meet their intended goals, industry is paying a high price for this lack of understanding. We created The Logistics Institute to raise the level of understanding of logistics concepts and to increase the likelihood of logistics projects yielding their intended results through logistics professional development.

Another observation I made in working with our clients is that a very small minority of the professionals working in logistics have any kind of formal education in logistics. The ones that do are in high demand. As a result, the turnover of logistics professionals (especially in logistics services companies) is extraordinarily high. The key to maintaining high levels of logistics performance is keeping high performing logistics professionals on the job. The key to keeping high performers on the job is to challenge them professionally. The key to challenging them is to continue to develop their education and skills in logistics.

The very best logistics organizations maintain formal career paths and development programs for their logistics professionals. (This is the best way we have found to combat logistics naivety.) We have worked with a variety of logistics organizations that maintain dedicated human resources staff to focus solely on developing the logistics workforce. We worked with another large organization to develop an internal logistics institute to help the logistics professionals maintain their cutting edge understanding and implementation of advanced logistics concepts (see Figure 10-23).

10.6   HUMAN-FRIENDLY LOGISTICS

One of the most basic of all human instincts is to flee in the presence of real or perceived danger. Another basic human instinct is seek out a higher quality of working life. Because logistics work (in warehousing and transportation in particular) is some of the most dangerous work in all of industry and offers a low quality of working life in many organizations, it should not come

FIGURE 10-23   **Internal logistics professional development program.**

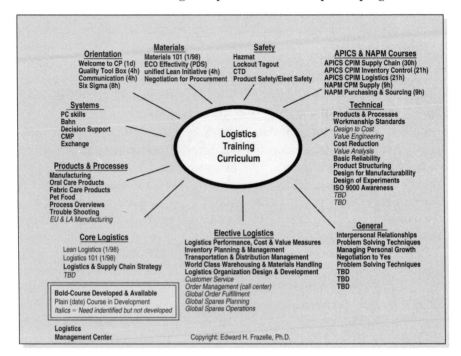

as a surprise that turnover in the logistics workforce is perhaps the greatest barrier to productivity improvements. The effect is aggravated in times of low unemployment as is the case today. In most warehouses today, it is difficult to keep someone on-post for more than three months. The truck driver shortage is so severe that a shortfall of over 100,000 truck drivers is expected in the United States within the year.

World-class logistics organizations understand that they are competing with other disciplines and other industries for the best employees. A common theme in those same organizations is an attempt to develop human-friendly logistics policies and procedures. Human-friendly logistics is based on the Golden Rule—treat people the way you would like to be treated. I encourage our clients to think of themselves or their children working in the positions and work environments they are creating. That mindset is required to invoke the disciplines of human-friendly logistics. Those disciplines include

- Human-friendly transportation
  - Driver routes and schedules that minimize time away from families
  - On-board communications

- Speed governors to eliminate the temptation to speed
- Loading and unloading aids for heavy and/or awkward loads
- Human-friendly warehousing
  - Golden zoning to keep most picking activity at or near waist level
  - Lifting aids to reduce back injuries
  - Waist-level handling and lifting aids to reduce back injuries
  - Natural light and color coordination
  - On-the-job time for housekeeping and problem resolution
  - Safety and ergonomic training and aids to reduce injuries of all kinds

These human-friendly logistics practices will probably never make logistics the most preferred work in all of industry, but they will help make logistics safe, pleasant, and satisfying work, and will help attract and keep high-performers gainfully employed in the logistics workforce.

10.7 COMMUNITY-FRIENDLY LOGISTICS

I am sad to admit that my profession, logistics, is one of the most environmentally harmful industrial activities. Consider these examples of the impact of logistics activity on the environment:

- I was shocked one day when a professional in the packaging industry shared with me that nearly half of all material in U.S. landfills is logistics related (primarily discarded packaging and dunnage).
- My friend and mentor, Professor Jun Suzuki's work in Japan has demonstrated the link between inefficient logistics practices and excessive CO^2 emissions.
- $7 \times 24 \times 365$ logistics operations increase noise and light pollution as trucks move around the clock and warehouse operations keep their lights on all hours.
- Home delivery and inefficient load planning contribute to traffic congestion in all major metropolitan areas.

The situation is so severe in Atlanta and throughout Georgia that several large corporations have selected surrounding states to locate major manufacturing operations. The newly elected Governor Roy Barnes even included logistics reform as a part of his election campaign.

I believe that logistics does not have to be a drain on the environment, but instead can work to preserve (and even replenish) natural resources and protect (and even improve) the environment. The key to the turnaround is what we call community-friendly logistics. The disciplines of community-friendly logistics include

- Returnable and reuseable containers
- Recyclable and decomposable dunnage
- Strategic reverse logistics management
- Regional transportation authorities
- Regional traffic management systems
- Intelligent vehicle highway systems
- Off-peak routing and scheduling

Some recently announced programs by the U.S. Department of Transportation will yield significant improvements. Operation Timesaver aimed at reducing average commute times by 15 minutes is one example. The Intelligent Vehicle Highway System initiative, incorporating collision-avoidance technology and automated traffic management systems, is another example. State governments are also beginning to appreciate the benefits of improving their own logistics. The *Georgia Regional Transit Authority* (GRTA) incorporating the concerns of the major transportation authorities and corporations is another example. These programs will take time to implement, and in the meantime, logistics professionals will have to take the responsibility (which is theirs to take) of including environmental impact in their logistics decision making. The typical push-back is the false assumption that community-friendly logistics practices are more expensive. My experience is just the opposite.

ACRONYMS AND ABBREVIATIONS

ACR	asset carrying rate (percent/year)
AD	annual demand (units per year)
ADS	annual dollar sales (dollars per year)
ADT	average daily traffic
AFE	average forecast error
AGVS	automated guided vehicle system
AI	allocated inventory (units)
AIL	average inventory level (units)
AIV	average inventory value (dollars)
AMS	automated manifest system
ANSI	American National Standards Institute
APS	advanced planning system
ASP	application service provider
ASRS	automated storage and retrieval system
ATP	available to promise
AUS	annual unit sales (units per year)
AWB	airway bill
AWH	annual working hours
BO	backorder
BOA	basic order agreement
BOL	bill of lading
C	unit cube (cubic feet/unit)
CAD	computer-aided design
CAM	computer-aided manufacturing

C&F	cost and freight
C/E	country of export
CF	cubic feet
CFM	continuous flow manufacturing
CI	commercial invoice
CIV	commercial invoice value
CIF	cost, insurance, and freight
CIM	computer integrated manufacturing
C/L	carload
CLM	Council of Logistics Management
CO	customer order
COD	cash on delivery
COO	country of origin
CPFR	collaborative planning, forecasting, and replenishment
CPU	central processing unit
CR	customer response
CRP	continuous replenishment program
CRS	customer response system
CRT	cathode ray tube
CSL	customer service level (percentage)
CSR	customer service representative
DC	distribution center
DCC	distribution center capacity (units)
DCO	distribution center operations
DDP	delivered duty paid
DDU	delivered duty unpaid
DOH	days-on-hand (days)
DOS	days of supply (days)
DRP	distribution requirements planning
DSD	direct store delivery
DTS	dock to stock
EAN	European article number
ECR	efficient consumer response
EDI	electronic data interchange
ELQ	efficient logistics quantity (units per order)
EMI	efficient manufacturing inventory
EOQ	efficient order quantity (units per order)
ERP	enterprise resource planning
ETA	estimated time of arrival
ETD	estimated time of departure

EVA	economic value added
EXW	ex-works
FAA	Federal Aviation Administration
FAD	forecasted annual demand (units per time period)
FAS	free alongside ship
FCL	full container load
FHA	Federal Highway Administration
FIFO	first-in, first-out
FIT	facility inventory turnover
FLD	forecasted lead-time demand (units per lead time period)
FOB	free on-board
FTE	full-time equivalent
FTFR	first-time fill-rate (percentage)
FTL	full truckload
FTZ	free (or foreign) trade zone
GATT	General Agreement on Tariffs and Trade
GLIB	global logistics and international business
GM	gross margin
GMROI	gross margin return on inventory
HazMat	hazardous materials
HOV	high-occupancy vehicle
HSR	high-speed rail
ICC	International Chamber of Commerce
ICC	Interstate Commerce Commission
ICC	inventory carrying cost (dollars per year)
ICR	inventory carrying rate (percent per year)
IMF	international monetary fund
IMS	inventory management system
INCOTERMS	International Commercial Terms
IP&M	inventory planning and management
ISO	International Standards Organization
IT	information technology
IT	inventory turnover
ITR	inventory turnover rate (turns per year)
IVHS	intelligent vehicle highway system
JIT	just-in-time
KD	knock down
KG	kilogram
KPI	key performance indicator
L	leadtime (time in hours, days, weeks, months, or years)

LAN	local area network
LAV	logistics asset value
LB	pound
L/C	letter of credit
LCL	less than container load
LCPO	logistics cost per order
LD	leadtime demand (units per leadtime period)
LFR	line fill rate (percentage)
LIFO	last-in, first-out
LIS	logistics information system
LKPI	logistics key performance indicator
LLP	lead logistics provider
LOG	logistics
LPH	lines per hour
LSC	lost sales cost (dollars)
LTL	less than load (less than full truckload)
LWR	logistics wage rate
MAD	mean absolute deviation (units)
MHE	material handling equipment
MOS	method of shipment
MRP	manufacturing requirements planning
MTBF	mean time between failure
NAFTA	North American Free Trade Agreement
NIP	net inventory position (units)
NVOCC	Non-Vessel Operating Common Carrier
OC	ordering cost (dollars per order)
OCZ	order completion zone
OE	order entry
OFR	order fill rate (percentage)
OP	order processing
OPH	orders per hour
OR	operations research
OS&D	over, short, and damaged
OUL	order up to level (units)
P	popularity (requests/month)
PD	physical distribution
PDA	personal digital assistant
PDP	perfect delivery percentage
P&D	pickup and deliver
PFD	personal, fatigue, and delay

PFE	percent forecast error (percentage)
PI	pipeline inventory
P/L	packing list
PO	purchase order
POC	purchase order cost
POCT	purchase order cycle time
POCTV	purchase order cycle time variability
POD	proof of delivery
POE	port of entry
POO	port of origin
POP	perfect order percentage
PPOP	perfect purchase order percentage
PTL	pick-to-light
PTS	picker to stock
QR	quick response
RF	radio frequency
RFID	radio frequency identification
RFI	request for information
RFP	request for proposal
RFQ	request for quotation
ROI	return on investment
ROP	reorder point (units)
RTP	review time period (hours, days, weeks, months, or years)
SCIS	supply chain information system
SCM	supply chain management
SD	storage density
SDFD	standard deviation of forecast demand (units)
SED	shipper's export declaration
SF	shortage factor (percentage)
SLI	shipper's letter of instructions
SP	selling price (dollars per unit)
SKU	stock keeping unit
SS	safety stock
STP	stock to picker
SUC	setup cost (dollars/setup)
SUP	supply
T	turnover (units/month)
T&D	transportation and distribution
TAC	total acquisition cost (dollars per year)
TEU	twenty-foot equivalent unit

TFS	total floorspace
TIC	total inventory cost (dollars per year)
T/L	truckload
TLC	total logistics cost (dollars per year)
TMS	transportation management system
TRC	total response cost (dollars per year)
TTC	total transportation cost (dollars per year)
TSC	total supply cost (dollars per year)
TWC	total warehousing cost (dollars per year)
UFR	unit fill rate (percentage)
UIV	unit inventory value (dollars per unit)
UN	United Nations
UOB	units on backorder (units)
UOM	unit of measure
UPC	universal product code
UPH	units per hour
USP	unit selling price (dollars per unit)
V	volume
VAH	vehicle available hours
VMI	vendor-managed inventory
VOH	vehicle operating hours
WAN	wide area network
WERC	Warehousing Education and Research Council
WH	warehouse
WIP	work in process
WOCT	warehouse order cycle time
WTO	world trade organization
WMS	warehouse management system
WWR	warehouse wage rate
XD	cross-dock
Y	yield
Z	zone

Index

About the Author

EDWARD FRAZELLE, PH.D., is president and CEO of Logistics Resources International, founder of The Logistics Institute at Georgia Institute of Technology, and director of the school's Logistic Management Series. As the former president of the International Material Management Society and a pioneer in today's logistics movement, Dr. Frazelle has trained more than 50,000 logistics professionals and helped more than 100 corporations and government agencies in the United States, Asia, Europe, and Latin America pursue and achieve logistics excellence. He has written or co-authored seven books, including Supply Chain Strategy, and numerous articles on logistics. His Website **www.LRILogistics.com** is recognized as one of today's most comprehensive and valuable resources for logistics information and instructional materials.